POETICS:
THEORY AND PRACTICE
IN MEDIEVAL
ENGLISH LITERATURE

The theme of the 1990 Bennett Memorial Lectures in Perugia, 'Poetics: Theory and Practice', invited a wide variety of approaches: for instance, the search for a late-medieval poetics in texts by commentators and philosophers; the study of an internal, implicit theory of poetry in the poetic texts themselves; and the application of modern literary theories to medieval works. The principal emphasis is on Chaucer: eight of the eleven contributors focus on aspects of his poetics, from appropriation of the reader's role to the symbolism of his landscape; there is material for Arthurians (is there a 'basic' English Arthurian verse romance?); and the Christian version of the Platonic ideal in *Pearl* and a discussion of the interaction of poetic and civil authority in poets from Chaucer to Spenser complete this collection.

Piero Boitani / Anna Torti (eds.)

POETICS:
THEORY AND PRACTICE
IN MEDIEVAL
ENGLISH LITERATURE

The J.A.W. Bennett Memorial Lectures
Seventh Series
Perugia, 1990

D. S. Brewer

First published 1991 by D. S. Brewer, Cambridge

D. S. Brewer is an imprint of Boydell & Brewer Ltd
PO Box 9, Woodbridge, Suffolk IP12 3DF, UK
and of Boydell & Brewer Inc.
PO Box 41026, Rochester, NY 14604, USA

ISBN   0 85991 331 7

British Library Cataloguing-in-Publication Data
Poetics: theory and practice in medieval English
literature. – (J.A.W. Bennett memorial lectures)
   I. Boitani, Piero   II. Torti, Anna   III. Series
   821
   ISBN 0–85991–331–7

Library of Congress Cataloging-in-Publication Data
Poetics : theory and practice in medieval English literature / Piero
   Boitani, Anna Torti, eds.
         p.   cm.
   'The J.A.W. Bennett memorial lectures, seventh series, Perugia,
1990.'
   Includes bibliographical references and index.
   ISBN 0–85991–331–7 (alk. paper)
   1. English poetry – Middle English, 1100–1500 – History and
criticism – Theory, etc.   2. English poetry – Middle English,
1100–1500 – History and criticism.   3. Chaucer, Geoffrey, d. 1400
– Technique.   4. Rhetoric, Medieval.   5. Poetics.   I. Boitani,
Piero.   II. Torti, Anna.
PR313.P64   1991
821'.109 – dc20   91–22612

This publication is printed on acid-free paper

Printed in Great Britain by
St Edmundsbury Press Ltd, Bury St Edmunds, Suffolk

Contents

Contributors

Jill Mann	University of Cambridge
A.J. Minnis	University of York
Charles A. Owen Jr.	University of Connecticut
A.S.G. Edwards	University of Victoria, B. C.
Paul B. Taylor	University of Geneva
Helen Cooper	University of Oxford
Paule Mertens-Fonck	University of Liège
David Wallace	University of Minnesota
Eugene Vance	University of Washington
Joerg O. Fichte	University of Tübingen
V.A. Kolve	University of California, Los Angeles

Preface

This volume contains the papers delivered at Perugia during the Symposium held there on 26–28 April, 1990 to commemorate J.A.W. Bennett (the J.A.W. Bennett Memorial Lectures, seventh series). The theme, 'Poetics: Theory and Practice in Medieval English Literature', was open to a wide variety of approaches – for instance, the search for a late medieval poetics in texts by commentators and philosophers; the study of an internal, implicit theory of poetry in the poetic texts themselves; the application of modern literary theories to medieval works.

The present book bears witness to the freedom and diversity with which our contributors understood the theme itself of the Symposium. Jill Mann focuses on the author-audience relationship in Chaucer. His role as reader of others' work is a covert surrogate for our own role as readers of his own. His representations of the reading process constitute an acknowledgement of the essential role played by the reader in the creation of literary authority, and show his interest in some of its important implications for the writer. Alastair Minnis examines commentaries to the *Roman de la Rose*, and hence the appropriations and adaptations of conventional critical discourse that took place in the *querelle de la Rose*.

Charles Owen turns to the fictional levels of the *Canterbury Tales*, and finds in their interplay a poetics of voice and genre. A.S.G. Edwards' essay is devoted to the 'challenge' that the representation of the spoken word presented to Chaucer and to the general scepticism about the possibility of effective utterance that resulted from Chaucer's preoccupation about the way in which characters do things with words. Paul Taylor sees the *Legend of Good Women* as a 'catalogue of the complicity of sight in the tragedy of love', which belies the theory that words can reveal to the inner eye of understanding the invisible forms behind visible shapes.

Using Dante's *Convivio* as a model, Helen Cooper examines the interaction of secular, philosophic, moral, and poetic authority in English literature from Chaucer to Spenser. In Paule Mertens-Fonck's article the problem of 'life and fiction' in the *Canterbury Tales*, already examined by Charles Owen, is viewed through the lens provided by the Prioress's name, 'Eglentyne', in the General Prologue to the *Canterbury Tales* as well as by a scene in the *Knight's Tale*. Mertens-Fonck's historico-philological approach finds its counterpart in David Wallace's search for a 'historicist' poetics. In his essay, 'Lumbardye' becomes a powerful spatial metaphor for a tyrannical state of mind, which affects the poetic text as well as its relationship with the political present. Eugene Vance discusses the type of inherent claims made for poetic discourse when the *Pearl*-poet employs the word, 'perle', both as the sign of an inanimate jewel and as a proper name to address a perfect maiden. He proposes that we turn to the Christian version of the Platonic idea of participation in order to find a satisfactory explanation to this problem.

Joerg Fichte tries to grapple with Arthur. He seeks to establish a heuristic model which will serve as the basis for the entire corpus of middle English romance, and offers a paradigm comprising four major categories. By reading the *Franklin's Tale*'s central subject, that of magic, V.A. Kolve leads us to meditate on the poetic art itself as conceived by Chaucer: thus, the rocks, the garden, and the study – the *loci* of the Tale – suggest a true poetics of illusion.

We hope that readers will find the debate in this volume as stimulating as we found the discussions between contributors during the Symposium. For these to take place, we are particularly indebted to the session chairmen, Patricia Shaw, David Benson, and Przemysław Mroczkowski. Scholarship owes an even greater debt to the Regional Council of Umbria, the City of Perugia, and the British Council for making the Symposium possible.

4 February 1991   Anna Torti
                                                       Piero Boitani

THE AUTHORITY OF THE AUDIENCE IN CHAUCER

JILL MANN

The authority of the literary text seems, by the laws of etymology, to belong to the author. 'Auctour' glides insensibly into 'auctoritee'; indeed, the word 'auctour' itself can mean 'a source of authoritative information or opinion, an authority' (MED 2a). And as a natural result the problematic aspects of literary authority, much discussed in recent years,[1] have been generally considered in relation to the author – have been considered, indeed, first and foremost as a problem *for* the author. Jacqueline Miller's recent study of 'Authority and Authorship' in medieval and Renaissance literature, for example, identifies the central concern of Chaucer's *House of Fame* as the pressing need felt by 'Chaucer and many of his contemporaries . . . to define the (often uneasy) relationship between the status of their individual authorial positions and the authorizing principles of their art – to find the proper balance between their claims for poetic independence and their reliance upon the sanction of traditional *auctoritee*'.[2] This author-centred approach to the *House of Fame* goes back to J. A. W. Bennett's book on the poem, which sees it as 'the one work of the poet that dwells on the nature and rewards of poetic achievement . . . the work in which [Chaucer] presents himself as a seeker after fresh poetic inspiration, new poetic "tidings" '.[3] John Norton-Smith describes the *House of Fame* as delineating 'the hidden sources which urge him, as a poet, to both write and think about certain problems'.[4] Piero Boitani's magisterial study of the poem likewise climaxes with the questions: 'What gives a poet his inspiration? What makes him a poet?'[5]

With none of this have I any quarrel. Yet as Piero Boitani also observes elsewhere, when Chaucer gives us a self-portrait, he represents himself as a 'fanatic bibliophile'[6] – that is, not as a writer but as a *reader*. The vivid and intimate picture of Chaucer's everyday life which is given us by the eagle in the *House of Fame* describes him coming home from his daily work only to bury himself in his books.

---

[1] See especially Alastair Minnis, *Medieval Theory of Authorship: Scholastic Literary Attitudes in the Later Middle Ages* (London, 1984).

[2] *Poetic License: Authority and Authorship in Medieval and Renaissance Contexts* (New York and Oxford, 1986), p. 35. Chapter II incorporates Miller's earlier article, 'The Writing on the Wall: Authority and Authorship in Chaucer's *House of Fame*', *Chaucer Review* 17 (1982–3) 95–115.

[3] *Chaucer's Book of Fame: An Exposition of 'The House of Fame'* (Oxford, 1968), p. 3.

[4] *Geoffrey Chaucer* (London and Boston, 1974), p. 39.

[5] *Chaucer and the Imaginary World of Fame* (Cambridge, 1984), p. 216.

[6] 'Old books brought to life in dreams: the *Book of the Duchess*, the *House of Fame*, the *Parliament of Fowls*', pp. 39–57 in *The Cambridge Chaucer Companion*, ed. Piero Boitani and Jill Mann (Cambridge, 1986), at p. 40.

'For when thy labour doon al ys,
And hast mad alle thy rekenynges,
In stede of reste and newe thynges
Thou goost hom to thy hous anoon,
And, also domb as any stoon,
Thou sittest at another book
Tyl fully daswed ys thy look;
And lyvest thus as an heremyte,
Although thyn abstynence is lyte.'

(652–60)

Nor is this an isolated case. In the *Parliament of Fowls*, Chaucer represents himself as busy all day in reading, not in writing. In the *Book of the Duchess*, his relation to books is not that of the creative writer, but that of the casual bedtime reader. True, in the *Legend of Good Women*, his role as a writer is brought into play by the God of Love's accusations against him, but even so it is as an assiduous reader, perpetually poring over his books, that he first introduces himself. The idea of linking the dream-vision to the reading of a book was, indeed, as A. C. Spearing has observed, Chaucer's special contribution to the genre.[7] The much-discussed Narrator of *Troilus and Criseyde* ought perhaps to be called not the Narrator but the Reader, since he reminds us at every stage that he is getting all this out of a book and is unable to alter the story he is telling or fill in its lacunae. These persistent intrusions of a reading presence within the text dramatize not only Chaucer's relationship to a literary past – to the authors whose influence must be reconciled with his own creative independence – but also his relationship to a literary future – to the readers on whom the continuing life and meaning of his work depends. That is, Chaucer's role as reader of others' works is a covert surrogate for our own role as readers of his own. His representations of the reading process constitute – I shall argue – an acknowledgement of the essential role played by the reader in the creation (or destruction) of literary authority, and show his interest in some of its more important implications for the writer.[8]

The reinstatement of the reader as the neglected third in the 'triangle of author, work and public' has been an important project in twentieth-century criticism – in, for example, the work of Stanley Fish, of Wolfgang Iser, and in the 'reception-theory' outlined by Hans Robert Jauss.[9] In this triad, writes Jauss, the reading public 'is no passive part, no chain of mere reactions, but rather itself an energy formative of history'.[10] Jauss, like Mikhail Bakhtin before him, stresses the 'dialogical character of the literary work',[11] which enables it to acquire new significances as new historical contexts – in practice, new readers –

---

[7] *Medieval Dream-Poetry* (Cambridge, 1976), p. 58.

[8] The subject is broached by Susan Schibanoff, 'The New Reader and Female Textuality in Two Early Commentaries on Chaucer', *Studies in the Age of Chaucer* 10 (1988) 71–108, at pp. 96–103.

[9] See Stanley Fish, *Is There a Text in This Class? The Authority of Interpretive Communities* (Cambridge, Mass. and London, 1980); Wolfgang Iser, *The Implied Reader: Patterns of Communication in Prose Fiction from Bunyan to Beckett* (Baltimore and London, 1974); id., *The Act of Reading: A Theory of Aesthetic Response* (Baltimore and London, 1978); Hans Robert Jauss, *Toward an Aesthetic of Reception*, trans. Timothy Bahti (Brighton, 1982).

[10] *Aesthetic of Reception*, p. 19.

[11] Ibid., p. 21. On Bakhtin, see Tzvetan Todorov, *Mikhail Bakhtin: The Dialogical Principle*, trans. Wlad Godzich (Manchester, 1984).

bring to light new structures of meaning. 'A literary work', says Jauss, 'is not an object that stands by itself and that offers the same view to each reader in each period. It is not a monument that monologically reveals its timeless essence. It is much more like an orchestration that strikes ever new resonances among its readers and that frees the text from the material of the words and brings it to a contemporary existence . . .'.[12] In approaching Chaucer's work with these words in mind, it is no part of my intention to congratulate him for having cleverly anticipated modern reception-theory; his own analysis of the reading process, though equally sophisticated, is animated by different interests and aims. Nor am I proposing to apply reception-theory to Chaucer's work. There is the world of difference between analysing the representations of the reading process in Chaucer's text, and analysing the reading processes that his text itself implies or provokes – an excellent subject but one for another paper. I wish only to draw attention to Chaucer's various imagined representations of the reader's role; and if reception-theory has a part to play, it is perhaps that it has prepared us to appreciate Chaucer's interest in this subject, and to recognize the originality, the honesty, and above all magnanimity, which mark his reflections on it.

Let us go back to the conversation between Chaucer and the eagle in the *House of Fame*, and in particular to the point where the bird offers to identify all the different constellations for the airborne poet, so that when he next reads about them in books he will be able to relate his reading to what he has seen. Chaucer nonchalantly rejects this kind offer, because, he says, he believes everything the books say without having to verify it, and what is more, it might hurt his eyes to look at the stars directly.

> 'No fors,' quod y, 'hyt is no nede.
> I leve as wel, so God me spede,
> Hem that write of this matere,
> As though I knew her places here;
> And eke they shynen here so bryghte,
> Hyt shulde shenden al my syghte
> To loke on hem.'
>   (1011–17)

Every author must at times have wished for a reader like this – docile, credulous, ready to take on trust everything the books tell him. This is, if you like, the passive reader whose existence is rejected by Jauss. And likewise, of course, by Chaucer, for his appearance here is nothing other than a joke, his acknowledgement that the passive reader has no existence outside of this comic fantasy.

How a typical reader is actually likely to behave we can see in the immediately preceding passage, where Chaucer, in direct contrast to his stated attitude, immediately begins checking off what he sees around him against the information he has gathered from his reading. Looking back through the heavens at the world he has left behind, he thinks first of Boethius's account of Philosophy's imaginary flight through the spheres on the wings of thought (973–8; cf. *De Cons. Phil.* IV m.1). Then he thinks of Martianus Capella's *Marriage of Philology and Mercury* and Alan of Lille's *Anticlaudianus*, and observes that they too have accurately described the celestial regions.

---

[12] *Aesthetic of Reception*, p. 21.

And than thoughte y on Marcian,
And eke on Anteclaudian,
That sooth was her descripsion
Of alle the hevenes region,
As fer as that y sey the preve;
Therfore y kan hem now beleve.   (985–90)

The implications of this passage for the truth-claims of literature have been thoroughly discussed in Chaucer criticism. What is important about it as an illustration of the reading process is not only that it shows us the constant interaction between literature and life in which the reader is engaged, but also that it shows us books *meshing with other books* in the mind of the reader. As Gillian Beer puts it in her Introduction to *Arguing with the Past*: 'Books once read do not stay inside their covers. Once in the head they mingle, forming networks of allusion with other reading and other experiences of the time'.[13] Chaucer's heavenly flight draws Boethius, Martianus and Alan into a collage whose significance is created and sealed by the experience of the moment.

This observation is not negated but given an extra dimension of complexity by the circumstance that in this particular case the 'experience' which serves as the nodal point of literary meaning is of course one that no human being has ever had outside the pages of a book. The 'network of allusion' in this case makes no contact with reality; it remains a purely literary phenomenon. And yet in a strange way, to find something repeated in *another* book carries something of the same evidential power as finding it confirmed in experience. Reading about an ascent through the cosmos in Boethius, Martianus and Alan – and one might add, in other authors such as Dante, whose influence on this scene is palpable even though he is not named – leaves the same kind of residue in the memory as experience itself.[14] 'A thousand tymes have I herd men telle / That ther ys joy in hevene and peyne in helle' says Chaucer at the opening of the *Legend of Good Women* (F 1–2), and he proclaims his willingness to believe it; but nevertheless he also knows that there is no living soul who has ever been to either place. So when at the end of Book I of the *House of Fame* he refers us, if we want a detailed description of Hell, to Vergil or Claudian or Dante, it is as if the correspondences between these three separate reports must inevitably arise from and bear witness to the independent reality of what they describe – whereas what they in fact testify to is nothing other than a chain of literary influence (that is, both Claudian and Dante model their descriptions on Virgil). Chaucer focuses the question of literary truth on these 'non-existent' experiences not only, I think, because of his concern with the kind of belief that literature can command, but also because of his awareness of the *priority* of books over experience – his interest in the way that they prepare us to recognize experiences when we have them, to give them a predetermined shape and name. We shall certainly recognize Hell if we ever see it. To see literature performing this preparatory role with experiences that people have never had, makes it easier to see it performing the same role with the ones that they do have. Love,

---

[13] *Arguing With the Past: Essays in Narrative from Woolf to Sidney* (London and New York, 1989), p. 9.

[14] Iser quotes Henry James's observation that reading gives us the illusion 'that we have lived another life' (*The Act of Reading*, p. 127).

for example. At the opening of the *Parliament of Fowls*, Chaucer tells us that he 'knows not Love in deed', but the poem nevertheless constitutes a packed storehouse of impressions on the subject, garnered from innumerable books and awaiting the confirmatory experience that will activate them.

It is in the *Parliament of Fowls* that we find the best and fullest example of books mingling with each other and forming networks of allusion in the reader's head. What we enter in this poem is not so much a garden of Love as a reader's mind, in which Macrobius and Cicero, Boccaccio, Dante, Alan of Lille and the *Romance of the Rose* mesh and entangle themselves into a bizarre configuration. It is rather like those films that begin with a hand turning the pages of a book, whose pictures suddenly begin to move and fill the screen with their own autonomous reality. Jauss speaks of the reader approaching each new work he reads with a 'horizon of expectations' created by a knowledge of pre-existing literary works – a horizon whose boundaries may be confirmed or dramatically thrown open by the act of reading.[15] The *Parliament of Fowls* could be seen as a sort of animated version of one reader's 'horizon of expectations'. But the mental world that lies within this horizon is not such a tidy and well-ordered affair as one might suppose from Jauss's account of it; it is more like a literary Disneyland. Books collapse into each other in an unpredictable and undisciplined sort of way, forming unexpected alliances and idiosyncratic patterns; they are linked by haphazard association rather than by the laws of genre or subject. Cicero's Africanus seems to have assimilated himself to Dante's Virgil; the gate to Dante's Hell does not open on to a world regulated by divine justice but on to the amoral frivolities of Guillaume de Lorris's garden. The texts take on a life of their own: the birds depicted on Nature's robe in Alan of Lille's *Complaint of Nature* come to life and start squabbling at her feet.[16] What is more, this variegated literary kaleidoscope could at any moment be shaken into a new pattern by the arrival of a new book on the horizon, creating a new network of allusions with those already in place and changing expectations yet again.

This is all great fun for readers. But it creates certain problems for writers. Iser discusses the 'asymmetry' in the dialogic relation between text and reader arising from the fact that the text cannot answer back, and is therefore in some sense at the mercy of the reader's ability to make sense of it. For Iser, this potential imbalance is regulated by controlling mechanisms in the text: 'the reader's activity must be controlled in some way by the text'.[17] The multi-textual jumble of *The Parliament of Fowls* shows that the reader's activity is not so easily regimented. We have here no disciplined concentration on the individual literary work as a thing-in-itself, carefully analysed in terms of the rules it establishes for itself, its relations with other literary material and with life scrupulously curtailed and regulated by notions of literary decorum and methodological consistency. This is not professional reading, this is *real* reading, producing a mish-mash of half-remembered words and images whose arrangement is orchestrated by the reader rather than the writer.

---

[15] *Aesthetic of Reception*, p. 25.
[16] The point is made by Peter Dronke, 'Chaucer and the Medieval Latin Poets: Part A', pp. 154–72 in *Writers and their Background: Geoffrey Chaucer*, ed. Derek Brewer (London, 1974), at pp. 164–5.
[17] *The Art of Reading*, p. 167.

That Chaucer was conscious of the potential problems in the dialogic relation between writer and reader can be seen, I think, from the various cases where he imagines different sorts of dislocation in this relation, cases where one voice in the dialogue could be said to drown out the other. Let us start with an example where the problem is on the reader's side: *Troilus and Criseyde*. Here it is the writer – the fictional Lollius – who assumes dominance over the reader – the dramatized projection of Chaucer himself. Knowing the outcome of the story from the beginning, Chaucer nevertheless represents himself as being drawn in by the moment-by-moment excitement of the reading process to an emotional identification with the happiness of the two lovers which gives way – like theirs – to a progressive dismay at the way the story is going in the last two Books. In Book III, the reader's passionate involvement in the story instantly realizes the words on the page as a scene of dramatic immediacy:

> Criseyde, which that felte hire thus itake,
> As writen clerkes in hire bokes olde,
> Right as an aspes leef she gan to quake . . .   (1198–200)

So far from being felt as an intrusion that breaks the illusion of present experience, the reference to 'bokes olde' makes us aware of how live an experience reading can be, the words filling themselves out with our imagined participation (as Chaucer appeals to his readers to fill out his report of the scene with their own experience of love). Yet by Book V, the story has become distasteful to the reader, and Chaucer's disaffection from what he reads registers itself in the terse reportage with which he rehearses its bare essentials.

> And after this the storie telleth us
> That she hym yaf the faire baye stede
> The which he ones wan of Troilus . . .
>
> I fynde ek in stories elleswhere . . .
>
> But trewely, the storie telleth us,
> Ther made never womman moore wo
> Than she, whan that she falsed Troilus . . .   (V, 1037–9, 1044, 1051–3)

'The story telleth us' but we don't really want to hear it, because the information is at odds with the matrix of meaning we have been encouraged to prepare by the ecstasies of Book III, and are reluctant to discard for another, gloomier version. Trapped by the story he reads, the reader finds it too late to retract his commitment to the characters and experiences it has offered, and can only respond by throwing the book away altogether. The ending of the poem rejects not only human love but also reading.

> Lo here, the forme of olde clerkis speche
> In poetrie, if ye hire bokes seche.   (V, 1854–5)

Chaucer's role here is not that of the writer revealing to us the hidden meaning of the story he has told; it is rather that of the reader, registering his disgust and disappointment with the story he has read, and regretting that he ever started on it.

In *Troilus* it is the reader who is alarmed by a lack of control, his role curtailed and restricted by the unpalatable nature of the text. Elsewhere in Chaucer it is the writer's inability to control what the reader does with his text that is a potential cause of alarm. Chaucer is possibly the only English poet to have been more troubled by the anxiety of *exerting* influence than by the anxiety of undergoing it; the burden of the future can be more worrying than the burden of the past.[18] Consider, for example, the relationship between Virgil and Dante from Virgil's rather than (as is more usual) Dante's point of view, and it becomes apparent that for all Dante's reverence and love for his the poet who is his 'maestro' and 'autore' (*Inferno* i,85), he is neverthless making Virgil *mean* something that the Roman writer not only never conceived of but would have actively disliked. Virgil would doubtless have been as uncomfortable with his role as a forerunner and guide to Christianity as St Bernard would be were he to return from the grave and find he had been made a precursor of Islamic fundamentalism.

Chaucer's own anxieties, as least as he dramatizes them, centre particularly on the effect of his writings on women. In the God of Love's accusations against him in the Prologue to the *Legend of Good Women*, he projects a concern that reading *Troilus and Criseyde* might reinforce men in a low opinion of women:

> And of Creseyde thou hast seyd as the lyste,
> That maketh men to wommen lasse triste,
> That ben as trewe as ever was any steel . . .   (F, 332–4)

Already in *Troilus and Criseyde* itself, Chaucer shows Criseyde ruefully prophesying that when her story becomes known, women will hate her most because her actions will be used to discredit the sex as a whole (V, 1063–6). It is of no use for Chaucer to protest, as he does at the end of *Troilus*, that it is not his intention to blacken women's reputation; an author's intentions, as every modern critic knows, cannot control the meaning of his work. And if this axiom allows for the free play of critical subtlety, it also allows for a crude reductivism that can turn the story of Criseyde into an anti-feminist anecdote. We can see the problem in the famous *querelle* over the *Roman de la Rose*: the male humanists vainly appealing to literary subtleties – to Jean de Meun's urbane irony, or his use of dramatic monologue in order to distance himself from anti-feminist points of view, while for Christine de Pisan all this means nothing beside the simple fact that the text is *read* as anti-feminist; one husband, she says, used to read the poem aloud to his wife and shower her with blows as he did so.[19] Chaucer gives us a similar situation in his picture of the Wife of Bath forced to endure her fifth husband reading aloud day and night from his 'book of wikked wyves'. Loath as I am to say a good word for St Jerome, it must I suppose be admitted that his *intention* in writing the treatise *Against Jovinian* was to persuade his readers to celibacy, not to encourage them to torment their wives. But to the Wife of Bath this is a distinction she is not in a position to appreciate; she might be forgiven for thinking, like Hilaire Belloc's illiterate Sarah Byng, that the sole function of literature is to breed distress. Her response to Jankyn's onslaughts is not to suggest he take a course in literary criticism, but simply to attempt to destroy the book.

---

[18] For these terms see W. Jackson Bate, *The Burden of the Past and the English Poet* (London, 1971), and Harold Bloom, *The Anxiety of Influence: A Theory of Poetry* (London, Oxford and New York, 1973).

[19] Christine de Pisan, Jean Gerson, Jean de Montreuil, Gontier et Pierre Col, *Le Débat sur Le Roman de la Rose*, ed. Eric Hicks (Paris, 1977), pp. 139–40.

We can reject Jankyn's use of literary texts as immoral, but it is less easy to prove that it is illegitimate. If meaning is determined by interpretive communities, as Stanley Fish tells us it is, then men must surely make up one of the largest and most cohesive communities of this sort, whose interpretative values were accepted without protest and indeed without notice for centuries. But Chaucer, with his sharp eye for the way literature interacts with life, noticed them. In the figure of Pluto in the *Merchant's Tale*, he gives us a brilliant vignette of the male reader observing life through the spectacles of literature – spectacles which have special blinkers on the side. Seeing May and Damian about to commit adultery in the tree, Pluto comments sententiously not on Damian's ungrateful betrayal of his kind master, but on the general and deplorable treacherousness of womankind. He supports these strictures with reference to 'ten hundred thousand tales' of women's 'untrouthe and brotilnesse' (2240–1), and also to the anti-feminist proverbs in the Solomonic books of the Bible. Pluto assumes that experience provides the evidence and literature plays a merely confirmatory role ('Th'experience so preveth every day / The tresons whiche that wommen doon to man': 2238–9). But it is of course the other way round: it is the anti-feminist material he has read, converging with his personal bias towards his own sex, that shapes his expectations and conditions him to respond to experience in a particular way. As in the *House of Fame* and the *Parliament of Fowls*, reading is *prior* to experience and disposes us to approach it selectively, preparing us to recognize familiar forms while unfamiliar ones fall outside the range of vision. Pluto is blind not only to Damian's role in the adultery but also to his own past: the wife whom he so pompously lectures on the treasons women inflict on men was won by a rape, as Chaucer reminds us by referring to Claudian's *De Raptu Proserpinae*, and its account of how he 'ravysshed' her on the slopes of Mount Etna, when he introduces the pair. The reading of Pluto's own story might suggest that a few remarks on the brutalities men inflict on women might not come amiss. Proserpina does not point this out directly, but she mounts a parallel attack on Solomon, whose 'auctoritee' as a critic of women is similarly undermined by the facts of his personal life, since he was a 'lecchour and an ydolastre' (2298). Like the Wife of Bath commenting on St Jerome, she unearths the personal 'auctour' buried in the impersonal 'auctoritee', as an interpretative strategy which will reveal masculine bias. Moreover, she claims that when Solomon said he had never found a good woman, what he *meant* was that nobody is truly good but God alone. We might be tempted to dub this last simply a *mis*interpretation, but Proserpina has lifted it from the entirely sober context of the *Melibee* (1076–80), where it is less easy to ascribe to female unscrupulousness in argument. As with the Wife of Bath's cavalier handling of biblical and patristic authorities in defence of multiple marriages, it is not possible to distinguish intrinsically between the creative exegesis practised by men (and therefore taken seriously) and the creative exegesis practised by women (and therefore regarded as unlicensed); St Jerome, Pluto, the Wife of Bath and Proserpina all use identical interpretative methods.[20]

If these last examples of the reading process have shown its potential reduc-

---

[20] See E. Talbot Donaldson, 'Designing a Camel; Or, Generalizing the Middle Ages', *Tennessee Studies in Literature* 22 (1977) 1–16, at pp. 5–7, and David Aers, *Chaucer, Langland and the Creative Imagination* (London, Boston and Henley, 1980), p. 86.

tivism, we can turn back to the *House of Fame* for an example of its more creative aspects, and see them, what is more, exercised in women's favour rather than to their detriment. Chaucer's picture of Dido in Book I is, as has often been pointed out, a blend of Virgil and Ovid; emerging from a narrative summary of the *Aeneid*, her lament over Aeneas's departure swells to proportions that remind us of Ovid's *Heroides*, and insensibly persuades us to see it from the female point of view – that is, as an act of treacherous desertion rather than a self-sacrificing submission to a heroic destiny. The immediate cause of this emotional involvement in Dido's position is not, however, Ovid (who makes surprisingly little contribution to the *material* of Dido's lament), but the fact that her story makes contact with certain proverbial commonplaces in the mind of the narrator. Or rather, here again we should say in the mind of the reader, for in narrating the train of images he 'sees' on the wall of the temple Chaucer is also 'reading' a written text, as his opening quotation of Virgil's words makes clear; as in any reading process, the words transform themselves insensibly into a series of vivid pictures to which the reader imagines he is responding directly. Dido's trust in Aeneas's seeming goodness thus activates in him a whole stream of generalizations that relate her story to his own store of ideas on life.

> Allas! what harm doth apparence,
> Whan hit is fals in existence!
> For he to hir a traytour was;
> Wherfore she slow hirself, allas!
> Loo, how a woman doth amys
> To love hym that unknowen ys!
> For, be Cryste, lo, thus yt fareth:
> "Hyt is not al gold that glareth."
> For also browke I wel myn hed,
> Ther may be under godlyhed
> Kevered many a shrewed vice.
> Therfore be no wyght so nyce
> To take a love oonly for chere,
> Or speche, or for frendly manere,
> For this shal every woman fynde,
> That som man, of his pure kynde,
> Wol shewen outward the fayreste,
> Tyl he have caught that what him leste;
> And thanne wol he causes fynde
> And swere how that she ys unkynde,
> Or fals, or privy, or double was.
> Al this seye I be Eneas
> And Dido, and hir nyce lest,
> That loved al to sone a gest;
> Therfore I wol seye a proverbe,
> That "he that fully knoweth th'erbe
> May saufly leye hyt to his yë" –
> Withoute drede, this ys no lye.   (265–92)

This interpretation of Dido as simply one in a long line of female victims of male heartlessness and an example of the need to look before you leap liberates Chaucer from the Virgilian original; when he returns to Dido and reports her long lament, he emphasizes its independence from any 'auctour', locating its origin in the imaginative autonomy of the dream.

> In suche wordes gan to pleyne
> Dydo of hir grete peyne,
> As me mette redely –
> Non other auctour alegge I.   (311–14)

The Dido passage has been discussed – most notably by Sheila Delany – in terms of 'Chaucer's experience as a poet', illustrating his sense of 'the validity of conflicting truths' and the unreliable basis of literary authority.[21] This it doubtless is, but what particularly interests me is what it has to tell us of the reading process. For the importance of Ovid to Chaucer is not simply that he offers us another version of Dido – as if he and Virgil were presenting alternative accounts of the same historical events; it is that his version of Dido is recuperated from a *reading* of Virgil's text. As the text frees itself into images in the reader's mind, so it assumes a quasi-reality, permitting it to be restructured into a new meaning. So Virgil's Dido is reconstructed as Ovid's Dido, and both are read in the light of Chaucer's own knowledge of the everyday experience stored in proverb and commonplace, until Dido takes on a different form again, rooted in the authority of the reader, and 'non other auctour'. The dialogical character of the literary work is here seen in action; literary authority passes from the author to the reader.

Dido miserably foresees her imprisonment within a literary text – 'alle myn actes red and songe / Over al thys lond' (347–8), the meaning of her story fixed as simply the tale of a loose woman liable to give herself to anybody. In imagining Dido and Criseyde foreseeing their own after-life in story, Chaucer implicitly confronts the writer's responsibilities towards the human subjects whose living complexities he reduces to the outline of a meaning. But what frees him from the full weight of these responsibilities as writer is the autonomy of the reader, who can always read *through* the story to recuperate a structure of meaning unperceived by the author. If Chaucer's reading is not faithful to Virgil, it is at least faithful to Dido.

Chaucer's reading of Dido perhaps qualifies as an instance of creative misprision, in Harold Bloom's terms; I want to end by looking at some examples of less dignified kinds of misreading. The first is in the *Book of the Duchess*, in Chaucer's reading of the story of Ceyx and Alcyone. This is, in Ovid, a pathetic and moving tale, but in Chaucer's re-telling, as has often been noted, the pathos is oddly muted by passages of brisk summary or bluff comedy, especially in the account of Juno's messenger visiting the cave of Morpheus and having to bellow in the god's ear to wake him up.[22] Although Chaucer tells us that Alcyone's grief at the loss of her husband affected him so much that he felt bad about it all the next morning (95–100), this is not represented as being his immediate reaction to the story. What primarily interests him about it is that there is such a thing as a god of sleep, a fact in which his present insomnia gives him an overriding interest. He promptly vows to the god a sumptuous feather-

21 *Chaucer's House of Fame: The Poetics of Skeptical Fideism* (Chicago and London, 1972), p. 57.

22 A. C. Spearing notes the imbalances of tone created by these comic elements; *Medieval Dream-Poetry*, p. 71.

bed, and gold-leaf decoration for his cave, if only he will send him to sleep – and of course his prayer is instantly granted. Modern critical theories are rarely, in my experience, so honest about the reading process as Chaucer is here, but we are all familiar, I think, with the kind of tangential reaction he is describing. In the twentieth century it is perhaps easier to illustrate in relation to films: we all know the men who never seem to see anything in a film but the cars or the guns ('Did you *see* that 1959 Cadillac?'). We weep buckets as we watch Anna Karenina prepare to throw herself under the train, reflecting all the while that a little fur muff like hers is just what we need for next winter. The undisciplined and arbitrary nature of the reader's response must be the despair of the writer; his best efforts will be negated or unbalanced by the reader's immediate needs and obsessions – or even simply indelibly coloured by them, as Gillian Beer reports that her reading of *Anna Karenina* is permanently intertwined with 'the plains of Yugoslavia and the bleak clangour of Tottenham Court Road' in the 'repertoire of memory'.[23]

Yet although Chaucer's first response to the story of Ceyx and Alcyone is thus both contingent and tangential, the story nevertheless seems to work its way into his mind, metamorphosing itself into his dream of the Black Knight's grief for his lost mistress, and hanging over his thoughts and feelings all next day. Again the story expands within the reader's mind, taking on its own life and fashioning itself into new shapes, realizing its effects obliquely and over time.

Finally, what of the *Canterbury Tales*? In the oral tale-telling of the pilgrims, the reading process seems to disappear entirely; and yet it could be said that this is also a means of bringing the writer into direct confrontation with his audience, providing direct access to their response. When we examine these responses, it becomes clear that the Canterbury pilgrims react to literary fiction in a manner fairly typical of the Great British Public: they want above all to be entertained, and are restive with the unrelieved solemnity of the *Monk's Tale* (they like their pathos simple, as in the *Prioress's Tale*). Their interest in a story is focused by their individual circumstances: the main point of the *Miller's Tale* in the eyes of the Reeve is that it is about a carpenter (because he is one); the Clerk's final ironic advice to wives to let their husbands 'weep and wail' strikes a chord with the unhappily-married Merchant; the Franklin is struck by the Squire's eloquence because it contrasts with the graceless behaviour of his own son. The spokesman for the pilgrims' reactions to the tales is most often Harry Bailly, whose literary responses are well described by Alan Gaylord: 'When Harry reacts to a story, he never treats it as a thing-in-itself; it serves rather to mirror his own likes and dislikes, or to point to something which is already known'.[24] Adapting Marianne Moore's observation that the poet gives us 'imaginary gardens with real toads in them',[25] Gaylord says of Harry that 'He expects to hear about real toads in real gardens; he is most pleased if it turns out the toads and the gardens belong to someone he knows, and if what is said about them confirms what he had always thought about gardening. To the

---

[23] *Arguing With the Past*, p. 2.
[24] Alan T. Gaylord, '*Sentence* and *Solaas* in Fragment VII of the *Canterbury Tales*: Harry Bailly as Horseback Editor', *PMLA* 82 (1967) 226–35, at p. 232.
[25] 'Poetry', in *Collected Poems* (London, 1951), p. 41.

extent that the stories remind him of familiar things he is willing to respond with familiar emotions'.[26]

This, then, is how Chaucer imagines his readers to be, how he imagines them responding to what he writes. One might suppose this to be no more than humorous condescension on his part, were it not that in the *Book of the Duchess* he has represented himself as just such a reader. And these are the readers whose authority over the text he is willing to acknowledge, with the magnanimity I mentioned earlier. When the time comes for Chaucer to tell his own tale, he modestly obliges with the rhyme of *Sir Thopas*, which he says is the only one he knows (708–9). After two hundred lines of bathetic tail-rhyme, he is stopped in his tracks by the Host's inability to endure any more, and is told in words of one syllable and four letters exactly what his 'drasty rymyng' is worth. He is then grudgingly allowed to tell a tale in *prose*, whose importance, as he stresses, lies in its 'sentence' rather than in its verbal felicities. The authority of the audience here becomes absolute; the author is not simply misinterpreted or under-appreciated but actually hooted off the stage. The best commentator on this passage is still G. K. Chesterton, who emphasizes that the joke here is of far larger scope than a satire on bad romances; it is a joke encompassing Chaucer's entire relation to his literary creation and his audience. 'Chaucer is mocking not merely bad poets but good poets; the best poet he knows; "the best in this kind are but shadows" '.[27] This last comment is of course a quotation of Theseus's remarks on the play produced for his wedding in *A Midsummer Night's Dream*, and Bottom and his mechanicals getting to work on the story of Piramus and Thisbe are probably the authentic heirs of Chaucer's pilgrims in their roles as literary critics. But the conclusion of Theseus's comment is relevant too: 'The best in this kind are but shadows; and the worst are no worse, if imagination mend them'. And Hippolyta answers: 'It must be your imagination then, and not theirs' (V.i.211–14). It is in the reader's imagination that the literary work finds the fullness of its meaning. For Chaucer, the literary process is not completed with the production of a literary work. It is not complete without the reader – that is, until it has been absorbed by a living consciousness into a pattern formed by experience and other books that will give it meaning – not a fixed meaning, but one that will shift and grow with new readings. The authority of the writer is realized in the effect of his work on the reader, but however great that authority is, it is incapable of controlling precisely what that effect will be. The creative autonomy – or plain cussedness – of the reader must be the despair of the writer, but it must also be, on the other hand, his abiding consolation.

---

[26] '*Sentence* and *Solaas*', p. 232.
[27] *Chaucer* (1932; repr. London, 1962), p. 21.

THEORIZING THE ROSE: COMMENTARY TRADITION IN THE *QUERELLE DE LA ROSE*

A. J. MINNIS

The *Roman de la Rose* has caused considerable controversy since Jean de Meun took up and completed the original work of Guillaume de Lorris sometime between *c*.1269 and 1278. During the period 1401–3 occurred the famous *querelle de la Rose*, in which Jean Gerson, august theologian and powerful chancellor of Paris university, and the proto-feminist Christine de Pizan, were ranged against three 'early humanists' (as they sometimes have been styled), the Col brothers, Pierre and Gontier, and Jean de Montreuil, Provost of Lisle. The very same battles have been fought over again during the past twenty-five years, Jean de Meun having found vigorous advocates in the persons of D.W. Robertson Jr. and John Fleming, who have followed their fifteenth-century counterparts in taking the line that the *Roman* functions as a powerful *remedium amoris*, the voice of the author being the voice of reason – and specifically, of Jean's character Raison.[1]

---

[1] D.W. Robertson, in his *A Preface to Chaucer: Studies in Medieval Perspectives* (Princeton, N.J., 1962), p. 364, laments that an 'irate woman' and a 'zealous reformer' were 'not to be silenced by reason', and regards their views as essentially anti-humanistic. Similarly, John Fleming, in *The Roman de la Rose: A Study in Allegory and Iconography* (Princeton, N.J., 1969), p. 47, declares that Christine de Pizan's 'part in the quarrel has been rather inflated, one suspects, by modern feminists and should probably not be taken too seriously'. Like Robertson, he believes that in the history of criticism of the *Roman* the rot set in with Jean Gerson's misunderstanding: 'He was the first modern critic of the *Rose*, the first person to whom it must patiently be explained that Jean de Meun was a "true catholic, the most profound theologian of his day, versed in every science which the human kind can grasp" ' (p. 29). The quotation is from Gontier Col: see *'La Querelle de la Rose': Letters and Documents*, trans. Joseph L. Baird and John R. Kane, North Carolina Studies in the Romance Languages and Literatures, No. 199 (N. Carolina, 1978), p. 57. The *Roman* is, on Fleming's reading, charged with 'considerable moral seriousness' (p. 237); Jean de Meun set about 'pillorying, mocking and condemning his "hero" [i.e. Amant], mercilessly and without sympathy, through thousands of lines of mordant verse' (p. 247). The opponents of the *Rose* have, however, been ably defended by J.L. Baird and J.R. Kane, 'La Querelle de la Rose: In Defense of the Opponents', *The French Review* 48 (1974) 298–307. Douglas Kelly, in his *Medieval Imagination, Rhetoric and the Poetry of Courtly Love* (Madison, Wisconsin, 1978), p. 262 n. 23, and P.-Y. Badel, *Le Roman de la Rose au XIVe siècle* (Genève, 1980), pp. 411–82, take a balanced view. 'There was a certain amount of bad rhetoric on both sides', suggests Kelly, 'and ignorance and misunderstanding of what both Guillaume de Lorris and Jean de Meun intended . . .'. The bibliography on Christine is vast, and is expanding rapidly under the influence of gender studies; important work having been done by, among others, Maureen Curnow, Sheila Delany, Nadia Margolis, Gianni Mombello and Charity Willard. Their interests and objectives are, however, different from those of this article; suffice it to say that I am in broad agreement with the views of Susan Schibanoff, 'Taking the Gold out of Egypt: The Art of Reading as a Woman', in *Gender and Reading*, ed. E. Flynn and P. Schweikehart (Baltimore, Maryland, 1986), pp. 83–106, and Beatrice Gottlieb, 'The Problem

The position of the attackers of the *Rose* has been supposed to mark 'a most decisive break with the traditions of medieval humanism': 'From this time forward humanists would find themselves frequently put on the defensive by the attacks of the righteous'.[2] This approach is, however, somewhat misleading, in that both Jean's friends and foes actually drew on one and the same corpus of literary theory, the product of late-medieval scholasticism, as found in the commentaries on classroom authorities. It is the function of this paper to explore that common ground, and hence to illuminate the meaning of the various appropriations and adaptations of conventional critical discourse which occurred in the *querelle*. The standard medieval criticism of Ovid is very much at the centre of this inquiry, since it is evident that those who loved the *Roman* and those who loathed it could at least agree on one thing – that Jean de Meun was a 'Medieval Ovid', for better or worse as it were. However, one of Jean's advocates, the eloquent Pierre Col, was not content to bracket his author with the ancient *praeceptor amoris*: he endeavoured to go one better by invoking the precedent of Biblical lovers, a daring – but certainly not unparalleled – move, which shall involve us in a brief foray into scriptural exegesis. But it seems right and proper that we should begin with a consideration of *persona* theory in the *querelle de la Rose*, since this matter has received special attention in both the old controversy and the new.

1. *In propria persona, in persona aliorum*: Authors and Characters

According to Robertson, Christine de Pizan fundamentally misunderstood the way in which Jean de Meun had deployed his *personae*:

> Her accusation against Raison refers to lines 4377ff., where the idea that it is better to deceive is attributed by Raison to lovers and certainly not advocated by Raison herself. La Veille, Jalousie, and Genius all speak in character; no one of them represents the views of the author.[3]

Of Gerson he says: 'it is easy to see how a man who assumes that the *Roman* is an autobiography and who attributes the views of all *personae* to the author would be horrified by the poem'.[4] Similarly, John Fleming regards the 'psychomachic architectonics' of the poem as 'commonplace', and finds it 'difficult to explain why so few critics have grasped them'. The underlying 'critical principle here enunciated' is identified as

> the very ancient one of literary decorum: the actions and speeches of fictional characters should consistently reflect their feigned natures. The obligation which this principle implies for the critic is that he must carefully distinguish between creature and creator, unless there is substantial reason to think that the two share a common point of view . . . Yet the prevailing critical abuse of Jean's poem observes no such amenities, however elementary. The inanities of a befuddled lover, the lewd guffaws of an aging prostitute, the ludicrous self-

of Feminism in the Fifteenth Century', in *Women of the Medieval World*, ed. J. Kirshner and S.F. Wemple (Oxford and New York, 1985), pp. 337–62.

2 Robertson, *Preface*, p. 364.
3 Robertson, *Preface*, p. 361.
4 Robertson, *Preface*, p. 363.

exculpation of an evil friar, the ravings of a jealous husband – all this, and
more, is passed off as the personal opinions of Jean de Meun. . . . Even Gerson
knew better, in theory, than to ascribe to a poet the postures of his purely
fictional creations. Pierre Col, who shared Gerson's theory but, unlike the
Chancellor, actually practised it, never forgot; and his reminder that the Lover
in the *Roman* talks like a lover, the Jaloux like a *jaloux*, and so forth, is one
with which all serious criticism of Jean's poem must begin, wherever it intends
to end.[5]

But how did this 'critical principle' develop, and in what forms did it come to
the Cols and Gersons of the late-medieval world?

Our point of departure is provided by the medieval distinction between three
styles of writing (the *characteres scripturae*), which goes back to the fourth-
century commentary by Servius on Virgil's *Bucolics*. The style of a work can be
called 'exegematic' when the author speaks in his own person; 'dramatic', when
he speaks in the persons of others; and 'mixed', when both these styles are used.[6]
This classification was applied to both secular and sacred writings. According to
Isidore of Seville (d. *c*.450), in Virgil's *Georgics* only the poet speaks, while in
tragedies and comedies, wherein the dramatic mode is employed, only the
characters speak. In the *Aeneid*, he continues, Virgil speaks sometimes in his
own person and sometimes through characters, this being a mixture of the
narrative mode and of the dramatic mode.[7] Writing over two centuries later in his
De arte metrica, the Venerable Bede declares that 'In the dramatic or active type
the characters (*personae*) are presented speaking without any intervention by the
poet, as is the case with tragedies and fables', and he proceeds to identify the
Song of Songs as having been written in this way.[8] In his Psalter commentary
(*c*.1144–69) Gerhoh of Reichersberg says that in the Pentateuch, Moses speaks
in his own person, in the Song of Songs, the introduced persons speak, while in
the Apocalypse and in the *Consolatio philosophiae* the author speaks both in his
own person and through others.[9] A twelfth-century Ovid commentator argues
that in the *Heroides* Ovid employs the dramatic method because there characters
are used, without 'an invocation, nor does he set out what his subject is to be. If
he were to do that he would be using the exegematic method'.[10]

Some scholars built on these commonplaces an interpretative method capable
of distinguishing between types of literary responsibility and of placing the
responsibility for the diverse statements made in a given work where it belonged, whether to a specific character or to the author speaking *in propria
persona*. Boethius commentary is a major focus for such theory – as one would
expect, given the way in which Boethius conveyed his philosophy on fate and
free will through two major characters, the lamenting and limited Boethius-
persona (who is not to be confused with the author himself) and Dame Philosophy, in whose mouth Boethius put his own most profound insights. Writing in

5   Fleming, *Allegory and Iconography*, p. 107.
6   Servius, *In Vergilii carmina commentarii*, ed. G. Thilo and H. Hagen (Leipzig, 1881), iii.1.
7   *Etymologiae*, viii.7.11, ed. W.M. Lindsay (Oxford, 1911).
8   Ed. H. Keil, *Grammatici Latini*, vii (Leipzig, 1880), p. 259.
9   Migne, *PL*, cxci.630–1.
10 *Accessus ad auctores, Bernard d'Utrecht, Conrad d'Hirsau*, ed. R.B.C. Huygens (Leiden,
    1970), p. 32. Cf. the discussion in A.J. Minnis, *Medieval Theory of Authorship: Scholastic
    Literary Attitudes in the Later Middle Ages*, 2nd edn. (Aldershot, 1988), pp. 22, 57–8.

the late thirteenth century, William of Aragon explained that in this work two *personae* are feigned ('duplex persona confingitur . . .'), namely, the learned and the learner, or the sufferer along with the physician.[11] This account enjoyed a wide dissemination in the Romance world, since part of William's prologue to his commentary – wherein it is to be found – was translated and incorporated in the prologue to Jean de Meun's French translation of Boethius, and in its turn Jean's prologue was taken over by those responsible for the 'revised mixed version' of the *Consolatio* to serve as the preface to what turned out to be the most popular of all medieval translations of this work.[12] Similarly, in his widely influential commentary on the *Consolatio* (a.1304), Nicholas Trevet distinguished between the *persona indigens*, the person in need of consolation, and the *persona afferens*, the person effecting that consolation. The first metre of the *Consolatio* is said to present the former, the sorrowing Boethius lamenting his misery in elegiac verses, whereas the first prose presents the latter, the figure of Dame Philosophy.[13] What is especially interesting about these accounts is the recognition of the fictionality of the characters and their distance from the author himself.

This emerges even more clearly in the efforts of scriptural exegetes to preserve the reputations of inspired authors in the face of certain unacceptable or dubious statements which appear in their writings. In his highly popular commentary on Ecclesiastes (written 1254–7), St Bonaventure had asked, if its putative author Solomon was a wicked man, can this work be said to have any authority?[14] Drawing on a passage in St Gregory's *Dialogues*,[15] Bonaventure explains that here sometimes Solomon speaks in his own person and sometimes in the persons of others. When he speaks in the person of the foolish man, he does not approve of this foolishness but rather abhors it; when he speaks as a wise man his words are to be to be taken as directly conducive to good behaviour. Solomon's own views are made clear by the *sententia* which is clearly stated at the end of his work; this epilogue, it would seem, provides us with a measure with which to judge the ways in which doctrine is being communicated throughout the book.

Vernacular writers drew on these methods of assigning, devolving – or indeed avoiding – responsibility. In the Latin commentary which (it would seem) John Gower wrote to accompany his Middle English *Confessio amantis* the distance between the passions of the narrator and the wisdom of the author is emphas-

---

[11] The Latin text of this prologue has been edited by R. Crespo, 'Il prologo alla traduzione della *Consolatio philosophiae* di Jean de Meun e il commento di Guglielmo d'Aragonia', *Romanitas et Christianitas: Studia I. H. Waszink oblata*, ed. W. den Boer *et al.* (Amsterdam and London, 1983), pp. 55–70. Cf. Jean de Meun's version, as ed. by V.L. Dedeck-Héry, 'Boethius's *De Consolatione* by Jean de Meun', *Mediaeval Studies* 14 (1952) 168–71.

[12] Cf. A.J. Minnis, 'Aspects of the Medieval French and English Traditions of the *De consolatione philosophiae*', in *Boethius: His Life, Thought and Influence*, ed. Margaret Gibson (Oxford, 1981), p. 314.

[13] From the complete but unfinalized edition of Trevet's commentary on the *De consolatione philosophiae* on which Professor E.T. Silk was still working at the time of his death. I am grateful to him for kindly providing me with a typescript of that edition.

[14] The relevant passage is translated in A.J. Minnis and A.B. Scott, *Medieval Literary Theory and Criticism c.1100–c.1375: The Commentary Tradition* (Oxford, 1988), pp. 231–2.

[15] *Dialogi*, iv.4, pr. Migne, *PL*, lxxvii.321–5.

ized. Gower is not speaking *in propria persona*, but rather is conveying the emotions of others, according to the key gloss:

> Hic quasi in persona aliorum, quos amor alligat, fingens se auctor esse Amantem, varias eorum passiones variis huius libri distinccionibus per singula scribere proponit.[16]

And at the end of the *Confessio* (just as at the end of Ecclesiastes) the author reasserts himself in his proper role, leaving behind all the limited *personae* through whom he had spoken during its course. Amans gives way to the author-moralist John Gower; *amor*, now revealed in all its ephemerality and relativity, is bettered – at least according to the Latin gloss – by *caritas*.[17]

In the *querelle de la Rose*, the supporters of Jean de Meun sought to defend him by arguing that certain controversial statements in the *Roman de la Rose* were made not by the writer himself but by *personae* of limited standing or indeed of reprehensible character. In his 1402 *Traité contre le Roman de la Rose*, Jean Gerson imagines someone making such a defence, which takes its precedent from sacred Scripture, one of the crucial texts being the book of Ecclesiastes. What evil is there, such an advocate might say, if Jean de Meun, a man of great perception, learning and fame, should have wished to compose a book that features characters (*personnaiges*) which speak according to their respective natures? After all, the prophet David, speaking in the person of a fool, said there is no God (Psalm 13:1 and Psalm 52:1), and wise Solomon composed the whole book of Ecclesiastes in such a manner. Why, then, cannot Jean de Meun be allowed to do likewise?

> Et quel mal est ce, dit l'ung des plus avisés, quel mal est ce, je vous pry, se cest home de tel sens, de tel estude et de tel renon a volu composer ung livre de personnaiges ouquel il fait par grant maistrise chascun parler selond son droit et sa proprieté? Ne dit pas le prophete en la persone d'ung fol que Dieu n'est pas? Et le sage Salemon ne fist il en especial tout son livre *Ecclesiastes* en ceste maniere, par quoy on le sauve de cent et cent erreurs qui la sont en escript?[18]

But, Gerson retorts, 'to a fool his own foolishness must be made manifest': the folly of the lover is not adequately revealed in the text. To say that the author does not himself speak but others who are there introduced is 'too slight a defence for so great a crime'. If someone were to call himself an enemy of the king of France and make war on him, this title would not save him from being punished as a traitor. If one were to write erroneous things against Christianity in the person of a heretic or Saracen, this would not excuse him. (Gerson proceeds to ask which is worse, for a Christian clerk to preach against the faith in the person of a Saracen, or for him to bring forth a real Saracen speaking or writing against the Faith? While the latter is not to be borne, the former is actually the worse, he answers, because the 'secret enemy' is more injurious

---

[16] *The English Works of John Gower*, ed. G.C. Macaulay, EETS ES 81 and 82 (1900–1), i.37.

[17] These few sentences do not do justice, of course, to the elaborate ending of the *Confessio amantis*. I investigate the matter in more detail in my forthcoming article, '*De Vulgari Auctoritate*: Chaucer, Gower and the Men of Great Authority'.

[18] *Le Débat sur le Roman de la Rose*, ed. Eric Hicks, Bibliothèque du XVe siècle, xliii (Paris, 1977), p. 64; cf. Baird and Kane, *Letters and Documents*, p. 74. Throughout this article I draw on the translations of Baird and Kane, occasionally making minor alterations.

than the open one). If someone defames others by means of the characters which he introduces in his book, he is legally held to be wicked and deserving of punishment. In sum, the author is responsible for what his characters say; he cannot hide behind his *personae*.

What, then, of the argument that, since holy Scripture presents Solomon and David as having been foolish lovers, Jean de Meun is perfectly justified in portraying Amant as such?[19] Gerson's retort is that the Bible uses these characters to reprove evil, 'in such a way that every man might perceive that condemnation of evil and that approbation of good, and (what is most important) that all those things could have been done without excessive frivolity'. Jean de Meun, by contrast, does not provide clear condemnation of immoral speeches in the relevant contexts:

> Mais j'entens bien ce que vous murmurés ensemble: vous doctes, comme par avant l'ung de vous allega, que Salemon et David ont ainssy fait. C'est ycy trop grant outraige pour excuser ung fol amoureulx, accuser Dieu et ses sains et les mener a la querelle; mais ne se puet faire: je voulroie bien que ce Fol Amoureulx n'eust usé de ces personnaiges fors ainssy que la sainte Escripture en use, c'est assavoir en reprouvant le mal, et tellement que chascun eust apperceu le reproche du mal et l'aprobacion du bien, et – qui est le principal – que tout se fist sans excés de legiereté. Mais nennin voir. Tout semble estre dit en sa persone; tout semble estre vray come Euvangille,[20] en especial aux nices folz amoureulx auxquelz il parle; et, de quoy je me dueil plus – tout enflamme a luxure, meismement quant il la samble reprouver: neis les bien chastes, s'ilz le daingnoient estudier, lire ou escouter, en vaurroient pis. [21]

To sum up these objections, Gerson clearly feels that in the *Roman* there is no clear distinction between *personae* and poet. To say that he does not fully understand the theory of *personae* would be simplistic and indeed inaccurate; his criticism of Jean de Meun is on quite different grounds, i.e. that 'immoral speeches – without clear, unambiguous disapproval in the context – are to be condemned, whoever says them' (to borrow the clear formulation by Baird and Kane).[22] This is, of course, what happens in, for example, Ecclesiastes, as interpreted by Bonaventure – a reading of that text with which Gerson is obviously in general agreement. Gerson goes beyond this type of argument, however, when he remarks that Jean seems to say everything *in propria persona* and, even when he seems to reproach lechery, actually is inciting his readers to it; hence the chaste could well be corrupted by the poem.

But Pierre Col, writing at the end of Summer 1402 in defence of the *Roman*, pressed home the argument that it is a fully 'dramatic' work (in the sense defined above) and hence the opinions of the characters must not be confused with those of the author. Ovid, in his *Ars amatoria*, may have spoken *in propria*

---

[19] This aspect of the *débat* is treated in more detail in the final section of this article.

[20] The Evangelists were regarded as the first-hand witnesses for the life of Christ, so presumably Gerson's point is that Jean de Meun, in similar fashion, stands by and is responsible for what he says in the *Rose*, rather than having *personae* express views with which he is not in agreement.

[21] Hicks, *Le Débat*, p. 74.

[22] Baird and Kane, 'In Defence of the Opponents', p. 302.

persona, 'sans parler per personnaiges',[23] but that was certainly not Jean's method. 'I say that Master Jean de Meun in his book introduced characters (*personnaiges*), and made each character speak according to what appertains to him, that is, the Jealous Man as a jealous man, the Old Woman as an old woman, and similarly with the others'. It is wrongheaded, he continues, to say that the writer thinks of women in the same way as the Jealous Man does. Jean merely reports (*recite*) what a jealous man always says about women in general, in order to demonstrate and correct the very great irrationality and disordered passion which exist in people like him.

This concept of objective reporting in contradistinction to personal affirmation had, of course, been used by Jean de Meun himself in the *apologia* to the *Roman*. There, however, it concerned the repetition of what Jean's authors had said (about women), not what his *personae* had said.[24] The logical distinction between *reportatio* and *assertio* had for long been part and parcel of the system whereby medieval writers reconciled their apparently discordant authorities: in his *Sic et non* prologue, Peter Abelard had warned that the views expressed in an author's citations of other men's books should not be attributed to the author himself.[25] This became a commonplace of scriptural exegesis. To take but one example among many, in his *Summa quaestionum ordinariarum* the Paris-trained theologian Henry of Ghent (*c.*1217–93) brings his discussion of the apparent fictions and falsehoods in Scripture to a close with the statement that 'whatever lies are found in Scripture, it does not proffer to us as being true by positively asserting (*asserendo*) their truth and commending them, but in reporting (*recitando*) them in the text solely for our instruction'.[26] Moreover, the great compilers of the late Middle Ages had declared that they were 'reporting' the opinions of the authors who were their sources rather than 'affirming' their own views.[27] Jean, and his defenders and attackers, appear to have followed such usage.

Worthy of special note is the fact that Pierre Col, on Jean's behalf, is disavowing authorial responsibility for statements made by the characters in the *Roman*, a use of the distinction which had been anticipated, around a decade earlier, by Geoffrey Chaucer's rejection of personal blame for what his Canterbury pilgrims had to say. I pray you, Chaucer's narrator asks the audience, not to regard as churlishness my plain speaking in telling the pilgrims' tales in their own words. For whoever repeats another man's tale must report ('reherce') his every word as accurately as he can (*Canterbury Tales*, Gen. Prol. I (A) 725–33).[28] Characters like the Miller and Reeve are certainly churls, and hence speak in a churlish manner – and herein lies Chaucer's defence of his inclusion of

---

23 Letter *Aprés ce que je oÿ parler*, ed. Hicks, pp. 105, 100; cf. Baird and Kane, *Letters and Documents*, pp. 108, 103–4.

24 See especially ll. 15216–24; ed. E. Langlois, SATF (Paris, 1914–24), iv.95.

25 The relevant passage is translated in Minnis and Scott, *Medieval Literary Theory and Criticism*, pp. 90–92.

26 Trans. Minnis and Scott, *Medieval Literary Theory and Criticism*, p. 266. Henry became a canon at Tournai (1267) and later archdeacon successively of Bruges (1276) and Tournai (1278). His complete works are now being edited under the direction of Dr. Raymond Macken.

27 Cf. Minnis, *Medieval Theory of Authorship*, pp. 191–203.

28 All Chaucer references are to *The Riverside Chaucer*, 3rd edn by L.D. Benson *et al.* (Oxford, 1988).

their tales. He is obliged to 'reherse / Hir tales alle, be they bettre or werse', but he himself is not saying anything 'of yvel entente' (I(A) 3172–4).

The distinction between reporting and asserting forms the basis of Col's challenge (in his letter of the end of the Summer of 1402), to Gerson's argument about the enemy of the King of France and the Saracen not being able to avoid blame by appealing to their roles (cf. p. 17 above). Powerful counter-examples are brought forward.[29] If Sallust recites the conspiracy of Catiline against the Republic of Rome, is he guilty for this? If Aristotle recites the opinions of the ancient philosophers which contain philosophical errors, does this make him an advocate of errors? If Holy Scripture recites the abominable sins of Sodom and Gomorrah, does it exhort one to commit such sins?[30] Vices have to be declared in order to be denounced, as is common practice among preachers. Read Jean de Meun's own justification, Col urges his opponents, for there and only there does he speak 'as author' ('la seulement parle il come aucteur et la come aucteur dit . . .'), as one who is personally responsible for what is said.[31] And what he says there – that nobody ought to despise a woman, that his intention was not to speak against the clergy, that his bawdy or foolish expressions are required by his subject-matter, that he writes under the correction of Holy Church – is unexceptionable.

But neither of those two formidable opponents of the *Rose*, Christine de Pizan and Jean Gerson, were impressed, and held to the view that 'truth and honour must be preserved in fictional characters'.[32] To the end, Gerson persisted in his belief that there was little distinction between Jean's characters and Jean himself. Genius, he declares, praises lechery, saying that it follows nature, 'and afterwards the author in his own person says the same thing even more disgust-

---

[29] Letter *Aprés ce que je oÿ parler*, ed. Hicks, pp. 101–2; cf. Baird and Kane, *Letters and Documents*, p. 105.

[30] There was a theological tradition of analysis of the apparent fictions and falsehoods in Scripture. For brief discussion and references see Minnis and Scott, *Medieval Literary Theory and Criticism*, pp. 209–11.

[31] Hicks, pp. 110–11; cf. Baird and Kane, *Letters and Documents*, p. 113.

[32] Gerson, sermon 'IVa Dominica Adventus: *Poenitemini*' (24th December 1402), ed. Hicks, p. 182; cf. Baird and Kane, *Letters and Documents*, p. 183. Christine de Pizan's most direct responses to the issue are as follows. The first occurs in her letter *Reverence, honneur avec recommandacion* to Jean de Montreuil, where she complains that 'Many people attempt to excuse' Jean de Meun 'by saying that it is the Jealous Man who speaks and that in truth Meun does no more than God himself did when He spoke through the mouth of Jeremiah!' (Hicks, p. 15; Baird and Kane, p. 50). Here the main point seems to be that, according to Jean's supporters, his strictures on women should be taken with the same seriousness as Jeremiah's social criticism; both discourses may be partial, but they stem from a higher source. Clearly, she is indignant that the *Rose* should be aggrandized by such a comparison with Scripture. Instead of exploring the technical distinction between *auctor* and *personae*, however, she concentrates on the poem's content, bringing out the 'glaring contradiction' in the characters' view of women (as interpreted by Jean's defenders), namely that men are ordered to flee what they should pursue and to pursue what they should flee. Christine's second, and fuller, response forms part of her later letter to Pierre Col, *Pour ce que entende-ment*. Jean de Meun is responsible for what his characters say: 'the will of the player manipulates such instruments to his own purpose'. Besides, he is so concerned to slander women that he has some of his characters attack them even when such sentiments are not appropriate to their natures (Hicks, p. 132; Baird and Kane, p. 130). Col's appeal to the Bible's 'reportage' of evils is summarily dismissed on the grounds that in Holy Scripture whenever such matters are recounted, they are condemned unequivocally (Hicks, pp. 133–4; Baird and Kane, p. 131), which is not done in the *Rose*.

ingly in the end of the work'.[33] This, one may add, is the exact opposite of what Solomon had done in Ecclesiastes – for at the end of that work he made his own moral viewpoint utterly clear, as Bonaventure had explained (cf. p. 16 above). The material which has been offered above makes it abundantly clear, I hope, that late-medieval theologians were thoroughly aware of the principle of literary decorum and well used to practising it in their scriptural exegesis.[34] Gerson was at least as adept in putting this principle into practice as Pierre Col was; the difference consisted simply in the fact that in Gerson's opinion the *Rose* could not be rescued by such means. This was 'too slight a defence for so great a crime'.[35]

The different positions are, then, fundamentally irreconcilable – and as well as 'bad rhetoric on both sides' there were plenty of good arguments on both sides.[36] It should be remembered that Geoffrey Chaucer, that great advocate of the principle that *personae* should be allowed to speak according to their different natures (the author being free of blame for what he reported of their speech), at several points in his *oeuvre* evinced a certain skepticism concerning

---

[33] Gerson, sermon '*Poenitemini V*: La Chasteté Conjugale', ed. Hicks, p. 184; cf. Baird and Kane, *Letters and Documents*, p. 168.

[34] This interpretative principle was bolstered by other exegetical ideas, including the notion that knowledge of the 'circumstances of the letter' was essential for the understanding of a given passage. See M.-D. Chenu, *Toward understanding St Thomas*, trans. A.-M. Landry and D. Hughes (Chicago, 1964), p. 144; P.C. Spicq, *Esquisse d'une histoire de l'exégèse latine au moyen âge*, Bibliothèque thomiste, xxvi (Paris, 1944), pp. 250–1. Then there was the distinction between words considered in themselves (*de vi vocis*) and words as they functioned within a passage (*de vi sermonis*), on which see A.J. Minnis, ' "Authorial Intention" and "Literal Sense" in the Exegetical Theories of Richard FitzRalph and John Wyclif', *Proceedings of the Royal Irish Academy*, vol. 75, sect.C, No. 1 (1975) 27–9.

[35] Gerson, *Traité*, ed. Hicks, p. 72; cf. Baird and Kane, *Letters and Documents*, p. 80. Cf. the argument in Baird and Kane's article, p. 302. It should be added that *persona* theory also features in the extensive Middle French commentary on the *Echecs amoureux* (both texts seem to date from the late fourteenth century), a poem which was heavily influenced by the *Rose*. The author, declares the commentator at the outset, followed the precedent of the ancient poets in that he wished to offer profit and delight (the commonplace Horatian tag: cf. p. 24 below). The commentator's own emphasis is on the profit, as is indicated by his version of a conventional apology for poetry: 'the principal intention (*entente*) of the author in question and the end (*fin*) of his book is to concentrate on virtue and good works and to flee from all evil and all foolish idleness'. With this end in view, the commentator is anxious to establish some distance between the author and the *personae* he deploys, including the *persona* of the amorous young man who plays the chess of love with his lady. 'We should know first of all', he declares, 'that the author of this poem . . . feigns (*faint*) and says many things that are not to be taken according to the letter (*a la lettre*), although they may be lifelike (*formablement*), and that there may be some truth secretly hidden beneath the letter and the fiction . . . And because of this he feigns and introduces several characters (*personnes*), each of whom speaks in his turn as is appropriate to his nature, in the manner of feigning used in *The Romance of the Rose*. And no doubt one can sometimes well feign and speak figuratively and in fable (*faindre . . . et parler par figure et fabuleusement*)'. Joan Morton Jones, '*The Chess of Love* [Old French Text with Translation and Commentary]', Diss. University of Nebraska, 1968, p. 31. A fuller discussion is included in my article 'Authors in Love: The Exegesis of Late-Medieval Love Poets', forthcoming in the memorial volume for Judson B. Allen, which is being edited by Charlotte Morse, Penelope Doob and Marjorie Woods. The use which modern defenders of the *Rose* have made of the *Echecs amoureux* commentary has been judiciously criticized by Douglas Kelly, *Medieval Imagination*, pp. 107–8.

[36] Cf. Douglas Kelly's comment as cited in n. 1 above.

the efficacy of such a defence. For example, the Nun's Priest brings together two versions of the reporter's defence – that on the subject of women he is merely repeating what his authors say, and he is merely repeating the words of his character Chaunticleer – in a context which makes the whole business seem rather ludicrous:

> Wommennes conseils been ful ofte colde;
> Wommannes counseil broghte us first to wo
> And made Adam fro Paradys to go,
> Ther as he was ful myrie and wel at ese.
> But for I noot to whom it myght displese,
> If I conseil of wommen wolde blame,
> Rede auctours, where they trete of swich mateere,
> And what they seyn of wommen ye may heere.
> Thise ben the cokkes wordes, and nat myne;
> I kan noon harm of no womman divyne.   VII, 3256–66

In particular, his attempt to put the blame for his own jolly misogyny onto the cock is blatantly – and amusingly – unfair, since Chaunticleer certainly did *not* utter the words for which he is here made responsible. The implication would seem to be that here the buck stops with the Nun's Priest. Then there is the infinitely more complex case of *The Manciple's Tale*, in which Chaucer, *inter alia*, revisits the 'very ancient principle of decorum' as he had formulated it in the General Prologue.[37] This tale features a reporter (albeit the reporter of an event – the adultery of Phoebus's wife – rather than of speech) who is severely punished by his impetuous master. The lot of a messenger is not a happy one; his claim of 'reporter status' will not always ensure his safety. Similarly, no author can be confident of devolving all his moral responsibility to his *personae*; he may be brought to book by a reader who feels that his 'crime' far exceeds the bounds of such a 'defence'. And who among us would give universal consent to the principle that a statement in a literary text, no matter how offensive or repugnant it may be, must be allowed its say if it is put in the mouth of a character who may not express the personal views of the author? The views of Christine and Gerson on this issue are certainly not as philistine or incomprehending as some modern defenders of the *Rose* would have us believe.

At the very least, it would seem that the medieval literary theory of *personae*, as disseminated in the commentary tradition, had far-reaching implications and resonances, which became abundantly clear when scholastic hermeneutic terminology and techniques were applied to controversial vernacular texts. We may now turn to the attempts of the disputants in the *querelle de la Rose* to comprehend and evaluate their controversial modern text with reference to controversial ancient ones, namely the minor works of Ovid, particularly the *Ars amatoria*.

---

[37] See especially the repetition of the *sententia* of 'the wise Plato' that 'the word moot nede accorde with the dede' (IX (H) 207–10); cf. General Prologue, I (A) 741–2.

2. Jean de Meun as Medieval Ovidian

Christine de Pizan and Jean Gerson saw Jean de Meun as a modern Ovid not least because he was duplicating Ovid's great fault, namely, he had written an 'art of love' which offended against public morality.[38] Reading books which stimulate lust is particularly dangerous, declares Gerson in a sermon (preached on 17 December 1402); men who own them should be required by their confessors to tear them up – books like Ovid's, or Matheolus, or parts of the *Roman de la Rose*.[39] In a later sermon (24 December 1402) he declares that, had he the only copy of the *Roman*, worth a thousand pounds, he would burn it rather than have it published in its present form.[40]

In similar vein, Christine considered if the *Roman* has any *utilité*. 'I do not know how . . . to consider this book useful in any way', she exclaims in a letter written in the summer of 1401 to Jean de Montreuil (author of a lost treatise in defence of Jean de Meun).

> Ainsi, selon ma petite capacité et foible jugement, sans plus estre prolixe en lengage, non obstant que asséz plus pourroit estre dit et mieulx, ne sçay considerer aucune utilité ou dit traictié . . .[41]

Apparently she is using the term in the technical sense which the Latin form *utilitas* bears in the *accessus ad auctores*, as designating the didactic effect and moral worth which one requires in an authoritative work of literature.

More specifically, *utilitas* was one of the headings characteristic of the 'type C' academic prologue (as designated by the late R.W. Hunt), a prologue which had its origin in late-antique Greek commentaries on Aristotle's works.[42] Hence the medieval version of this paradigm, as one would expect, emphasized the philosophical credentials of a literary text, regularly identifying the 'part of philosophy' to which it pertained as ethics and describing its usefulness in

---

[38] Blanche H. Dow speaks of Christine's 'intellectual as well as temperamental' unanimity with Gerson; of 'a complete communion of ideas between them': *The Varying Attitude toward Women in French Literature of the Fifteenth Century: The Opening Years* (New York, 1936), p. 142. However, the position of D. Catherine Brown seems to be more accurate; she indicates the differences between the two opponents of the *Rose*, emphasizing that 'Gerson's attack . . . is much more that of the moralist than the feminist': *Pastor and Laity in the Theology of Jean Gerson* (Cambridge, 1987), pp. 224–5. My method in the following section, however, inevitably emphasizes their similarities – for they certainly shared a distaste for Ovid as love poet and for any defence of the *Rose* which was based on traditional Ovid criticism. But it should be noted that Christine's charge that Ovid was a defamer of women was far more specific than Gerson's concern about his alleged incitement to sexual misconduct.

[39] Ed. Hicks, *Débat*, p. 179; cf. Baird and Kane, *Letters and Documents*, p. 158.

[40] Sermon 'IVa Dominica Adventus: *Poenitemini*', ed. Hicks, *Débat*, p. 182; cf. Baird and Kane, *Letters and Documents*, p. 164. Cf. Gerson's statement in his letter *Responsio ad scripta cuiusdam* (to Pierre Col, winter 1402–1403), ed. Hicks, *Débat*, p. 172; cf. Baird and Kane, *Letters and Documents*, p. 151.

[41] Letter *Reverence, honneur avec recommandacion*, ed. Hicks, *Débat*, p. 20; cf. Baird and Kane, *Letters and Documents*, p. 54. Cf. the earlier formulation, 'To what purpose or to what profit (*a quel utilité ne a quoy prouffite*) is it that the hearers of this book have their ears assailed by so much sinfulness?': Hicks, p. 15; Baird and Kane, p. 49.

[42] See the seminal articles by R.W. Hunt, 'The Introductions to the *Artes* in the Twelfth Century', *Studia medievalia in honorem R.M. Martin, O.P.* (Bruges, 1948), pp. 85–112, and E.A. Quain, 'The Medieval *Accessus ad auctores*', *Traditio* 3 (1945) 228–42.

behavioural and pedagogic terms (the emphasis often being placed on its claim to moral edification). For example, Arnulf of Orléans, commenting on Lucan, declared that the *Pharsalia* is very useful in that it reveals the horrors of civil wars, thereby warning men not to engage in them.[43] The *utilitas* of the Roman satirists was usually located in their harsh reprehension of vice and recommendation of virtue: the censures by Juvenal and Persius of 'poets writing to no purpose' (*poetas inutiliter scribentes*) won much approval.[44] Other commentators picked up Horace's dictum that poets aim to profit or delight (*aut prodesse volunt aut delectare poetae*; *Ars poetica* 333).[45] It could be exploited in praising those poets who managed to combine both functions, as in this *accessus* to the fables of Avianus:

> intentio eius est delectare nos in fabulis et prodesse in correctione morum, utilitas [eius] est delectatio poematis et correctio morum. Ethicae subponitur, quia tractat de correctione morum.[46]

Alternatively, poems could be categorized in terms of whether they offered profit, or delight, or both, as in the 'Bernard Silvestris' commentary on Virgil, where Horace is cited in support of the view that 'Some poets write with a useful purpose in view, like the satirists, while others, such as the writers of comedies, write to give pleasure, and yet others, for example the historians, write to a useful end and to give pleasure'.[47] Occasionally in *accessus ad satiricos* the Roman satirists are aggrandized at the expense of those who supposedly wrote to give pleasure only – and sometimes Ovid appears in that group. 'It should be known', declares a fifteenth-century *accessus* to Juvenal, 'that certain poets direct themselves towards usefulness alone, like Horace and this Juvenal; others to delight alone, like Ovid'.[48] Could Christine de Pizan have been influenced by such a comment? Certainly she seems to have in mind not only Horace's dictum but also its importance as a basis for categorizing different kinds of poet:

> car oeuvre sans utilité et hors bien commun ou propre – poson que elle soit delictable, de grant labour et coust – ne fait a louer.[49]

This reinforces her earlier point that Jean should have been able to write a far better book, more profitable and of higher sentiment ('plus prouffitable et de sentement plus hault').

On rare occasions a scholiast will indicate the pleasure-giving function of Ovid's poetry, without any apparent wish to denigrate it thereby, as in an

---

[43] See Minnis and Scott, *Medieval Literary Theory and Criticism*, p. 155.

[44] From an *accessus* printed in P.O. Kristeller *et al.*, *Catalogus translationum et commentariorum: Medieval and Renaissance Latin Translations and Commentaries* (Washington, 1960–), i.192–3, 195, 198; iii.225–7.

[45] For examples see Huygens, *Accessus ad auctores, etc*, pp. 26, 45, 63, 84, 86, etc.

[46] Huygens, *Accessus ad auctores, etc*, p. 22. The series of *accessus* here edited is found in full in Munich, Clm 19475 (twelfth century; Tegernsee), and in part in two other manuscripts, both dating from the end of the twelfth or the beginning of the thirteenth century.

[47] Minnis and Scott, *Medieval Literary Theory and Criticism*, p. 152.

[48] Kristeller, *Catalogus*, i.192; cf. the citation and relevant discussion in A.J. Minnis, ' "Moral Gower" and Medieval Literary Theory', in *Gower's 'Confessio amantis': Responses and Reassessments*, ed. A.J. Minnis (Cambridge, 1983), pp. 55–56.

[49] Hicks, *Débat*, p. 21; cf. Baird and Kane, *Letters and Documents*, p. 55.

accessus to the *Amores* which Ralph Hexter has edited from Munich, Bayeri-sche Staatsbibliothek Clm 631: 'Vtilitas est delectio, uel apud Corinnam sui ipsius commendatio'.[50] But, as Hexter says, normally medieval Ovid critics 'paid little attention to' literary delight, concentrating instead on didactic func-tion.[51] This did not necessarily entail a specifically ethical reading,[52] but very frequently that was precisely what was emphasized, particularly in the intro-ductions to Ovid's *Heroides*. Here one of the most common formulations of literary *utilitas* was that this poetry showed its audience both what to do and what to avoid. Having seen the advantages of lawful love and the disasters and disadvantages which result from unlawful and foolish love, the readers of the *Heroides* 'may reject and shun foolish love and adhere to lawful love'.

> Finalis causa talis est, ut visa utilitate quae ex legitimo procedit et infortuniis quae ex stulto et illicito solent proseque, hunc utrumque fugiamus et soli casto adhereamus.[53]

The same ideas are reiterated in *accessus* after *accessus*, to such an extent that we may take this as the standard medieval view of the *Heroides*:

> Utilitas vel finalis causa secundum intentiones diversificantur, vel illicitorum vel stultorum amorum cognitio vel quomodo aliquae per epistolas sollicitentur vel quomodo per effectus ipsius castitatis commodum consequamur. Vel finalis causa est ut per commendationem caste amantium ad castos amores non invitet vel ut visa utilitate quae ex legitimo amore procedit visisque infortuniis vel incommoditatibus quae ex illicito et stulto amore proveniunt, et stultum et illicitum repellamus et fugiamus et legitimo adhereamus.[54]

Christine anticipates Jean de Montreuil offering a similar defence of the *Roman*: 'I know well that you will excuse it by replying to me that therein he enjoins man to do the good but to eschew the evil'. But this justification is unaccept-able, she declares: 'There is no point in reminding human nature, which is naturally inclined to evil, that it limps on one foot, in the hope that it will then walk straighter'.

> Mais je sçay bien que sur ce en l'excusant vous me respondréz que le bien y est ennorté pour le faire et le mal pour l'eschiver. Si vous puis souldre par meilleur

---

50 Ralph J. Hexter, *Ovid and Medieval Schooling. Studies in Medieval School Commentaries on Ovid's 'Ars Amatoria', 'Epistulae ex Ponto', and 'Epistulae Heroidum'*, Münchener Beiträge zur Mediävistik und Renaissance-Forschung, 38 (München, 1986), pp. 16 n.4, 103, 224. This particular item dates from the fourteenth century. Cf. the first *accessus* to the *Amores* edited by Huygens, *Accessus ad auctores, etc*, p. 36: 'Intentio est delectare'.
51 Hexter, *Ovid and Medieval Schooling*, p. 212.
52 Hexter, *Ovid and Medieval Schooling*, pp. 16–17, 25, 156–8, 213.
53 Huygens, *Accessus ad auctores, etc*, p. 30; trans. Minnis and Scott, *Medieval Literary Theory and Criticism*, p. 21. In these early *accessus* the term *finalis causa* is either used as a synonym for *utilitas* or as a term which helps to elaborate some aspect thereof. In the later 'Aristotelian Prologue', which came into vogue in the thirteenth century, *finalis causa* referred to the ultimate end or objective in writing; that is to say, it came to cover material hitherto included under discussions of *intentio* and/or *utilitas*. See Hexter, *Ovid and Medieval Schooling*, pp. 46–7, 103, 111, 147, and Minnis, *Medieval Theory of Authorship*, p. 29; cf. Huygens, *Access-us ad auctores, etc*, pp. 28, 30, 32, 33, 37.
54 Huygens, *Accessus ad auctores, etc*, p. 32; trans. Minnis and Scott, *Medieval Literary Theory and Criticism*, p. 23.

raison que nature humaine, qui de soy est encline a mal, n'a nul besoing que on lui ramentoive le pié dont elle cloche pour plus droit aler . . .[55]

Why, Christine continues, should the good in this book be praised (for she is prepared to admit that it contains some good things), when one can find far more virtuous things, and more profitable to the decorous and moral life, in the works of certain philosophers and teachers of the Christian faith like Aristotle, Seneca, St Paul, and St Augustine? The fact that Christine offers this argument immediately after her protestation that the *Roman* lacks *utilité* strengthens the suggestion that throughout this entire excursus she had stock medieval Ovid criticism in mind, even though Ovid himself is not named here.

The connection between the *praeceptor amoris* and Master Jean de Meun is, however, made quite explicit in Jean Gerson's reaction to these same critical ideas. In his 1402 treatise against the *Roman*, Gerson imagines a supporter of de Meun saying that, while there is some evil in the book it contains much more that is good, and so 'praingne chascun le bien et laisse le mal!' ('Let every man receive the good and reject the evil').[56] Gerson retorts, are the evil things in the book thereby deleted? Indeed not – a hook does not injure the fish less if it is covered in bait; a sword dipped in honey does not cut less deeply. Indeed, the good things contained in the book actually make it more dangerous. One should recall how Mohammed, in order to attract Christians more readily to his own law and to cover his own outrages, mixed in some Christian truths with his own impure errors. St Paul (I Corinthians 15:33), Seneca and experience all teach that evil speaking and writings corrupt good morals.

This argument naturally leads Gerson to consider the salutary example of Ovid's exile.[57] The *Tristia* is cited as proof that he was exiled on account of his wretched *Ars amatoria*; even his refutation of its false teaching, the *Remedium amoris*, could not save the poet from this fate. This is standard *accessus* fare. In the introduction to the *Tristia* edited by Huygens, several opinions are given concerning the reason for Ovid's exile, one of which is that 'he had written a book, *On the Art of Love*, in which he had taught young men how to deceive and attract married women. This gave offence to the Romans, and it was for this reason that he is alleged to have been sent into exile'.[58] Similarly, in the extensive *vita Ovidii* found at the head of Giovanni del Virgilio's commentary on the *Metamorphoses* (c.1322–3), the composition of the *Ars amatoria* is described as having incurred Octavian's wrath, 'and according to some, this is why [Ovid] was exiled from Rome, because he had taught unchaste [love] . . .'.[59] The *Remedium amoris* was commonly regarded as an attempt by Ovid to make up for this great mistake. 'Afterwards he regretted what he had done', states the *accessus* to the *Remedium amoris* edited by Huygens, 'and, being anxious to be reconciled with those he had offended, he saw that the best way

---

[55] Hicks, *Débat*, p. 22; cf. Baird and Kane, *Letters and Documents*, p. 55.
[56] Hicks, *Débat*, p. 65; cf. Baird and Kane, *Letters and Documents*, p. 75.
[57] Hicks, *Débat*, p. 65; cf. Baird and Kane, *Letters and Documents*, p. 75.
[58] Huygens, *Accessus ad auctores, etc*, p. 36; trans. Minnis and Scott, *Medieval Literary Theory and Criticism*, p. 27. See further the extensive materials from Ovid commentary cited by Hexter, *Ovid and Medieval Schooling*, pp. 87–97, 136, 211, 213.
[59] Trans. Minnis and Scott, *Medieval Literary Theory and Criticism*, p. 362.

of achieving this was to discover the antidote for the love which he had proffered to them'.[60] According to Giovanni del Virgilio, the *Remedium* was one of a series of books which he wrote in exile. The *Fasti* having failed to mollify Caesar, 'Ovid wrote his fifth book, *Ovid on the Remedy for Love*, so that he should remove the reason for his having been sent into exile. But because he saw that this was of no avail, he wrote his sixth book, *Ovid's Sorrows . . .*'.[61] Gerson was of the opinion that Octavian was absolutely right – and that his example could teach present-day rulers a thing or two. How amazing it is, he declares, that a pagan and infidel judge (obviously a reference to Octavian) should condemn a book which incites to foolish love, while among Christians such a work is supported, praised and defended![62]

Despite such outrage, the 'take the good and leave the evil' defence of literature survived, and appeared in a variety of forms and in many different contexts. In the preface to his English 'Moral Ovid' (1480), William Caxton quotes Romans 15:4 ('All that is written is written for our doctrine'), and explains that the good is written to the end that example should be taken of those who do well, and the evil to the end that we should keep ourselves and abstain from evil.[63] Caxton also applied this argument to a famous collection of prose tales, Malory's *Morte Darthur*, which he printed in 1485: 'Doo after the good and leve the evyl . . . al is wryton for our doctrine . . .'.[64] The problem about this defence is, of course, that it can be used to justify practically anything – any genre, form or style; any text whatever, whether it be edifying, innocuous or offensive.[65] Christine and Gerson saw the inherent weakness in its argument with clarity and total conviction. 'Good people', pleads the latter in his sermon of 24th December 1402, 'take these books [i.e. Jean, Ovid, Matheolus] away from your daughters and children! For they will take the evil and leave the good' ('Car ilz prandront le mal et laisseront le bien').[66]

If Jean de Meun's resemblance to Ovid could cut both ways, so also could the notion that he had surpassed Ovid. For the poem's opponents, the fact that it was more comprehensive and thoroughgoing than the *Ars amatoria* made it all the more dangerous. 'It is clear', declares Gerson in his *Traité contre le Roman*, 'that this work is worse than that of Ovid', because the *Roman* contains not only Ovid's *Ars amatoria* but also other books 'which are not any the less dishonest or dangerous', books 'which are there translated, brought together, and drawn in by force and to no purpose'. Gerson proceeds to argue that Jean de Meun had less scruples than his Roman predecessor. Ovid clearly stated in the

---

60 Huygens, *Accessus ad auctores, etc*, p. 34; trans. Minnis and Scott, *Medieval Literary Theory and Criticism*, p. 25.
61 Minnis and Scott, *Medieval Literary Theory and Criticism*, p. 363.
62 Hicks, *Débat*, pp. 75–7; cf. Baird and Kane, *Letters and Documents*, pp. 82–4.
63 *The Metamorphoses, translated by William Caxton, 1480* (New York, 1968), i, unfol. More-over, Romans 15:4 is echoed at the very beginning of the Middle French moralization of the *Metamorphoses*, the *Ovide moralisé*, a work which Christine certainly knew (cf. n.99 below). See Minnis, *Medieval Theory of Authorship*, pp. 205–6.
64 *Malory: Works*, ed. E. Vinaver, 2nd edn. (Oxford, 1971), p. xv. Cf. the similar use of Romans 15:4 in the prologue to Caxton's second edition of *The Game and Playe of the Chesse*, ed. W.J.B. Crotch, *The Prologues and Epilogues of William Caxton*, EETS OS 176 (1928), pp. 10–11.
65 Cf. the discussion in Minnis, *Medieval theory of Authorship*, pp. 204–8.
66 Hicks, *Débat*, p. 182; cf. Baird and Kane, *Letters and Documents*, p. 163.

Ars that he is not writing about good matrons or of ladies joined in marriage, nor of those who could not be loved lawfully (cf. *Ars amatoria* 1,31–4; 2,599–600). But the *Roman* is no respector of persons: 'it mocks all, blames all, despises all without any exception'.[67]

But for the poem's supporters, the fact that Jean had surpassed Ovid made his poem all the more praiseworthy, as may be seen from Pierre Col's ingenious amplification of a common defence of Ovid and its application to the *Roman* (written in the summer of 1402).[68] By describing the way in which the Rose's castle was captured, he claimed, Jean de Meun was actually aiding its defenders. Because they then knew how their fortress could fall, in the future they would block the gap or place better guards there and thus lessen the chances of the assailants. Moreover, Jean made this information widely available by writing in 'the common language of men and women, young and old, that is, in French ('en franssois')'. By contrast, the 'fin' of the *Ars amatoria* was exclusively to teach men how to assault the castle – being in Latin this work was not available to women. Ovid, then, served only the assailants, whereas Jean de Meun has taken the side of the defenders in preparing them for the stratagems which they will face.[69]

Here *fin* is used in the technical sense carried by *finis* or *finalis causa* in the *accessus*.[70] Moreover, in the introduction to the *Ars amatoria* printed by Huygens – described by Hexter as the 'canonical' introduction to that work – Ovid's aim for the first two books only is expressed, as if the entire work were addressed to men only, and its final cause is analysed simply in terms of Ovid's male addresses.[71]

> Intentio sua est in hoc opere iuvenes ad amorem instruere, quo modo debeant se in amore habere circa ipsas puellas, materia sua est ipsi iuvenes et puellae et ipsa precepta amoris, quae ipse iuvenibus intendit dare. . . . Finalis causa est ut perlecto libro in mandatis suis, quid tenendum sit in amore ipsius iuvenibus enucleatum sit.[72]

Could Pierre Col have been influenced by a comment such as this, wherein the contents of the *Ars amatoria* are misrepresented? By contrast the *accessus* in Copenhagen, Kongelige Bibliotek Gl. Kgl. S. 2015 4° (late twelfth century?), maybe the work of the scholar Fulco who was criticized so roundly by Arnulf of Orléans,[73] declares with far greater textual justification that Ovid sought to teach

---

[67] Hicks, *Débat*, pp. 76–7; cf. Baird and Kane, *Letters and Documents*, pp. 83–4.

[68] Hicks, *Débat*, pp. 104–5; cf. Baird and Kane, *Letters and Documents*, p. 108.

[69] This, of course, was the standard view of Ovid's *Remedium amoris*, i.e. that it reveals the stratagems of love, thereby forewarning and forearming people against them. See for example the *accessus* edited by Huygens, *Accessus ad auctores, etc*, p. 34, and translated in Minnis and Scott, *Medieval Literary Theory and Criticism*, p. 25. Though Col does not mention the later Ovid poem here, his assumption seems to be that the *Rose* is a bigger and better *remedium amoris* than the one provided by Jean's Roman predecessor. Cf. Col's subsequent argument, as described on pp. 29–30 below.

[70] For uses of *finis* in twelfth-century *accessus* and also in later commentaries, see Minnis, *Medieval Theory of Authorship*, pp. 20, 29, 31, 32, 41, 52, 92, 93, 120, 126–7, 129–30, 132, 147–8, 174, 179, 217, 240n.

[71] Hexter, *Ovid and Medieval Schooling*, pp. 46–7.

[72] Huygens, *Accessus ad auctores, etc*, p. 33.

[73] For brief discussion and references see Hexter, *Ovid and Medieval Schooling*, p. 43.

both young men and women in the art of love, a view reiterated in his account of the work's *materia*:

> Hic itaque Ouidius intendit iuuenes et puellas in amorem instruere, de amore agit. Amor enim principalis materia, circa quam eius principaliter uersatur intentio, et hac de causa scribit. Vel materia eius sunt iuuenes et puelle, quos uult docere et instruere in arte amandi.[74]

And in the *accessus* to the *Remedium amoris* which has been edited by Huygens,[75] it is noted that Ovid had not only taught young men how to acquire and keep mistresses but also given girls the corresponding instruction. Clearly, Col does not reflect this tradition of glossing. His remark that Ovid's work was inaccessible to women because they could not read Latin (a quite understandable development of the view that the poem's intended audience was exclusively male) is a total anachronism, of course, which reflects conditions in the France of his own day rather than those appertaining in Ovid's Rome, wherein the *Ars amatoria* would have been just as available to high-born people of whatever sex as was Jean de Meun's vernacular poem in its late-medieval milieu.

At this point in his letter Pierre changes tack, and argues that Ovid was unfairly maligned;[76] obviously he realizes that if this case is made convincingly he will be in a good position to defend the ancient poet's modern counterpart. To this end he accuses the Roman husbands who objected to the *Ars*, thereby causing Ovid's exile, as being excessively and unreasonably jealous. Little has changed, he continues, for nowadays it is said that the wife of the least jealous Italian husband is more strictly watched than the wife of the most jealous French one. The upshot of all this is that the national characteristics of the French equip them to take the *Roman* in the spirit in which it was meant, in contrast with the Romans, who were congenitally disposed to react violently against the *Ars amatoria*. Not that the exile of the poet did any lasting damage to the poem's posterity, adds Pierre, for it endures, will endure and has endured in all Christendom. Besides, Ovid recanted by writing the *Remedium amoris*. Viewed in the light of these facts – that the controversial book itself did not suffer (they would have served their interests better by burning it), and that the poet repented – the exiling of Ovid is seen to be unjustifiable by reason, and must have been motivated by enormously cruel jealousy.

What, then, of the argument that Jean drew on works other than the *Ars amatoria*? This made the work even more effective, Pierre declares, in forewarning the defenders of the castle.[77] The more varied the forms of attack that he describes the better he teaches the defenders to guard the castle: and it was for this purpose ('fin') that he wrote it. To amplify Pierre's point through the scholastic critical idiom which he is using, the *finis* of the *Roman* excels that of the *Ars amatoria*. He bolsters his argument by citing the case of a friend who borrowed his copy of the *Roman*: largely due to his reading of the poem, this man managed to disentangle himself from foolish love. The obvious implication is that the *Roman* is a very effective *remedium amoris*. To be more precise, Col

---

[74] Ed. Hexter, *Ovid and Medieval Schooling*, p. 219.
[75] Huygens, *Accessus ad auctores, etc*, p. 34.
[76] Hicks, *Débat*, p. 105; cf. Baird and Kane, *Letters and Documents*, pp. 108–9.
[77] Hicks, *Débat*, pp. 105–6; cf. Baird and Kane, *Letters and Documents*, p. 109.

is claiming that the *Roman* does something which generations of *accessus* to the *Remedium amoris* had claimed for that book of Ovid's. It would seem, then, that some of the stock justifications of Ovid's poetry have been appropriated in the defence of the *Rose*.

But Christine de Pizan was not convinced. Pierre Col's claim that Jean was on the side of the defenders of the castle was, in her view, 'mervilleuse' (incredible). Master Jean, she retorted in a letter dated 2 October 1402, does nothing at all to help the defenders in closing up the gaps, for he does not speak to them at all and is not of their counsel; rather, he aids and abets the attackers in every form of assault.[78] If you were to suggest that the poet is simply recounting how the castle fell rather than recommending it, she warns Pierre Col, she would reply that a man who described an evil way of making counterfeit money would be teaching that method quite sufficiently. By introducing Ovid's *Ars amatoria*, she continues, Pierre has been caught in his own trap; it would have been better for his case if he had not mentioned it. The only way he could have cited it to good effect would have been to say that the *Ars*, wherein Ovid spoke of nothing but chastity, is the foundation and principle of the *Roman*, which is a mirror and exemplar of the good and chaste life – a proposition which is ridiculous. Christine's basic premiss here is that a bad work cannot be the foundation of a good one. Furthermore, she continues, when Pierre says that de Meun included in his poem the work of many authors other than Ovid, by his own reasoning it is proved that the poet is speaking only to the attackers, just like Ovid, from whom he borrowed. Here her point seems to be that, by supporting Ovid's *Ars* with other similar writings, Jean is quite clearly supporting the attackers rather than the defenders; a proliferation of evil material does not make for a good *fin*. But Pierre has said that the more diverse the methods of attack which are revealed to the guards the better they are taught the art of defence. This is tantamount to saying that a man who attacks you and tries to kill you is merely showing you how to defend yourself!

Christine does not question Col's assumption that the *Ars amatoria* was written exclusively for a male audience. Similarly, in her earlier *Epistre au dieu d'amours* (1399) she had declared roundly that Ovid, like many other men who held a grudge against women, set out to slander them.[79] Women do not chase after men: it is men who ardently pursue women, no matter how much privation and suffering their passion may entail. In order to show such men the means of tricking women, she continues, Ovid wrote the *Ars amatoria*. Far from teaching the code and traditions of noble love, he does the opposite, for this is rather a book of the art of sheer deceit and dissimulation.

This is very much of a piece with her 1402 letter to Pierre Col, to which we may now return.[80] Pierre gives further proof of having fallen into his own trap, Christine says, when he argues that Ovid was banished due to jealousy rather than reason. To refer to the poet's exile on account of the *Ars amatoria* is to make a dangerous admission; the Romans, who at that time governed their deeds with excellent judgement, had everything to fear from the dissemination of such a work. They wisely perceived 'the perverse and poisonous doctrine prepared in

[78] Hicks, *Débat*, pp. 136–7; cf. Baird and Kane, *Letters and Documents*, p. 134.
[79] Trans. Baird and Kane, *Letters and Documents*, p. 36.
[80] Hicks, *Débat*, pp. 137–9; cf. Baird and Kane, *Letters and Documents*, pp. 134–6.

order to sow in the hearts of the young the desire for dissoluteness and idleness, as well as the traps readied to deceive, capture, suborn, and undermine the virginity and chastity of their daughters and wives'. One may recall the somewhat sensationalist comment found in an *accessus* to the *Amores*, to the effect that when Ovid wrote the *Ars amatoria* he had 'made adultresses of almost all the married women and maidens', which, not unnaturally, 'made the Romans hostile towards him'.[81] Christine is prepared to give the ancients more credit for having anticipated the danger in advance – and, indeed, for the relative leniency (or indulgence) of the punishment they meeted out to the poet. The fact that they were acting rationally is emphasized by their attempt to suppress the book (there is no doubt that they burned it where they could find it, Christine says). But the root of a bad plant always survives. The *Ars amatoria* is mistitled, she concludes this phase of her attack, for it contains nothing of real love. 'It could well be called the art of the false and malicious business of deceiving women'. Thus Christine responded to Pierre Col's attempt to assign a good *fin* to Jean de Meun's poetry with the help of standard criticism of Ovid.

3. Beyond Ovid: The Precedent of Biblical Lovers

Finally, we may consider what was probably the most daring defence of the *Rose* to figure in the *querelle*. In the letter which he wrote at the end of the summer of 1402, Pierre Col went beyond all analogies with Ovid to appeal to the precedent of Biblical lovers.[82] In his *Traité* Gerson had attacked the *Roman* on the grounds that 'he who made it was a foolish lover'. Why then, Col retorts, does not Lady Eloquence – a personification in Gerson's work – first draw such conclusions against Solomon, David, and other foolish lovers, who lived long before Jean de Meun, 'whose books are made a part of holy Scripture and their words a part of the holy mystery of the Mass'. It was 'a foolish lover' (i.e. David) who 'caused Uriah the good knight to be killed by treachery in order to commit adultery with his wife'. It was 'a foolish lover' (i.e. Solomon) 'who caused the temples with the idols to be built for the love of strange women'.

Col proceeds to extol the advantages of knowing one's enemy by personal experience. Saints Peter and Paul were more firm in the faith after they had sinned, he declares; similarly, Jean de Meun, because he had been a foolish lover, was very firm in reason, for the more he knew by his own experience the folly which is in foolish love the more he was able to despise it and praise reason. When he wrote the *Roman* he was no longer a foolish lover, and had repented of having been one: 'quant il fist ce livre de la *Rose* il n'estoit plus fol amoureux, ains s'en repantoit de l'avoit esté.[83] This is manifest by the fact that

---

[81] Huygens, *Accessus ad auctores, etc*, p. 37; trans. Minnis and Scott, *Medieval Literary Theory and Criticism*, p. 28.

[82] Hicks, *Débat*, p. 94; cf. Baird and Kane, *Letters and Documents*, pp. 97–8.

[83] Col supports this argument by citing Jean de Meun's own *Testament*, in which, Col declares, Jean admits that in his youth he made 'many works through vanity', these being 'various ballades, rondeaux and virelais that we do not have in writing' – which are not to be confused with that later, mature work, the *Rose*. Hicks, *Débat*, p. 95; cf. Baird and Kane, *Letters and Documents*, p. 98. The scope of this paper is of course limited to the reception of the *Rose* in the *querelle*, but it may be suggested that Jean de Meun, in his *Testament* and indeed within

he speaks so well of reason, for a foolish lover is unable to do this. The voice of Reason, it would seem, is in large measure the voice of Jean de Meun – a point of view which has recently been echoed by such critics as Robertson and Fleming.[84]

This ingenious appeal to the Bible echoes a long-running controversy in scriptural exegesis, over how the sins of major scriptural *auctores* could be reconciled with their undeniable authority. Theologians had for generations attempted to cope with the unpalatable historical facts that King David, saint and supreme prophet, had committed adultery with Bathsheba and engineered the situation in which her husband Uriah was killed, and that King Solomon, the son of that mutual pair, had been led astray by his excessive love of women, even to the extent of worshipping strange gods.[85] Twelfth-century Biblical commentators had allegorized David as Christ, Bathsheba as the Church, and Uriah as the devil. Their successors, some of whom seem to have been worried by the obvious clash between the literal and spiritual meanings here, were willing to accept that David, Solomon (and, in a very different capacity, St Paul) had indeed sinned, but translated them into *exempla* of what to do and what to avoid. St Bonaventure, in the commentary on Ecclesiastes which we have had cause to cite earlier, affirmed that this work was written not by a sinner but by a penitent man who regretted his sins.[86] Similarly, the English Dominican Thomas Waleys, commenting on the Psalter in the early fourteenth century, described David and St Paul as having passed through a state of sin; they were writing not as sinners but as men who had once been sinners, and hence one can have confidence in what they wrote.[87] Arguments like this were obviously in Col's mind when he wrote the above passage. A writer's amatory experience, then, does not necessarily invalidate his work – providing that, like David or indeed like the exiled Ovid, he has put his *amours* behind him.

But what if a writer does *not* leave his love behind? That is a far more difficult proposition to defend. But Col, to his intellectual credit, tries to do just that in a later passage of this very same letter.[88] He turns from past love to

the *Rose* itself, had engaged in Ovidian self-fashioning, interpreting his own writings in a way which his later supporters were to adopt and amplify. Similarly, Giovanni Boccaccio 'constructed details of his own "vita" in accordance with what he found in Ovid's', as has been demonstrated by Robert Hollander, *Boccaccio's Two Venuses* (New York, 1977), pp. 112–16. He concludes that Boccaccio 'is the "new Ovid" in that he thinks of himself as the prime vernacular writer in the matter of love, but he wants simultaneously to keep himself separate from Ovidian sentiments that are only carnal' (p. 116). Chaucer was, as usual, the exception. Despite the Man of Law's profession that the English poet had wished to overgo Ovid (II (B[1]) 53–6), in all his major narrative works he ostentatiously denies any experience of love, whether in the past or in the present. See especially *Troilus and Criseyde* ii. 12–13, 'Forwhi to every lovere I me excuse, / That of no sentement I this endite . . .'.

84 Robertson, *Preface*, p. 199, argues that 'Raison speaks with the voice of Patristic authority, Boethius and Cicero. She is, as it were, Lady Philosophy, who is described by Guillaume as the Image of God. He who seeks Jean de Meun's opinions will find them here, not in the discourses of the other characters who, with Ciceronian decorum, speak as their natures demand'. Cf. Fleming, *Allegory and Iconography*, p. 107, who argues that Raison is 'associated in the poem with the *Sapientia Dei Patris* or Christ'; see also pp. 132–5.

85 For discussion and references see Minnis, *Medieval Theory of Authorship*, pp. 103–8.

86 Trans. Minnis and Scott, *Medieval Literary Theory and Criticism*, pp. 232–3; cf. the discussion on pp. 207–9.

87 *Postilla super primos xxxviii psalmos Davidicos Thomae Iorgii* (London, 1481), pp. 1–3.

88 Hicks, *Débat*, p. 97; cf. Baird and Kane, *Letters and Documents*, pp. 100–1.

present and indeed future love. Gerson had argued that Jean's character Raison should have suited his teaching to his audience (thereby following the rules of rhetoric), remembering that he was speaking to a Foolish Lover, who could easily be incited to carnality, rather than to a layman, clerk or theologian. Despite what Lady Eloquence says, Col replies, being a clerk, a philosopher or theologian is not irreconcilable with being a foolish lover – witness the examples of David, Solomon and others.

> . . . semble par ses paroles [i.e. of Lady Eloquence] qu'estre clerc, philozophe, ou theologien et fol amoureux ne se sueffrent pas ensemble, ains sont incompatibles. Hélas! il en va bien autrement, et est alé et ira – dont c'est dommages –, come de David et Salemon et autres . . .

Indeed, he adds, some clerics even say that Solomon wrote the Song of Songs on account of his love of Pharaoh's daughter. ('Scarcely a Catholic view', Gerson was to declare in his reply.)[89] One could bring forth, Col exclaims, 'more than a thousand examples of people who were clerks and at the same time foolish lovers'. These roles are as compatible with one another 'as being at once clerk and knight', as were Pompey, Julius Caesar, Scipio and Cicero.

Gerson's problem, Col continues, is that he believed everyone to be like himself: because *he* was a clerk, philosopher and theologian without being a foolish lover, he thought that all others were like him. This is manifestly not the case. Moreover, even if the great Gerson himself were, in the future, to become a foolish lover, this would not make him any the less a clerk – at least, at the beginning of this passion, the implication being that when it took proper hold it could well interfere with his proper functioning as a clerk, philosopher and theologian.

> Et n'est il pas possible que il meismes, ou tamps a venir, soit fol amoureux? Par Dieu si est! Si n'en seroit il ja moins clerc, au moins au commansement de la fole amour.

This vacillation is fascinating. On the one hand, Col does not want to set aside the argument that Jean wrote the *Roman* not as an actual lover but as a repentant one: 'when he made this book of the *Rose*, he was no longer a foolish lover, and had repented of being one' (cf. p. 31 above). On the other, he is tempted to brush it aside by claiming that even if Jean had written his poem while under the influence of foolish love, this would not have interfered with the text's clerkly, philosophical and theological achievements.

Col does not explain what lies behind that last argument, but one may speculate that he had in mind the notion, which has its source in Aristotle, that certain kinds of moral shortcoming do not impinge on one's intellectual ability. Knowledge (*scientia*) is not a moral virtue, declares an anonymous schoolman in Paris, Bibliothèque Nationale, MS Lat.3108, because, as Aristotle says, it does little or nothing to lead one to the virtues[90] – a reference to the seminal passage in Book 2 of the *Ethics*, 'Ad virtutes autem scire quidem parum aut nihil potest'.[91] To turn once again to Henry of Ghent's *Summa quaestionum*

---

89 Hicks, *Débat*, p. 168; cf. Baird and Kane, *Letters and Documents*, p. 149.
90 Text transcribed in J. Leclerq, 'Le magistère du prédicateur au XIIIe siècle', *Archives d'histoire doctrinale et littéraire du moyen âge*, 21 (1946) 129–30.
91 Quoted from Robert Grosseteste's version of the Latin text, as printed in *S. Thomae Aquinatis*

ordinariarum, there the argument is offered that someone can be said to be a teacher of theology by dint of the knowledge which he possesses and his consequent intellectual ability to teach.[92] Once this condition is established, Henry continues, it cannot be lost through immoral behaviour. In this sense a sinner may be regarded as a teacher of theology, for he is able to possess correct doctrine just like the righteous man, and indeed he may be better educated than the righteous man in terms of the technical knowledge which he possesses. Arguments like these figured largely in the debates over whether an immoral preacher can and/or should be allowed to preach: indeed, the passage I have cited from Paris, B.N. Lat.3108 appears in a quodlibet on the subject, 'Whether to preach in a state of mortal sin is itself a mortal sin or not'. The central ideas involved had a long life, appearing in many different guises. In the last lecture I had the pleasure of delivering here in Perugia I argued that they may lie behind the challenging question posed by Chaucer's Pardoner, can an immoral man tell a moral tale?[93] Applying all this to Col's enigmatic and convoluted statements, one may speculate that he is groping towards the hypothesis that, since the sound doctrine and knowledge of a well-educated cleric is not necessarily damaged by any vices to which he may fall prey, the issue of whether or not Jean de Meun was a foolish lover when he wrote the *Rose* is irrelevant to our consideration of the intellectual content of what he has written. It is hardly surprising that Col was reluctant to spell this out. He knew full well that it was far more difficult to reconcile the roles of clerk and lover than it was to reconcile the roles of clerk and knight.

Giovanni Boccaccio, it may be recalled, was even less keen to grasp this particular nettle. In his short treatise in praise of Dante, the *Trattatello* (first version *c.*1351–5), he agonized over whether Dante's persistent 'lust' – which found 'most ample space; and not just in his youthful years, but also in maturity' – devalued his writing.[94] Having shifted some of the blame onto the irresistible female sex (with the aid of ideas from Walter Map), and briefly referred to the power of love as demonstrated by classical mythology, Boccaccio then proceeds with a familiar argument about the sins of scriptural authors. 'David, even though he had many wives, only needed to see Bathsheba to forget, on her account, God, his kingdom, himself, and his integrity, becoming first an adulterer and then a murderer. . . And Solomon, to whose wisdom nobody, excepting the Son of God, has ever attained: did he not abandon Him who had made him wise and, to please a woman, kneel and adore Baalim?' In view of this

in decem libros ethicorum Aristotelis ad Nicomachum expositio, ed. R.M. Spiazzi (Marietti, 1949), p. 11. For full discussion of the implications of this *sententia* see the fourth section of my paper 'The *Accessus* Extended: Henry of Ghent on the Transmission and Reception of Theology', forthcoming in the proceedings of the conference '*Ad Litteram*: Authoritative Texts and their Medieval Readers' (University of Notre Dame, Indiana, April 2–4, 1989), which is being edited by Mark Jordan and Kent Emery.

92 This forms part of the *quaestio* 'Whether a sinner can be a teacher of theology', printed in *Summae questionum ordinariarum . . . Henrici a Gandavo* (in aedibus J. Badii Ascensii, Paris, 1520; rpt. by the Franciscan Institute, Louvain and Paderborn, 1953), fols 79v–81r.

93 A.J. Minnis, 'Chaucer's Pardoner and the "Office of Preacher" ', in *Intellectuals and Writers in Fourteenth-Century Europe,* eds. P. Boitani and A. Torti (Tübingen and Cambridge, 1986), pp. 88–119.

94 Trans. by David Wallace in Minnis and Scott, *Medieval Literary Theory and Criticism,* pp. 502–3.

evidence, Dante cannot be excused: but, given that he is in such distinguished company, his head need not hang 'so low as it would otherwise have done had he alone been at fault'.[95] The point is that Boccaccio could not blame the poet's sins on his youthfulness, in which age a man was physiologically prone to sexual passion. To be of mature age and be in love was much harder to defend (and to be an aged lover was to run the risk of being regarded as utterly ridiculous – witness the many medieval caricatures of the *senex amans*).

It would seem, then, that to go beyond the terms of reference of 'the Medieval Ovid' and look towards Scripture, as Col tried to do in defending Jean de Meun, and as Dante most certainly did in his *Comedy*, did not guarantee an escape from those problems regularly encountered by those Medieval Ovidians, both critics and authors, who sought to appropriate that (rather paradoxical) respectability enjoyed by the writer who was the great expert not only on human love but also on its rejection. Quite clearly, in medieval literary theory, *amor* sits uncomfortably with *auctoritas*.[96] When such theory is pressed into the moral defence of poetry which has human love as its central subject, the problems and paradoxes are many and various.

This inquiry has illustrated how, in the *querelle de la Rose*, a common body of ideas from commentary tradition was manipulated to serve two utterly opposed and irreconcilable points of view. I have tried to avoid taking sides in the modern re-enactment of this battle of the books, but my own assessment of the evidence would seem to indicate the speciousness of the argument that what separated Christine de Pizan and Jean Gerson from the *cognoscenti* who defended Jean de Meun was ignorance of, or lack of familiarity with, the literary issues involved. All the participants in the debate were aware of the terms of reference of the late-medieval 'ethical poetic', to borrow a term from the late Judson Allen. Given Gerson's education, and the regularity with which many of the fundamental issues and relevant methods of textual analysis occurred in the standard scriptural exegesis of his day, this is hardly surprising.[97] What, then, of

---

[95] Similarly, in his *Decameron* (Fourth day, Introduction) Boccaccio had used the same sort of argument in defence of his own liking for women and wish to please them in his writing. Feminine beauty, he points out, was 'much admired' by "Guido Cavalcanti and Dante Alighieri in their old age, and by Cino da Pistoia in his dotage". Then Boccaccio moves from the moderns to the ancients. He could pursue his case still further by citing history-books which are 'filled with examples from antiquity of outstanding men, who, in their declining years, strove with might and main to give pleasure to the ladies'. The point seems to be that if such distinguished men were still susceptible to female charm, then he, Boccaccio, can hardly be accused with utter severity. *Opere di Giovanni Boccaccio*, ed. C. Sergio (Milan, 1967), pp. 258–9; trans. G.H. McWilliam, *Boccaccio: The Decameron* (Harmondsworth, 1972), p. 329. See further my article 'Authors in Love' (cited above, no. 35). Cf. the strategy adopted by John Gower, who at the end of his *Confessio amantis* has his narrator (now revealed to be a *senex amans*) take encouragement from his visionary encounter with a company of lovers, particularly the group of old lovers which includes David, Solomon, Aristotle, Virgil and Ovid: 'I thoghte thanne how love is swete, / Which hath so wise men reclamed, / And was miself the lasse aschamed . . .' (viii.2720–22). This passage is discussed in my forthcoming article '*De Vulgari Auctoritate*: Chaucer, Gower, and the Men of Great Authority'.

[96] Cf. my articles 'Authors in Love' (cit. n. 35 above), and '*Amor* and *Auctoritas* in the Self-Commentary of Dante and Francesco da Barberino', *Poetica*, 32 (1990) 25–42.

[97] Moreover, anyone who suspects that Gerson's reaction to the *Rose* derived from deficient knowledge of 'humanistic' literary culture would do well to consider his assured declaration

Christine? Some modern defenders of the *Rose* have tried to devalue her contribution by impling she was insufficiently learned and hence unable to cope with the niceties of literary debate.[98] But Christine seems to have been knowledgeable about certain aspects of medieval literary theory, particularly the standard criticism of Ovid, which was after all quite easily available in the *accessus* and glosses which regularly appeared in medieval manuscripts of Ovid's works.[99] Whether she knew in detail all the criticism which has been cited above in elucidating some of the technical vocabulary found in the *querelle* is impossible to say, but I have demonstrated, I hope, that she knew *some* of it – and doubtless her quick wit helped her to grasp some of the principles underlying the rest, for there is no doubt that she was an adept manipulator of the ideas involved. Skilful exploitation of ideas is quite different in kind, and looks quite different, from semi-comprehension of them. Certainly in Christine's case, the skill implies the knowledge in at least some degree.

Whatever the truth of this specific matter may be, it seems possible to offer the generalization that when the opponents of the *Roman de la Rose* castigated it as worthless, or when its supporters affirmed its great value, they had in common certain paradigms, and revealed themselves to be influenced by certain principles, which figure largely in medieval commentary tradition, most relevantly in the *accessus Ovidiani*. Defenders and attackers alike turned to this corpus of criticism when they sought to theorize the *Rose*. Indeed, it may be no exaggeration to say that scholastic literary principles of the kinds illustrated above actually determined some of the parameters of the debate itself.

---

that he has read most if not all of Jean's sources: 'I first drank long ago in my youth at all, or almost all, those fountains from which the writings of your author have poured forth translated, like little streams: such as Boethius, Ovid, Terence, Juvenal, Alanus de Insulis, Guillaume de Saint-Amour, Abelard and Heloise, Martianus Capella, and many others. . . . Yet you believe us to be too brutish and too dense to be able to understand this book of yours'. Hicks, *Débat*, p. 172; Baird and Kane, *Letters and Documents*, p. 151.

[98] Hence Robertson speaks of her 'squeamishness' and 'dismay' at Jean's reference to Saturn's 'coilles', arguing that these same parts had 'frequently appeared with philosophical significance in the sober discussions of the mythographers': *Preface to Chaucer*, p. 21, cf. p. 85. However, a good discussion of Christine's learning, and a comparison of her culture with that of the Col brothers, is provided by Badel, *Roman de la Rose au XIVe siècle*, pp. 436–47.

[99] And she certainly knew the *Ovide moralisé*, which is a primary source for her *Épitre d'Othéa*. At one point (Hicks, p. 144, Baird and Kane p. 140) Christine cites the 'common proverb' about 'the glosses of Orléans which destroyed the text' – a reference to the exegetical practices of the school of Orléans, that great centre of classical studies in the twelfth century: *inter alia* it produced a substantial corpus of commentary on Ovid (Including that by Arnulf of Orléans). Cf. Alexander of Villa Dei's attacks on Orléans in general and Arnulf in particular in *The Ecclesiale of Alexander of Villa Dei*, ed. L.R. Lind (Lawrence, Kansas, 1958), pp. 2–3, 10–11; see further the debate between Arnulf and Fulco of Orléans which was referred to on pp. 28–9 and n. 73 above. Christine's point is simply that ingenious scholastic argument can twist the meaning of a text, which was (in her view) precisely what the defenders of the *Rose* were doing when they claimed it to be a morally edifying work. Like Chaucer, she mistrusted those who engaged in unscrupulous 'glosynge' which killed the 'lettre' (cf. *The Summoner's Tale*, III (D) 1788–94).

FICTIONS LIVING FICTIONS: THE POETICS OF VOICE AND GENRE IN FRAGMENT D OF THE *CANTERBURY TALES*

CHARLES A. OWEN JR.

My title, Fictions Living Fictions, is basic to life as well as to literature. For the effort we constantly make to assimilate what comes to us from outside through our senses results in fiction, and the shock we often get when we catch a glimpse of ourselves from an unexpected angle – in a mirror from another mirror for instance – reminds us that the image of ourselves we carry in consciousness has only elements of reality (if indeed the term reality has any validity). We are in our own consciousness, as well as in the consciousness of others, fictions, and what we think of as experience selective and at times inaccurate is really something we half create. We as well as the Canterbury pilgrims are fictions living fictions.

The world we live in is in our consciousness. Despite the assumptions of some modern critics the sign systems of language are not self-referential, nor are they intermediate between consciousness and reality.[1] They find their 'signifieds' in consciousness, which fits together the diverse sets of signals our senses provide us into a mental image of the world. We have no way of testing the accuracy of this image other than by trial and error. For most people in the middle ages a guarantee for accuracy (though not for completeness) existed in God, who created mankind in his own image. We have accumulated enough data over the generations to know that there are important areas of 'reality' which our senses do not convey to us, that in fact our image of the world is a fiction, but a fiction which works much of the time. The image seems furthermore to be one we in large part share with other human beings. We assume it to

---

[1] For a criticism of the tendency to self-referentiality in post-modernist criticism, see Gabrielle Spiegel, 'History, Historicism, and the Social Logic of the Text in the Middle Ages', *Speculum* 65 (1990), 61 ff, and Lee Patterson, 'On the Margin: Postmodernism, Ironic History, and Medieval Studies', *Speculum* 65 (1990), 106. For language as intermediate see Hayden White, *Tropics of Discourse* (Baltimore, 1978), p. 125 f: 'We do not know the origin of language and never shall, but it is certain today that language is more adequately characterized as being neither a free creation of human consciousness nor merely a product of environmental forces acting on the psyche, but rather the instrument of mediation between the consciousness and the world that consciousness inhabits'. The signs of language always have their signifieds in consciousness. Consciousness is thus the mediator between language and the 'other'. The interaction between language and consciousness refines and modifies that primary world of images. P. Ricoeur (*Time and Narrative* (Chicago, 1985) addresses the problem of the two times, psychological and objective, time as we experience it in consciousness and time as objectively measured, and reviews all the efforts to bridge the two, to mediate between or relate the two. Actually objective time and its measurements are a part of our consciousness, an effort to create a parallel for what we conceive to be 'out there'. That we have trouble reconciling the two concepts of time is not surprising. Both exist as creations in our consciousness, just as the particle and wave theories of light in physics do.

be inherited, a part of our genetic make-up. At the same time a considerable portion of the world we see ourselves as living in is for each of us individual, shared with no other creature.

Part of the conviction Chaucer's vision of the pilgrims carries for us results from his handling of the levels in his fictional world. We recognize many of the characteristics as present in our lives. This used to be called realism. We should perhaps coin a new term like fictisimilitude to express our skepticism about the completeness and accuracy of the messages our senses convey us. The enveloping fiction in the *Canterbury Tales* is that Chaucer is recounting for us an episode in his own life, a segment of his autobiography.[2] This segment includes the biographical sketches in the Prologue. But the biographical sketches have no special authority, they interact with what transpires in the rest of the autobiographical segment. They are like all biography fictional, an effort to assimilate the details of what we experience of a person into a comprehensible construct. Chaucer's sketches are partial, selective, each with its own principle of organization. They include exaggerated claims for completeness 'al the condicioun' (A 38), a specious economy in the employment of time 'whil I have tyme and space' (35), a sophisticated mocking of value judgments 'And I seyde his opinioun was good' (183), sudden deflations of pretense 'mous' (144) 'shaply' (372), oblique confirmations of worth 'bismotered' (76) 'shiten' (504), a freedom from system that the author attributes to his own dimwittedness (746).[3] They put us on our mettle, alert us to a play with meanings, prepare us for a complexity of relationships between us and our autobiographer, between him and his fellow pilgrims, between the fictions that people live and between them and the fictions that they tell, on every level. They prepare us especially for interpretation and misinterpretation, for response to what we and the pilgrims hear and hear about, for the cloud of potential witnesses and the relative quality of their observation and response.[4]

We discover at the end of the biographical sketches that the telling of stories is to be one of the elements, perhaps the main element, in the fiction that is a section of Chaucer's autobiography. We might think that these stories will be non-consequential whether the assumption is that they happened or not. For the stories we tell, even those that have a basis in what we call actuality, don't have the immediate results that the image we carry of our physical surroundings does. Unawareness or even insufficient awareness of elements in the world we

---

2   The segment of autobiography presents little information about Chaucer directly. He describes his fellow pilgrims in the Prologue, and then adopts the role of reporter. The Man of Law speaks about Chaucer's poetry without knowing that the poet is in his audience, and none of the other pilgrims appears to know who their companion is. In calling on him for a tale, the Host comments humorously on his appearance. When he interrupts Sir Thopas, he orders the narrator to stop rhyming and say something in 'geeste' or in prose. At another point the Host assumes that 'the substaunce is in me,/ If any thyng shal wel reported be' (B 3993–4). Chaucer is clearly incognito in his fiction and plays off his characters' ignorance against what he assumes will be his audience's knowledge.

3   Quotations from Chaucer in this paper are from *The Riverside Chaucer*, ed. Larry Benson (Boston, 1987).

4   The fiction that Chaucer's autobiography is not a fiction gives the characters that Chaucer creates an apparent freedom from authorial control. Creatures' freedom from their creator's control was a point of deep interest for Chaucer as shown in *TC*, IV 958–1078 and *CT*, B 4424–40. Emphasis on voice and the use of dialogical structure enhanced the impression of freedom in Chaucer's major fictions.

see ourselves as living in can carry heavy penalty. Storytelling is both escape from and unpenalized exercise in the fiction-making our lives depend on. Small wonder that humans at every level of civilization and sophistication take pleasure in the creation of fictions and that these fictions whether mathematical or aesthetic have value in the fictions we take to be our lives.[5] Chaucer the poet has created in the *Canterbury Tales* a fiction that will imitate this partially shared, genetically transmitted image of a world developed and elaborated individually by each one of us.

A collection of the stories we tell each other, about our past, about what we value, enjoy, and dread, about the nature of the world we live in, how it came into existence and what its future is likely or ordained to be, defines our culture. Sometimes such a collection becomes an actual book – the Bible, the *Iliad*, the *Divine Comedy*. The collection of fragments Chaucer called the 'Tales of Caunterbury' was recognized as such a book and was fitted together by those who read it after his death.[6]

Despite its inconsistencies and even contradictions they saw it as defining their world for them. The book that resulted from their efforts, in what amounted to two somewhat different arrangements of the fragments, misrepresented the way Chaucer's own vision of his work had developed.[7] But it made manifest the power of this particular frame and the range of stories the enveloping fiction with its own potential for development made possible.

The D fragment makes vivid use of this potential. The biographical sketches and the plan for storytelling enframe and impower a dialogical structure.[8] The Wife of Bath's performance and the fierce quarrel of the Friar and Summoner project a dialectic of voice and genre. The levels of fiction in the fragment interpenetrate with sudden shifts and interruptions and with the break-up of a

---

[5] This third level, beyond the mental image of the world and language, interacts with the other two and influences them. It includes what we view as historical, what we view as imaginary, what we view as scientific. Genres evolve in storytelling as levels of discourse do in language systems and jump across from system to system.

[6] Modern editions minimize the fragmentary character of the *CT*. They give the impression that the *CT* is much more nearly complete than it is. The fragments reflect the stages of a developing plan, no one of which came close to completion.

[7] The two arrangements are the *a*-Ellesmere, which has had the greatest influence recently, and the *c-d-b*, which Caxton and other early editors used. For the way these two arrangements evolved in the early fifteenth century, see Owen, 'Pre-1450 Manuscripts of the Canterbury Tales: Relationships and Significance', *Chaucer Review* 23 (1988) 1–29 and 95–116.

[8] See M.M. Bakhtin, *The Dialogic Imagination: Four Essays*, translated by Caryl Emerson and Michael Holquist (Austin, 1981), and *Problems of Dostoevsky's Poetics*, edited and translated by Caryl Emerson (Minneapolis, 1984). Bakhtin felt that Dostoevsky had discovered a 'new artistic sphere', the polyphonic novel, with roots in Socratic dialogue, Menippean satire and Carnival, with Rabelais and Cervantes as precursors. 'The dialogic relation between the characters is in effect developed to the point of including the relation between the narrator and his/her characters. The single and unified authorial consciousness disappears. In its place appears a narrator who converses with his/her characters and who becomes a plurality of centers of consciousness irreducible to a common denominator' (*Problems*, p. 6). When Bakhtin says of Dostoevsky, 'he does not seek expressive, graphic finalizing words – what he seeks above all are words for the hero, maximally full of meaning and seemingly independent of the author . . .' (*Problems*, p. 39), he might also be speaking of Chaucer in relation to the Wife of Bath. 'Authentic polyphony' (*Problems*, 178), the 'open structure of the great dialogue' (ibid., 177), the word as 'not a material thing but rather the eternally mobile, eternally fickle medium of dialogic interaction' (ibid., 202) might also be applied to Chaucer.

single level into sub-levels. The narrator, as everywhere in the *Canterbury Tales* except in the biographical sketches and in his own stories, is almost exclusively an auditor. In the 2294 lines of the fragment the narrator never once uses the first person, and he has only eleven lines of observation beyond the neutral introduction of speakers.[9] He is not only on an equal plane with the pilgrims but also with his audience. We hear what he hears. He thus encourages us to talk of the pilgrims as people we are watching and hearing with him. They are in the fiction free agents whose actions can surprise him – 'Up stirte the Pardoner and that anon' – for whom he cannot be held responsible any more than we. The elements have the hardness and independence of that impinging 'other', the outside world that we piece together from the signals our senses convey.

Chaucer has the Wife of Bath start out with her own attempt at autobiography. The account of her experience in five marriages first derails itself on a misreading of scripture, on the question of whether religious authorities sanction five marriages for one person; then on what the authorities and the Wife herself think about sex in marriage. In this Apologia what we experience is not her past but her voice, her domineering presence, as she marshals her authorities in support of her views and threatens the Pardoner who has the temerity to interrupt. Having come to terms with the Pardoner, she launches into the specifics of her five marriages. She creates a fiction to cover the first three marriages to old men, her 'good' husbands, a fiction that becomes a dramatic colloquy between the Wife and a composite of her three victims. The raw materials from which this colloquy evolves had themselves elements of fiction – the words never spoken that she accused her husbands of uttering, the supposed carrying-on with neighbour women, their libidinous passion for her *bele chose*, and her feigned jealousy at their sexual exploits, when in fact they were too sick to stand. The triumphant image of her self results from a simultaneity of levels. The pleasure she takes in conveying to her fellow-pilgrims (and to us) the tactical brilliance of her performance in this fiction, extending even and most daringly to the intimacy of sexual embrace, permits only a glimpse of the young girl's distaste (416–18). Her dominance, present in idiom and tone of voice, coopts both scenes, the scene described and the scene of the Wife describing.[10]

> Lordynges, right thus, as ye have understonde,
> Baar I stifly myne olde housbondes on honde
> That thus they seyden in hir dronkenesse;
> And al was fals, but that I took witnesse
> On Janekyn, and on my nece also.
> O Lord! The peyne I dide hem and the wo.   (379–84)

The fiction she creates of herself becomes more and more the image she projects. The long fourth marriage that lasts till she's forty takes up little space in her imagination. It appears chiefly as images of jealousy, the husband's death, and their separation. The Wife escapes from what must have been its

---

9 The eleven are D 163, 829, 832, 1265–9, and 1665–7.
10 Bakhtin in *The Dialogic Imagination* (see note 8) says, 'We might put it as follows: before us are two events – the event that is narrated in the event and the event of narration itself (we ourselves participate in the latter, as listeners or readers) . . . we perceive the fullness of the work in all its wholeness and indivisibility, but at the same time we understand the diversity of the elements that constitute it' (p. 155).

bitter disappointment into a stream-of-consciousness set of reminiscences, where she can be her ideal self. The transition here is abrupt. She gives three lines to her husband, a revelour who had a paramour. Then she's off

| And I was yong and ful of ragerye. | (455) |

| How koude I daunce to an harpe smale, | |
| And synge, ywis, as any nyghtyngale. | (457–8) |

| He sholde nat han daunted me from drynke! | |
| And after wyn on Venus moste I thynke. | (463–4) |

| But – Lord Crist! – whan that it remembreth me. | (469) |

The flour is goon; ther is namoore to telle;	
The bren, as I best kan, now mooste I selle;	
But yet to be right myrie wol I fonde.	(477–9)

The fiction of her husband's jealousy is at best exaggerated, for we learn of her absence on pilgrimage before his death and of his absence in London all one Lent. It perhaps makes tolerable the memory of her own jealousy:

I seye, I hadde in herte greet despit	
That he of any oother had delit.	
But he was quit . . .	(481–3)

Her claim not to have committed adultery – 'Nat of my body, in no foule manere' (485) – conflicts with her description of her sex life in a second stream-of-consciousness passage – 'I koude nought withdrawe / My chaumbre of Venus from a good felawe (617–8) . . . I ne loved nevere by no discrecioun' (622). Are we to believe that three pilgrimages to Jerusalem afforded her no opportunities?

She clearly wants to start talking about her fifth husband. It reflects not only the events on which her account is based but her own desires that she starts in before she has quite finished with her fourth:

Now of my fifthe housbonde wol I telle.	
God lete his soule nevere come in helle!	
And yet he was to me the moste shrewe.	(503–5)

The paradox of their love and their struggle, her age his youth, her property his poverty, her passion his learning, comes through in a constant mixing of levels. She is both with him and with the pilgrims and, beyond Chaucer's autobiography, drawing us into her fictions. Her account betrays at every point her emotional commitment, her voluble enthusiasm for the intensity of their life together. The pain and the pleasure, the past and the present merge. The simultaneity of levels permits description and comment to follow one another without transition. She feels strongly about what she's describing

| Who peynted the leoun, tel me who? | |
| By God, if wommen hadde writen stories. | (692–3) |

Her passion brings the past into the present. When Jankyn is reading from his book of wicked wyves, she responds to the stories as if she were hearing them afresh, as if she were present at the fictive occasions:

| Lo, heere expres of womman may ye fynde | |
| That womman was the los of al mankynde. | (719–20) |

> This sely man sat stille as he were deed.   (730)

> Fy! Spek namoore – it is a grisly thyng –
> Of hire horrible lust and hir likyng.   (735–6)

> Of Lyvia tolde he me, and of Lucye:
> They bothe made hir housbondes for to dye,
> That oon for love, that oother was for hate.   (747–9)

Her vivid recall of all that they shared strains against her sense that their relationship had its crucial moment of truth to give a natural form to her account. Immediately after hearing of their marriage we learn

> By God, he smoot me ones on the lyst,
> For that I rente out of his book a leef,
> That of the strook myn ere wax al deef.   (634–6)

And twice more (666 ff, 711 f) she reminds us of the climax to come, before she settles down to the drama of that night. We experience the rapt attention she gives her husband's reading and her growing impatience with his unawareness of her as the stories and the proverbs follow one another:

> And whan I saugh he wolde nevere fyne
> To reden on this cursed book al nyght.   (788–9)

The end comes the more quickly for the delay we experience before the outbreak of violence. It's the ending conventional to romance. They lived happily ever after in mutual love and care

> God helpe me so, I was to hym as kynde
> As any wyf from Denmark unto Ynde,
> And also trewe, and so was he to me.   (823–5)

The fiction of this life after Jankyn's knock-out blow is partial at best. It leaves out all word of his demise. It conflicts with her initial account of their life together, her feeling memory of his blows on her 'ribbes al by rewe', her equally vivid memory of his ability to 'glose' her, 'Whan that he wolde han my *bele chose*' (510). It agrees, however, with the ostensible genre of the tale she chooses to tell. The Wife of Bath sees herself as the heroine of a romance.

The Wife has not been telling what she thinks of as a story. Yet her account has been full of fictions, and her image of herself is patently a fiction. She is clearly a fiction living fictions, and in the fictional world Chaucer has created for us what she reveals goes beyond and sometimes counter to her intentions, which themselves are not entirely consistent. The extent to which genre impinges on her account and distorts her vision of what happened, emerges not only from the romance ending of her fifth marriage, but from the other fictions by which she projects her experiences. The colloquy with the composite of her first three husbands eliminates all distinction among them, and any change in her as well. Was the twelve-year-old virgin the same as the widow who married a third husband? The timeless stream-of-consciousness recall of an ideal self substitutes for the emptiness of her fourth and longest marriage. Her concentration on its end, her husband's tomb, his funeral, suggests what the end meant to her. Genre and voice thus interact to create a fiction in which a multiplicity of voices and genres are simultaneously present. The specific genre – social comedy, romance, stream-of-consciousness – occurs in the context of the Wife's autobiography, a part itself of Chaucer's. And Chaucer's voice subsumes all voices including his own as pilgrim in the General Prologue's portrait of the Wife, potentially present as undertone in everything the Wife says.[11]

With the Friar's comment, 'This was a long preamble of a tale!' (831), we must reposition ourselves, as indeed the pilgrims had to. No speaker holds our attention exclusively. Our absorption in a fiction is less secure. The only story-teller at the moment is Chaucer. The question inevitably arises: Why the Friar? What in Chaucer's mind motivates the Friar to comment on the length of the Wife's preamble? The Friar is the pilgrim whose associations with women keep returning in his portrait. He is thus the one to make the casual complacent comment that sums up what many in such an audience would have felt – amusement at the unexpected length and frankness of what the Wife has said. The Friar's comment brings back the pilgrimage, the possibilities of response, the listeners each of whom is a potential agent. The intrusion of the Summoner, however, has special impact. Chaucer ascribes to him an animosity that has an inner heat; it explodes with an intensity out of all proportion to the occasion. It finds at once what will later turn out to be its characteristic idiom, scatology:

> Lo, goode men, a flye and eek a Frere
> Wol falle in every disshe and eek mateere.   (835–6)

As in the tales he now threatens and will later tell, the Summoner ascribes to his enemy what is patently his own condition:

> For wel I woot thy pacience is gon.   (849)

The anarchic tendencies that threaten every community find a prospective release in storytelling, even before the Host's assertion of authority. With the Host the cast of speaking characters in the D fragment is complete, and each of the five voices is distinct.

The Wife of Bath responds to the interruption by taking on the Friar rather than the Summoner. The latter's violence had in a sense expressed support for her:

> Thou lettest our disport in this manere.   (839)

She perhaps senses in the Friar the contempt implicit in successful manipulation of women. She pays mock deference in asking his permission to proceed –

> If I have licence of this worthy Frere.   (855)

And she dedicates an eighteen-line improvisation at the beginning of her tale

---

11 The interaction between voice and genre is here in both directions. Paul Ricoeur, *Time and Narrative* (see fn. 1), vol. III, 246, puts the interaction as follows: 'The subject then appears both as a reader and the writer of its own life, as Proust would have it . . . As the literary analysis of autobiography confirms, the story of a life continues to be refigured by all the truthful or fictive stories a subject tells about himself or herself. This refiguration makes this life itself a cloth woven of stories told'. One might add, of stories untold but implicit, repressed, of which traces can be found. Hayden White makes a similar point about all history writing, *The Content of Form*, (Baltimore, 1987), p. 44. In *Tropics of Discourse* (see fn. 1), p. 127 f, he points out that even 'original descriptions of any field of phenomena are already interpretations of its structure'.

(864–81) to an ironic praise of his busy zeal in eliminating fairy threats to women's chastity:

> For ther as wont to walken was an elf
> Ther walketh now the lymytour hymself.   (873–4)

> Wommen may go saufly up and doun,
> In every bussh or under every tree
> Ther is noon oother incubus but he,
> And he ne wol doon hem but dishonour.   (878–81)

It is worth stressing, I think, that conscious storytelling draws the pilgrims into a different posture and a different idiom. The Wife responds to the Friar, it is true. Most of the eighteen-line section constitutes a modification of what she had planned to tell. But the language differs from her customary utterance. Storytellers not only bring their audiences into a fictional world, they enter it themselves. The nature of the story and the skill of the narrator will determine the extent of the difference from the person's normal posture and idiom. The genre's influence is not only on the imagined character the Wife of Bath, but on Chaucer as well. The influence of the genre on him will modify the imagined storyteller's skills as they present themselves in the fiction.[12] The Wife is represented as not only settling her score with the Friar at the beginning, but as having already chosen a fiction that will express the same concerns we heard more directly in her autobiographical segment. On the next to the deepest level her story furnishes an objective correlative for her vision of the future, her confidence that in her old age she can be for a young and handsome man the perfect wife and mistress. In the course of her performance she transforms to her purposes the genre of Arthurian romance, sending her protagonist off on a quest that deeply interests her, however inappropriate to the genre itself.

Her burning interest in what women most desire takes her out of her fiction completely – story and idiom both. We are back on the autobiographical level, away from the influence of genre, listening to her normal voice. The transition from the conscious fiction is at first merely pronominal, but it is almost at once complete:

> Somme seyde that oure hertes been moost esed
> Whan that we been yflatered and yplesed.
> He gooth ful ny the sothe, I wol nat lye.   (929–31)

We are back in the world of her prologue. She even takes us into another fiction to illustrate the point she has already made in describing what it was like to fall in love with her fifth husband while still married to her fourth – the difficulty women have in keeping secrets.

---

[12] This consideration has not been sufficiently recognized by those critics who have been critical of the dramatic reading of the *CT*. See for an excellent list of these critics C. David Benson, *Chaucer's Drama of Style: Poetic Variety and Contrast in 'The Canterbury Tales'* (Chapel Hill, 1986), p. 151, note 7. The distinction between dramatic monologue (as in the Wife's Prologue) and storytelling, where genre influences voice as well as meaning, has not been sufficiently recognized by either the proponents or the opponents of the dramatic reading.

> But that tale is nat worth a rake-stele.
> Pardee, we wommen konnen no thyng hele;
> Witnesse on Myda, – wol ye heere the tale? (949–51)

Her account of Mydas differs from every other, including the source in Ovid which she mentions. In fact it is the difference alone which makes her version relevant. Did someone substitute Mydas's wife for his barber in reading the story to Alysoun?

> Heere may ye se, thogh we a tyme abyde,
> Yet out it moot; we kan no conseil hyde.
> The remenaunt of the tale if ye wol heere,
> Redeth Ovyde, and ther ye may it leere.
> This knyght, of which my tale is specially. (979–83)

In contrast, the old hag's bed-lecture to her husband on true gentility and on the virtues of glad poverty does not tempt the Wife out of her fiction. Only at the end, with the two living out their happy lives and the pieties of the conventional blessing already in train, does she suddenly shift-shape. No modulation from storyteller to fellow-pilgrim for her! She will ask for no blessing on all the company. Instead she will ask for the things that support her ideal image of herself, that fiction she carries in her consciousness. She will ask for a young husband, sexual fulfilment, dominance, affluence, and long life.[13] The deepest levels of her needs, as Chaucer has imagined her, lie hidden from her consciousness. Chaucer permits them to emerge only obliquely from her performances, from the fictions she creates as an autobiography, from her choice of genre, and from the romance she tells as intentional fiction.[14]

What has been the effect of this autobiographical intrusiveness into the fiction the Wife is telling? It certainly makes less complete our absorption in the romance. At the same time it adds meaning, complexity to what we are hearing. The story itself is the more interesting for what it embodies of her interests and dreams and for what it tells us beyond her intentions. The contrast between the

---

13 What she prays for at the end of her original tale now assigned to the Shipman but not yet revised is 'Taillynge ynough unto oure lyves ende' (B 1624). As in the tale finally assigned her, her voice intrudes in another place, in the Shipman's Tale at the beginning, where the question of the husband's paying for his wife's proper attire comes up (a crucial issue later in the tale) and the narrator lapses into pronominal identity with her surrogate the wife of Seint-Denys and all other wives whose husbands are stingy: 'The sely housbonde, algate he moot us paye, / He moot us clothe, and he moot us arraye ... we ... oure ... us ...' (B 1201–9). Her voice is also recognizable in the Man of Law's endlink, where she first uses the expression 'My joly body' (B 1185), later used by the Wife of Seint-Denys as she offers her husband sexual repayment for the money she thought she had already earned with the Monk (B 1613). The speech in the endlink makes a perfect connection with her prologue to which it was originally attached (see Owen, *Pilgrimage and Storytelling in the 'Canterbury Tales'* (Norman, Okla., 1977), p. 16f and note 7, 220f). Chaucer heard her voice for the first time very early in his work on the *CT*. He and the Host were expecting to hear it on their return to the Tabard (E 2435–8), where the Host was also expecting to name the prize-winning narrator.
14 For instance, after getting her husband to agree that she has won of him 'maistrie / Syn I may chese and governe as me lest' (D 1237), 'she obeyed hym in every thyng / That myghte doon hym plesaunce and likyng' (D 1256). This contrast between theory and practice had earlier occurred in the romance ending of her fifth marriage. The old hag's second statement of what she wants of the knight (D 1066) comes closer to the Wife's ideal.

prologue and the tale is apparent when we consider Chaucer's role. Where the Wife's voice is dominant, we can see Chaucer as creator of the whole fiction in which the Wife appears; we can even sense stages in her development as he adds to her prologue and changes not just the tale but the genre of the tale she is to tell.[15] His presence in the prologue is through the fiction. We know the anti-feminist materials behind much of what he gives the wife to say. But we don't think of Chaucer as mocking anti-feminism in his autobiography. The situation changes in the tale. Here, except in the two instances of her intrusion, her voice is not so strong; it adapts to the world of genre. She becomes a romance storyteller at the same moment as her creator. When her surrogate the loathly lady sets out to answer her husband's complaint, 'Thou art so loothly, and so oold also, / And therto comen of so lough a kynde' (1100–1), Chaucer cannot resist injecting himself into the reply, at some expense to his fiction that it is the Wife's fiction.[16] He divides the least important third item into two parts and proceeds to indulge his interest in true gentility and 'glad poverte' for almost a hundred lines (1109–1206). Otherwise, the fusion of elements into the fiction that is the Wife of Bath is powerful enough to transform the materials out of which Chaucer creates her; her voice intrudes into the fictions on every level and sub-level that Chaucer gives her to tell.

With the tales of the Friar and the Summoner, the emphasis changes from autobiographical to biographical. The fabliaux the two men are heard as telling are exercises in hostile biography. What Chaucer has the two men seek to project in their tales is not an image of themselves but a pejorative image of the other. As with the Wife of Bath he allows them to fill the stage. The virulence he has them devote to the effort to vilify each other shows a great deal about the men themselves. The distinctions between the two performances are thus significant. The Friar, despite the 'louryng chere' he casts on the Summoner during the Wife's Tale, tries to control himself. He affects an attitude of objectivity, of viewing things from a superior point of view that gives his comments an air of authority. He starts off admonishing the Wife to leave 'scole matere' to the clericals:

> But, dame, heere as we ryde by the weye,
> Us nedeth nat to speken but of game.   (D 1274–5)

In this spirit he will tell a 'game' of a Summoner. In his choice of tale, a story that many would not consider a fabliau at all,[17] in the emphasis he puts on the dialogue between the witty fiend and the man who calls himself a 'bailly', in the

---

[15] See note 13. The wife was originally scheduled to tell a fabliau the Shipman's Tale instead of the romance now assigned her.

[16] An even clearer instance of Chaucer's intrusion at the expense of the tale occurs near the beginning of the Physician's Tale, where the upbringing of Virginia leads into thirty-three lines of apostrophe to governesses and parents on their responsibilities toward children, though Virginia herself has no governess and has no need of one (C 72–104). Chaucer's interest stems from a court scandal involving a daughter of John of Gaunt, whose governess was Chaucer's sister-in-law Katherine Swynford, later John of Gaunt's third wife and already mother of his children. The note on these lines in Robinson's second edition, 1957 (p. 727f), is superior to the note in the new *Riverside Chaucer* (p. 903).

[17] The Friar's Tale is called a fabliau in both Robinson editions (p. 8 in both editions), an exemplum in the *Riverside Chaucer*, p. 11, and a 'defamatory' story 'built around a folktale type' by Fisher (*The Complete Poetry and Prose*, New York, 1977, p. 106). Pearsall (*The

economy of the tale, the way image and incident make vivid the theology, the Friar maintains his position of authority: he intends to let his summoner and summoners in general send themselves to hell. But the Friar's habit of geniality, so useful in the confessional and in his associations with women and with the wealthy, cannot keep hidden his irritation at the Summoner. This irritation will intrude periodically into his fiction and make it autobiographical as well as biographical. It will provide the impetus for both interruptions, the Summoner's during his tale as well as his own during the Summoner's. It exposes the Friar to the extent that it emerges; it blemishes the playfulness he sees as proper to the storytelling; it will qualify the laughter he had seen his tale as occasioning at the very beginning of the quarrel (D 843). It is worth noting in detail how Chaucer makes the divided purposes underlying the Friar's performance plain.

A certain suspension of effect characterizes the Friar's Tale throughout. Part of the game is to make us wait. We wait a single line through the slight clash of legend's 'Whilom' with history's 'in my contree' for the mildly surprising subject of the tale's opening, – 'An erchedeken, a man of heigh degree'. We then wait twenty lines while the realistic background of the archdeacon's zeal in stamping out sin tips the scale in favour of history over legend. The picture we get of the archdeacon suggests an excessive severity, but not corruption. Finally we arrive at the Friar's promised victim-protagonist, the archdeacon's summoner, distinguished for us by one of Chaucer's negative superlatives – 'A slyer boye nas noon in Engelond' (1322). The 53 lines devoted to a description of the summoner's activities do four things. They put off even longer the start of the narrative. They show the summoner betraying his master's interests to advance his own. They depict a character whose energies flow exclusively into his professional activities, a slight difference from the 'good felawe', frequenter of taverns and privy 'puller of finches', described in the General Prologue. Finally they tempt the Friar out of even this pretence of storytelling into a direct expression of his feelings. The Friar's boast that he need fear no reprisal, for he and his brethren are out of the Summoner's jurisdiction, gives his rival an opening he is not slow to take advantage of –

> For thogh this Somonour wood were as an hare,
> To telle his harlotrye I wol nat spare;
> For we been out of his correccioun.
> They han of us no jurisdiccioun,
> Ne nevere shullen, terme of alle hir lyves.
> 'Peter! so been the wommen of the styves,'
> Quod the Somonour, 'yput out of oure cure!' (1327–33)

This stinging retort appears to anger the Friar into losing some of his poise. In his vituperative account of the summoner's activities the Friar cannot resist calling his victim names – 'This false theef, this somonour' (1338), a Judas in his thievery (1350), 'a theef, and eek a somnour, and a bawde' (1354), 'a dogge for the bowe' in his ability to smell out lechery in all its forms (1369 ff). This depiction of a corrupt extortioner, organizer of his own spy network, always on the lookout for victims to blackmail, hardly prepares us for the protagonist of

Canterbury Tales, London, Boston, Sydney, 1985, p. 166) associates both the Friar's Tale and the Summoner's Tale with the fabliaux, but calls them satirical anecdotes.

the narrative, vicious, grasping and conscienceless, it is true, but insatiably curious and deaf to all the warnings he gets of his own danger.

The Friar's delay in starting his own narrative has kept his audiences, the pilgrims and us too, suspended in a kind of limbo. We have only half left the world of the pilgrimage for the story world, for he keeps reminding us of his ulterior motive, sometimes dropping entirely the pretence of narrative and referring to himself as a part of a first-person plural group, us friars, indulging his hostility to summoners beyond anything justified in the fiction.

Once the Friar begins his narrative, almost all direct vituperation ceases. Even the echo of the name-association when his fiend and the summoner both introduce themselves as bailiffs:

> 'Artow thanne a bailly?' 'Ye,' quod he.
> He dorste nat, for verray filthe and shame
> Seye that he was a somonour, for the name.   (1392–4)

Even this unwillingness to acknowledge his calling has its part in the narrative strategy. The fiend turns out later to know the summoner's identity without being told. The tale makes a brilliantly comic synthesis of its disparate parts, the nice theological distinction between the way things and animals on the one hand and people on the other get successfully sent to the devil. The conversation between the summoner and the fiend suggests in a curious way a scene from a mock bildungsroman. We as audience catch all the implications; the summoner as innocent interlocutor hears only the facts. When he learns the real identity of his companion and how he would ride 'Unto the worldes ende for a preye' (1455), the slant rhyme 'sey ye' and the two punning ye's in the next line mock his insensitivity:

> 'A!' quod this somonour, 'benedicite! What sey ye?
> I wende ye were a yeman trewely.'   (1456–7)

Later the fiend can confidently call him 'leeve sire somonour' (1474) and tell him he will know enough of hell by direct experience to beat out Virgil and Dante for a professorship in the subject (1516 ff) without fear of alerting him to his danger. The colloquy has the leisurely quality of a game as it postpones the action and presents us with the anomaly of the fiend as witty underdog.

In fact it is the fiend who works under the harder taskmaster, the archdeacon's vigilance being somewhat slack in comparison with God's. The fiend is the one who feels under time pressure and wants to get on with the securing of his prey. The summoner, accustomed to seizing whatever is not too heavy or too hot (1436), points out to his brother what the carter seems to have given him, his horses, the wagon, and its contents. The devil of course knows better and instructs the summoner on the importance of 'entente'. This lesson out of the way, we are ready for the long-awaited climax, the visit announced at the beginning of the narrative to 'an old wydwe, a ribibe', where the summoner will feign an action 'for he wolde brybe' (1377 f). The summoner hopes to show his unsuccessful brother how to make a living 'as in this contree' (1579). He proceeds to demonstrate his technique – false accusation, naked extortion, pure aggression, without subtlety, without mercy:

> 'Nay thanne,' quod he, 'The foule feend me fecche
> If I th'excuse, though thou shul be spilt!'
> 'Allas!' quod she, 'God woot, I have no gilt.'   (1610–12)

The summoner's outrageous insistence that she is guilty not only now but in the past revives her spirit. She gives him the lie and consigns his body and her pan to the devil. This time there is no doubt as to intent. Her answer to the devil's question adds the one element still lacking for human damnation:

> 'The devil,' quod she, 'so fecche hym er he deye,
> And panne and al, but he wol hym repente!'
> 'Nay, olde stot, that is nat myn entente,'
> Quod this somonour, 'for to repente me
> For anything that I have had of thee.
> I wolde I hadde thy smok and every clooth!'   (1628–33)

By refusing to repent the summoner has sent himself to hell.

This brings us to another level, below the obvious fiction of Chaucer as pilgrim, of Chaucer as narrator, to the level of Chaucer as poet.

Chaucer's skill and his proclivities will figure in whatever he writes. His purpose, however, is to disappear himself. He wants us to see the actions of the pilgrims not as something Chaucer the poet invented but as something Chaucer the pilgrim observed. Motives, poetic effects, levels of discourse, narrative structures even, are presented as the choices not of Chaucer but of his fellow pilgrims. The Friar's divided purposes are a case in point. They can be seen as determining not only what happens in the tale but as extending beyond the blessing that brings the tale to an end:

> And God, that maked after his ymage
> Mankynde, save and gyde us, alle and some,
> And leve thise somonours goode men bicome!   (1642–4)

The Friar's sense of himself as having status in the community and performing dignified roles in its rituals takes over in an epilogue. He cannot quite forget the summoner, but if he could have, he would have spent time warning the pilgrims about the punishments of hell and the necessity for alertness against the temptations of Satan, who will not be permitted to tempt 'yow over youre myght'. On the one hand he is indulging in the 'scole-matere' he had criticized the Wife for discussing 'heere as we ryde by the weye' (1274 ff). On the other hand he is showing as a preacher might how the events of his tale apply to all men. By this sermonette he tries to diminish ex post facto the elements of hostile biography and turn his tale into an exemplum. In the end it becomes exemplary of his own frailty:

> And preyeth that thise somonours hem repente
> Of hir mysdedes, er that the feend hem hente.   (1663–4)

The Friar's self-control has been far from perfect. But in his epilogue Chaucer has had him show an awareness of the other pilgrims. His attack on summoners has been witty, effectively structured, theologically sound. It has enabled him at the same time to pray for their reformation. The Summoner's anger so dominates the transition as to eliminate everything else. As earlier, when the Friar interrupted the Wife of Bath, the Summoner's response is explosive as if he had in him some chemical reagent. As a result the quarrel becomes the major element of fiction. It fills the narrator's memory of events to the exclusion of all else. His description of the Summoner's anger in its physical manifestation is impressive. Stretching high in his stirrups is not enough. The Summoner quakes like an aspen leaf. But only for an instant is he incapacitated. His ire internalizes itself. He becomes an effective instrument of revenge, first courteously asking for his turn at storytelling and immediately seizing on the Friar's complacent claim in his sermonette to knowledge of the pains of hell:

> This Frere bosteth that he knoweth helle,
> And God it woot, that it is litel wonder;
> Freres and feendes been but lyte asonder   (1672–4)

And he goes on to tell his scatological anecdote of the friar who was comforted in a vision of hell by his inability to find there a single friar. An angel disabuses him by showing him twenty thousand swarming like bees 'Out of the develes erse' (1694). If hell was summoners' heritage in the Friar's Tale (1641), a special part of hell belongs to friars as their heritage 'of verray Kynde' (1706). It is characteristic of the Summoner to go the Friar one better in every aspect of his performance. If the Friar will tell a tale or two about summoners 'er that I go' (841), the Summoner will tell two or three about friars before they get to Sidyngborne (847). If the Friar prays for the reform of summoners, the Summoner will end his anecdote

> 'God save yow alle, save this cursed Frere!
> My prologe wol I ende in this manere.'   (1707–8)

The blessing underlines that this has been one tale about friars. The labelling it a prologue insures that he can continue telling stories. The Summoner in his anger has instinctively deconstructed the Friar's Tale, where the witty fiend as surrogate carries out the Friar's purposes and not proximity but identity is uncovered. The Summoner's Tale is in a sense all intrusion. He has designed a fiction not just to expose friars but to expose a particular friar very like the one on pilgrimage. He had earlier accused the Friar of losing his patience in his own impatient explosion at the Friar's interruption of the Wife of Bath. He will now tell a tale in which his own anger will recur on a number of levels. His victim-protagonist will end up almost as angry as he is himself at the conclusion of the Friar's Tale. No sense of dignity or status restrains the Summoner. He repeatedly mocks the Friar's social pretensions, and seems to understand that the lower his own position the greater the fall of the Friar since their struggle brings them both to the same level. Chaucer has devised a fiction for the Summoner with no source and no close analogues. Like the Friar's Tale it purports not to be a fiction. But the marshy country of Holderness in Yorkshire is more specific than the Friar's 'in my contree'; we get a more detailed picture of a rural community and its hierarchy of class; there is the same easy command of idiom and intercourse but no claim to ultimate judgment on the fates of any of the characters.

The outstanding feature of the Summoner's Tale is the way the friar's voice dominates. If the Friar tells a fiction in which a summoner sends himself to hell, the Summoner devises one in which the friar exposes himself by what he says. The statistics of the two tales are illuminating. In the Friar's Tale the fiend actually has more lines than the summoner, and the two together account for 197 lines or almost two thirds of the 344 lines of the tale. The friar in the Summoner's Tale accounts alone for more than three fifths of the 586 lines of the tale, and if we eliminate the scene at the lord's house, the proportion is almost four fifths or 336 out of 450.

The Summoner wastes no time on description but presents the friar in two short episodes, preaching and begging. In the first we hear him exciting the people to trentals and contrasting the lazy 'possessioners' who manage only a mass a day with the zeal of the friars, whose masses 'hastily ysonge' deliver the souls of friends and relatives from the punishments of the afterlife. From preaching the friar turns immediately to begging, hitting each house in turn, having his fellow write the names of the donors, 'Ascaunces that he wolde for hem preye' (1745), and putting whatever is given in a sack borne for them by a 'sturdy harlot' from the inn. This maximization of profit from preaching and begging reaches its climax when the companion friar 'planed awey' the names he had written in his 'tables'.

> 'Nay, ther thou lixt, thou Somonour!' quod the Frere.   (1761)

The Summoner has trapped the Friar into objecting only when the account threatens the profits. The interruptions underline the extent to which the quarrel is a no-win situation for the Friar. That he has put himself in the position of caring what a churl like the Summoner says about him demeans him. Each time he feels impelled to respond exposes him further.

With the friar's visit to the house of his friend Thomas his self-exposure intensifies. Here he can expect both relaxation and profit. His unbuttoned ease displays itself in a number of ways. He sends his companions on to the inn. He expresses his own sense of well-being despite Thomas's bedridden illness. He does not, as he will later do at the lord's house, reject the title of 'maister' by which both Thomas and his wife repeatedly address him. He freely displays his interest in the wife, embracing her, chirping with his lips as he kisses her sweetly, declaring himself to be her servant, praising her beauty above all the other wives in church, and finally taking her criticism of Thomas's irritability as reason for admonishing him to amend his ire.

The reflection of details from the Friar's portrait in the General Prologue extends even to the manner of speech. The Summoner's friar interposes French words 'To make his Englissh sweete upon his tonge' (A265). His response to the wife's question, 'What wol ye dyne?' epitomizes his effort at softening the impact of language:

> 'Now dame,' quod he, 'now *je vous dy sanz doute*,
> Have I nat of a capon but the lyvere,
> And of youre softe breed nat but a shyvere,
> And after that a rosted pigges heed –
> But that I nolde no beest for me were deed –
> Thanne hadde I with yow hoomly suffisaunce.'   (1838–43)

The negative conditionals in the form of questions, the five-syllable glide of identical plus rhyme in 'but the lyvere' 'but a shyvere' (with the reversal of stress on 'nat' in the second line syncopating the rhythm),[18] and the parenthetical exception disclaiming in his gourmet demands any request for special efforts on his behalf, help to give voice to the friar's ingratiating hypocrisy.

---

[18] Two other instances of identical plus rhyme occur in the Wife of Bath's Prologue, D 471f, and in the portrait of the Squire, A 97f. Each of the three has its own special quality.

His confidence that anything goes vis-a-vis these rustics leads him to respond to the word that their child has died since his last visit with the claim that he saw the death by revelation, he and two of his brothers. They had a vision of the boy's soul 'born to blisse', upon which the whole convent arose and sang a Te Deum. This transparent invention exemplifies the special efficacy of friars' prayers and introduces a disquisition on the subject the friar finds it hard to bring to a close. Repetitive as the four uses of the 'prayeres-freres' rhyme suggests, the passage keeps associating cleanness, fasting, poverty, and chastity with friars and has as its undercurrent the very different lives of lay folk and 'possessioners'. The insolence of the comparison matches the outreach of its allusions and imagery. Everything, even puns, can be seen as strengthening the position of friars. Dives and Lazarus, the ten commandments, the expulsion from Paradise, the beatitudes, the psalms of David contribute in turn to their special sanctity. Possessioners are like Jovinyan, who is like a whale and a swan, and 'Vinolent as botel in the spence' (1931). The friars' prayers like hawks springing up into flight make their 'sours' to God's two ears. Meanwhile Dives and divers (1877 f), chaced and chaast (1916 f), the buf of a belch and the Latin 'eructavit' (1934) add to the general effect of excess. All of this, the friar asserts, refers directly to Thomas, who could hardly thrive were he not a brother aided day and night by the chapter's prayers.

When Thomas points out how little he has benefited from the money he has spent on 'diverse manere freres', the friar dresses him down severely for dividing his support: 'Youre maladye is for we han to lyte' (1962). The discovery that he might have had much more from Thomas incites the friar into a paroxism of rebuke:

> A, yif that covent half a quarter otes!
> A, yif that covent four and twenty grotes!
> A, yif that frere a peny and lat hym go!
> Nay, nay, Thomas, it may no thyng be so!
> What is a ferthyng worth parted in twelve?
> Lo ech thyng that is oned in himselve
> Is moore strong than whan it is toscatered.
> Thomas, of me thou shalt nat been yflatered;
> Thou woldest han oure labour al for noght.   (1963–71)

This colloquy in which the friar does almost all the talking has as its silent component Thomas's growing anger. The double focus is especially strong, made possible by the vividness on both levels – within the story by the friar's complacent arrogance, on the pilgrimage level by the way this caricature of the Friar contributes to the Summoner's vengeance.

A sudden shift in the friar's discourse serves as an implicit stage direction. Aware of Thomas's response to his rebuke the friar remembers that he had earlier planned to say a word about 'ire' (1835):

> Ye lye heere ful of anger and of ire,
> With which the devel set youre herte afyre,
> And chiden heere the sely innocent,
> Youre wyf, that is so meke and pacient.   (1981–4)

The ensuing lecture-sermon on ire raises some interesting points. The Summoner's purposes have found expression up to now through his fictions. His protagonist has been setting himself up for the denouement, doing everything possible to anger Thomas and at the same time displaying qualities the Prologue portrait had ascribed to the Friar. The lecture on anger continues to carry out these purposes. It is calculated to infuriate its sole auditor in a number of ways. Occasioned by the wife's complaint, it veers from the sinfulness of ire to the danger of antagonizing a woman and it reiterates the friar's sensitivity to social distinctions that place Thomas not only low enough to be told his vices but low enough to be told by the friar that he can be told (2075 ff).

The exempla that take up more than half the lecture-sermon tell a different story. They stem from the friar's boast that he could go on speaking about the evils of anger for a whole day and from the casually related prayer that God send little power to 'an irous man' (2014). In the first of the exempla the angry judge sentences all three knights to death, though the only 'crime' committed is the failure to carry out the execution of an innocent man. The second follows without a line of transition. In it Cambises shows his vertuous counsellor how little drinking affects him by taking bow and arrow and shooting the counsellor's child. The third exemplum shows Cyrus the Persian emperor destroying the river Gysen because his horse drowned in it. Instead of exemplifying for Thomas the only auditor how sinful it is to yield to anger, each of the three exempla shows the protagonist triumphantly and destructively allowing his anger full rein. The friar's purposes in preaching to Thomas are quite different from the message implicit in these fictions. Here the Summoner's anger is finding an insidious release through sub-fictions that don't fulfil their ostensible function within his larger fiction.

The friar concludes his sermon by returning to the evils of anger – the devil's knife at Thomas's heart – and asks for his complete confession. Denied by Thomas who says he has just confessed to the curate, the friar moderates his demand to gold for the construction of their cloister. The subject inspires a passionate peroration on what friars contribute to the world (the sun being the only image sufficiently vital) and on what they have contributed since the Old Testament days of Elijah and Elisha. His plea for help brings him finally to one knee. The total effect of the friar's efforts infuriates Thomas. 'Wel ny wood for ire', he first establishes that he is a lay-brother and gets the friar to swear to divide among his fellows what he is planning to give. The generous fart he lets in the friar's groping hand has two effects. It successfully transmits Thomas's anger to the friar. The tale reflects the contagion of anger in the world created by the Summoner from the narrator to one and then the other of the two principal characters in his fiction. It also reiterates the limits of the Summoner's imagination. He sees as the ultimate punishment for his enemy his being subjected to some form of anal discharge.

The Summoner like the Friar finds it difficult to release his audience or his victim. He carries the friar of the tale, so furious he can barely speak, to the 'lord of that village' for vengeance. After recovering sufficiently to tell the lord and lady the insult and injury he, his order, and holy church have suffered, he sums it up:

> 'Madame,' quod he, 'by God I shal nat lye,
> But I on oother wyse may be wreke,
> I shal disclaundre hym over al ther I speke,

> This false blasphemour that charged me
> To parte that wol nat departed be
> To every man yliche, with meschaunce!'   (2210–15)

Any question of punishment for the churl dissipates itself in the lord's fascination with the problem in 'ars-metrik' posed by the equal division of the fart. The lord first ponders the issue, then comments on it. Clearly he has no intention of taking any action against Thomas: 'Now ete youre mete and lat the cherl go pleye.' Thus the way is clear for the 'wordes of the lordes squier' and a third indulgence, this on a purely intellectual plane, in anal vengeance on the part of the Summoner. The Summoner has devised a devastating response to the Friar. Self-exposure has the curious effect of enhancing his vengeance. The Friar has trapped himself into an engagement which can only besmirch him. The Summoner is so little interested in ultimates that he omits the blessing and substitutes the observation that he has carried out his threat:

> My tale is doon; we been almoost at towne   (2294)

In the dialectic of voice and genre it is the voice that is dominant at beginning and end. The D fragment starts out with a character created by Chaucer in full voice. It ends with a character's character whose voice dominates the character's tale. In each case the dominance of voice is intentional. Chaucer wants the Wife to dominate and he wants her to want to dominate. Chaucer wants the Summoner to want his character the friar to dominate and want to dominate. The Summoner also wants the friar to expose himself through what he says and the way he says it and at the same time to be recognizable as a satiric portrait of the Friar on the pilgrimage. The context in which the three fictions of the fragment occur is present within the three tales.

The intensity of self-absorption and self-exposure gives the D fragment its startling unity of impact. So strong had been the motivation of the pilgrims that it permeates all the levels of fiction, not only the level of the drama observed by Chaucer as pilgrim and reported by him as narrator but the stories the pilgrims tell as well, and in one instance the stories a character within a story tells. Interruptions in the fragment occur in practically every segment and remind us of the audience of pilgrims, our fellow listeners as it were. Only when we draw back and view the fragment as a whole do we appreciate the brilliance with which Chaucer has realized his vision. What he brought from his reading and experience, the skills he had acquired over his years as a poet coalesced in these moments of creation. Incorporated into the fragment but not confined by it, the dominating figure of the Wife of Bath was to cast its shadow beyond. The expansive enthusiasm with which she developed the fictions of her own life had its origins before the fragment was conceived and would have an influence beyond its confines; Chaucer perhaps had in mind for her a prominent role in the Day of Judgment at the Tabard. The quarrel of Friar and Summoner, despite its intensity, could have little effect on the other pilgrims. A disparate diptych, two fabliaux turned into hostile biographies, the quarrel brought the fragment to a triumphant close. The lofty conception inherent in the narrative the Friar 'chose' to tell suffered from his chronic inability to resist vituperation against the Summoner. The quarrel is a trap he wills himself into, as the summoner in his tale wills himself into hell. Meanwhile we experience the summoner's dialogue with the witty fiend who finds him deliciously impervious to his danger, the striking vignette of the carter who has no real intention of consigning his horses and his wagon to the devil, and the final scene at the widow's house, where the summoner sends himself to hell. The sermonette on the dangers of hell-fire instead of redeeming the Friar's Tale from its exclusive association with vilification of the Summoner provides his enemy with an opening for the first of his scurrilous and devastating attacks. The Summoner's anger infects his performance. The strategy of his revenge repeatedly covers his enemy the Friar with filth. But the baseness of the materials that go into the story soars to a kind of singing dissonance by the way its ingredients fit together. The voices and genres multiply. Fabliau, satire, biography, autobiography, the great frame narrative reflective of a culture, are simultaneously present in the episodes of the Summoner's Tale. The Summoner mimics through the voice of his protagonist the pilgrimage-Friar as he repeatedly subjects the friar to the filth of his revenge. Chaucer has the Summoner make his character express a comic hubris cosmic in scope in a series of startling events – the sermon on trentals, the intimate way he greets Thomas's wife, the ingratiating sweetness with which he orders his meal, the claim of vision and elaborate celebration when he hears of the death of Thomas's child, his panegyric on friars, the paroxysm of his reproach of Thomas for having given money to other friars, the sermon on anger, the groping for treasure, the fury of his departure, and the final scene at the lord's house with its lesson in ars-metrik. Only in the exempla of the sermon on anger and in the final scene does the emphasis shift from the extraordinary parodic imitation of the Friar. The surrealistic image of the wheel, with Thomas centred above and with friars' noses under every spoke and our protagonist's at the hub, beautifully combines vulgarity, justice, and geometry to serve as coda for tale, quarrel, and fragment.

Chaucer the pilgrim and Chaucer the narrator are present in this fragment in the resonance of the Prologue's pilgrim-portraits. Otherwise they are almost entirely silent. Not so Chaucer the poet. The pilgrims' voices have their origin in Chaucer's imagination. They incorporate his wit, his skill with words. They reflect his penchant for telling stories in a dramatic way. Implicit in the fragment is a poetics of voice and genre.[19]

---

[19] Voice and genre are in themselves complex and have a complex interrelationship. Voice draws on that segment of consciousness unshared with any other creature. Genre on the other hand is outside the personal. It represents the impingement from outside that occurs ordinarily through the senses. Voice and genre reflect the dichotomy of the two concepts of time discussed in Ricoeur's *Time and Narrative*, the dichotomy in physics of the wave and particle theories of light. They reflect too the relationship between sign and signified, between the poetics of sound (metrics) and the poetics of meaning.

CHAUCER AND THE POETICS OF UTTERANCE

A. S. G. EDWARDS

In recent years much has been written about the nuance and texture of Chaucer's language and its underlying rhetorical traditions and strategies.[1] But rather less explored has been Chaucer's own sense of the nature and implications of language itself. It is difficult to believe that he did not have some interest in the question. The issues of nominalist philosophy raised in the work of William of Ockham preoccupied Chaucer's contemporaries or near contemporaries, men like Fitzralph, Holcot, Bradwardine, Wyclif and Chaucer's friend 'philosophical Strode', Ralph Strode of Merton.[2] Chaucer's own philosophical interests would have made him conscious at least in a general way of what was in the air.

What would obviously have given a sharper focus to such interests was Chaucer's use for the first time of English verse as a cultivated medium for poetic utterance. When Hoccleve acclaimed him, in the generation after his death, as the 'firste fyndere of our faire langage',[3] he was pointing to a basic historical fact of which Chaucer himself was evidently acutely conscious from his earliest works. In these works, his dream visions, we usually see an affirmative sense of such utterance, often expressing itself in an exuberant virtuosity that seems to affirm, almost programmatically, the capacity of English poetry to match the French and Italian vernaculars.

But there is also evident, from fairly early on in Chaucer's poetic career, a different awareness of 'our faire langage', one that reveals a rather less optimistic sense of its creative possibilities, and which is, I think, consistently stressed in the *Canterbury Tales*. This sense is manifested in the ways characters in the Tales speak. The representation of the spoken word clearly provided Chaucer with a challenge that he found absorbing. We find the first fully realized response to it in the *Troilus*, in the brilliant renderings of dialogue and soliloquy to reflect complexities of emotion and motive. And, in the *Canterbury Tales*, we are frequently conscious of the dramatic interactions between various characters, and indeed, of the ultimate rationale of the Tales: that characters should talk, and tell tales of 'best sentence and moost solaas' (I, 798). We become keenly aware of the relationship between voice and subject, between who says what how. This awareness has led to an interest in the psychological problems of various narrators and the ways these affect their Tales. There has been

---

[1] For a helpful overview of such discussions see R.O. Payne, 'Chaucer and the Art of Rhetoric', in *Companion to Chaucer Studies*, ed. Beryl Rowland, rev. ed. (Toronto, 1979), pp. 42–64.

[2] See further on this point Russell Peck, 'Chaucer and the Nominalist Questions', *Speculum* 53 (1978) 745–60.

[3] In his *Regement of Princes*; cited from Caroline Spurgeon, *Five Hundred Years of Chaucer Criticism and Allusion* (Cambridge, 1925), I, 22.

correspondingly less interest in the ways characters within the Tales talk and what their utterances may imply. I do not mean to suggest something quite as simple as that speech reveals character. What I would suggest is that the character that is revealed through speech is often shown to possess some distinctive qualities that are often crucially related to what he or she seems to feel the spoken word can do. Speech becomes a way of demonstrating distinctive epistemological assumptions held by characters, assumptions that prove to be of crucial narrative significance. How characters do things with words within Tales seems to be a recurrent preoccupation of Chaucer's, so recurrent that I can do no more than sketch out a few of the more obvious demonstrations of it in a few Tales. I will also try and suggest that this preoccupation becomes ultimately related to a general scepticism about the possibility of effective utterance, not just within particular Tales, but through poetry at all, in a world where speech and its consequences seem so unstable.

It is, in fact, striking how often the narrative dynamic or dramatic force of a Tale depends on a failure of characters to grasp the full implications of what they say, so that speech actually imposes itself upon and defines the limits of physical action. We see such verbal constraints operating at the very beginning of the sequence of the *Canterbury Tales*, in the *Knight's Tale*. The plot of this Tale turns on the love of both Palamon and Arcite for Emily, a love that is occasioned while they are 'dampned to prisoun perpetually' (I, 1175–6 and I, 1342).[4] While they are in prison all they have is words. And it is out of words that they construct a more enduring prison than that which initially confines them. Their love for Emily, which shatters their stoic acceptance of their fate ('We moste endure it; this is the short and pleyn', I, 1091), is based on emotions separated from any contact with actuality. Theseus observes that 'She woot namoore of al this hoote fore / By God, than woot a cokkow or an hare' (I, 1809–10). One of the effects of Chaucer's changes to the *Teseida* is to emphasize this point. He completely eliminates the element of human contact between Emily and Palamon and Arcite at the first crucial encounter and changes the subsequent relationship between the two imprisoned lovers to introduce an intense and irrational mutual antipathy quite different from Boccaccio's rendering. And Chaucer goes on to stress Emily's lack of knowledge of and subsequent lack of interest in her two suitors in ways that are again quite different from Boccaccio where she is flirtatious and concerned for the well being of her admirers. In Chaucer, even when she becomes aware of their love, she remains indifferent, explicitly preferring the chaste charms of Diana, imploring her 'My mayden hede thou kepe and wel conserve, / And whil I lyve, a mayde I wol thee serve' (I, 2329–30).

Such changes to Chaucer's source serve to emphasize the gap between aspiration and object, between Palamon and Arcite's formulation of their love and the reality of Emily's feelings. These differences seem designed to stress a disjunctive relationship between speech and actuality. Because Palamon and Arcite assert something, therefore they feel it is, and act accordingly. Chaucer, on the other hand, seems concerned to stress the tragic irony of a form of love that exists only through the words of Palamon and Arcite and which leads them

---

4   All references to the text of Chaucer are to *The Riverside Chaucer*, general ed. L.D. Benson (Boston, 1987).

from their initial prison into one that becomes increasingly more comprehensive in its denial of freedom of action, so that, by the end of the poem prison has become a metaphor for life itself. 'The foule prisoun of this lyfe' (I, 3061) as Theseus terms it at the Tale's conclusion. In doing so he acknowledges the failure of his own efforts to contain the lovers' strivings, as he has consistently sought to do. In the end, Theseus can only exhort Palamon and Emily to 'maken vertu of necessitee' (I, 3042), after Arcite's death. His exhortation rings hollow, as indeed it must in a Tale that stresses the limitations of the spoken word to explain or control action. Both Palamon and Emily respond revealingly at the end . . . with silence.

If the Knight's Tale suggests that words cannot finally direct the course of human affairs, the Reeve's Tale suggests the world is not necessarily a better one where they can. The dynamic of the plot derives from perceptions about the power of words. The Miller mocks the clerks' skills in verbal analysis, in their ability to make what is small appear large:

> Myn house is streit, but ye han lerned art:
> Ye konne by argumentes make a place
> A myle brood of twenty foot of space.
> Lat se now if this place may suffise,
> Or make it rowm with speche . . .   (I, 4122–6)

Instead, through the narrowness of their physical circumstances in the Miller's 'owene chambre' (I, 4139), they confine words even more narrowly into the precise legal concept of 'esement'. 'Som esement has lawe yshapen us' (I, 4179), Aleyn asserts, and this provides the justification for his having sex with Malyn. And such precise notions of the law and its relationship to conduct, are thrown into relief by Malyn's only speech, after their night of lovemaking. She reveals to him the location of the 'cake of half a busshel' (I, 4244) that her father has stolen, concluding with the prayer that 'goode lemman, God thee save and kepe' (I, 4247). Her words provide the only instance in the Tale where speech expresses concerns beyond the narrowness of selfish preoccupation. But the moment is unique in the Tale. What the other characters say confirms their isolation from the possibility of such experience, either through the narrowness of legal formulation or the inflation of 'deynous Symkyn's' misplaced pride.

We see a different sense of verbal confinement in the Franklin's Tale, although once again, one with legal implications. It is obviously structured around a series of promises, forms of 'trouth,' that cannot all be faithfully adhered to: the marriage of Dorigen and Arveragus, the promise Dorigen makes to Aurelius and the agreement between Aurelius and the clerk. Its various endings emphasize the necessity for some of these forms of 'trouth' to be abrogated before any of the characters can achieve happiness. The Tale concludes with a demonstration of magnanimity extending through the social scale, in which squire and clerk show that they too, like Arveragus, can perform a 'gentil dede', deeds which exempt all the characters from the consequences of ill-considered verbal agreements none wishes to fulfil. The final question of the Tale: 'which was the mooste fre' (V, 1622), stresses the interconnection here between both meanings of 'fre', meaning both 'generous' and also quite literally 'free', liberated from the constraints that words have imposed.

Not all the consequences of a narrow sense of the spoken word are so fortunate. Chaucer seems to reserve his most sustained criticism of the constricting potential of speech for some of the clerical figures in the *Canterbury Tales*. The Friar's and Summoner's Tales are linked at various levels, most obviously at the immediate dramatic level of their quarrel, which recurs throughout the D Fragment and which makes their respective Tales a form of 'quiting'. Both Tales, it has been argued, also employ the same structural patterns.[5] And both draw on a common theme: the nature and consequences of insensate avarice in the ecclesiastical hierarchy. But the Tales are also related in more fundamental ways. The moral thrust of Chaucer's satire does not just depend on the recognition that these characters embody certain stock satiric traits that were typical of late fourteenth century attacks on ecclesiastical corruption. Chaucer seems more concerned to indicate the ultimate causes of such corruption, which he seems to perceive as stemming from a fundamental misunderstanding about the nature of utterance.

In the Friar's Tale, the tragedy of the summoner stems from the fact that he remains throughout an entrenched literalist. For him words only denote, never connote. When he first encounters the diabolic 'bailly' he sees no significance in his wearing a 'courtepy of grene' (III, 1382) or dwelling 'fer in the north contree' (III, 1413), details which are clearly intended to alert the audience to his diabolic origins.[6] And even when the 'bailly' does reveal himself as a devil, the summoner's response demonstrates the extent of his inability to perceive any moral implication to identity. His rejoinder

> . . . benedicite, what sey ye?
> I wende ye were a yeman trewely.
> Ye han a mannes shap as wel as I.
> Han ye a figure thanne determinat
> In helle, ther ye been in your estat?   (III, 1456–60)

expresses itself in a curiosity about externals, about the appearance of things, rather than with what such externals may imply. But for the summoner identity is a matter of surfaces. The question of the devil's 'figure determinat in helle' is unrelated to any interest in the nature of his 'estat'. For such an interest would lead inexorably to an interest in why he had sought the summoner's company at all. The articulation of identity, the naming of something or someone does not, for the Summoner, signify anything about the person or thing named. Such incuriosity extends to his own identity. The summoner never identifies himself to the devil; he 'dorste nat, for verray filthe and shame / Seye that he was a somonour, for the name' (III, 1393–4). And he is still maintaining 'I am a yeman, knowen is ful wyde' (III, 1524) just before the Tale's final action begins. He fails to notice that the devil has already, some time before, addressed him as 'sire somonour' (III, 1474). For him, identification does not intersect with actuality. Thus he confirms his agreement with the devil in terms he seems to feel are almost hyperbolically hypothetical:

---

[5] See Janette Richardson, 'Friar and Summoner: The Art of Balance', *Chaucer Review* 9 (1974–75) 227–36.

[6] See the references cited in *The Riverside Chaucer*, pp. 875–6, notes on lines 1380–3, 1413.

> For though thou were the devel Sathanas,
> My trouthe wol I holde to my brother,
> As I am sworn . . .   (III, 1526–8)

One might feel that a devil is a devil, whether or not he is Satan himself. But to comprehend such a word as 'devil' in any accurate way would require a sense that it possesses a moral component: it says something of more significance about the person thus identified. But for the summoner, knowing a devil is no more disquieting than being like a devil. The devil explains to him:

> My purchasyng is th'effect of al my rente.
> Looke how thou rydest for the same entente,
> To wynne good, thou rekkest nevere how,
> Right so fare I, for ryde wolde I now
> Unto the worldes ende for a preye.   (III, 1451–5)

And the summoner is quick to respond in stressing the affinities they share, and to insist: 'Of thyn aqueyntaunce I wolde praye thee / And eek of brether-hede . . .' (III, 1398–9). (Throughout, both summoner and devil emphasize terms that indicate such relationship and fidelity to it, words like 'brother', 'faithful', 'truly' and their cognates.)

Such a sense of words as bereft of any moral resonance and fixed in the narrow exactitude of the literal defines the summoner's fate. What he says is exactly what he means. And the Friar's Tale consistently stresses that he is destroyed, not through any diabolic stratagem, but through his own insistence that utterance is necessarily an exact reflection of intention, even when confronted with evidence to the contrary.

Thus, when the summoner and the devil meet the carter who cries to his stuck cart: 'The devel have al, bothe hors and cart and hey' (III, 1547), the summoner's response is immediate and literal minded:

> Herkne, my brother, herkne by thy feith!
> Herestow nat how that the cartere seith?
> Hent it anon, for he hath yeve it thee . . .   (III, 1551–3)

The devil, on the other hand, reaches a quite different conclusion:

> Heere may ye sen, myn owene deere brother
> The carl spak oo thing, but he thoghte another.
> Lat us go forth abouten oure viage.
> Heere wynne I nothynge upon cariage.   (III, 1567–70)

This view offers a radically different perception about the relationship between utterance, meaning and intention from that proposed by the summoner. The devil perceives that words do not necessarily reflect intended meaning through actual utterance: 'The carl spak oo thing, but he thoghte another'. The summoner's inability to grasp the truth of this view enables him to create his own damnation, without diabolic stratagem. The old woman who consigns him to 'the devel, blak and rough of hewe' (III, 1622) merely recalls the terms of his own shortsighted agreement with the devil. Even in her curse, she does not condemn him irretrievably, only 'but he wol hym repente' (III, 1629). But the notion of repentance requires a belief in the possibility of the spoken word to represent a state of being. But for the summoner's words lack any such metaphysical referents. His own predatory role requires that they remain fixed and literal. He is damned through a form of imaginative poverty that insists that speech is an exact reflection of intention.

The summoner in the Friar's Tale is punished because he believes that words can only mean one thing. The friar in the Summoner's Tale is punished because words mean nothing to him. This point of contrast between the two Tales seems to have generally gone unremarked. But it seems to lie at the heart of their respective preoccupations. In the Summoner's Tale, the friar's world is constructed around the efficacy of the gloss: 'Glosynge is a glorious thyng, certeyn / For lettre sleeth, so as we clerkes seyn' (III, 1793–4). And as the Friar's Tale has just demonstrated. But 'glosynge' does not invest the Summoner's friar with any moral superiority over the Friar's summoner. Rather, the opportunistic adaptability of his sermonizing demonstrates the connection between the crucial meanings of 'glose', both 'gloss' and 'lie'. The interrelationship of both activities is dramatized in the Friar's utterance where he glosses no text but demonstrates in his attempts at scriptural reference only his own 'glosynge', lying. His hypocritical exhortations about poverty, which are designed to gain him wealth, demonstrate his moral impoverishment, since his words have no fixed point of scriptural meaning.

Hence the 'maner glose' of his sermon becomes consistently self exposing, devoid of any applicability to its intended audience, the sick Thomas, while demonstrating the friar's own avarice. What is also enacted is the causality of his corruption, which is located in his corruption of language itself, so that his real sermon lies not in what he says but what his words show him to be. It becomes a form of self-referential utterance since he has no text and hence nothing to say that is not about himself and his greed. He does not interpret the Word of God, as a sermon might be expected to do. He seeks rather to interpret the word he has created, and in doing so he reveals the only truth he can reveal, the truth about himself.

And the nature of that selfhood is expressed in the fart, which is both dramatically and symbolically apposite. It matches one form of undifferentiated noise against another – the sermon itself. And the comment of the lord's squire 'on the departyng of the fart' extends the implications of this reciprocity of response by envisioning a form of requital whereby the friar will receive back in appropriate form the consequences of his own earlier eructations to the sick Thomas, where he will endure, with his brethren, a foulness of sound and smell that reflects his own spiritual flatulence, a foulness caused by his inability to perceive any connection between anything he says and anything outside of himself.

In the Friar's Tale we see words employed to create a moral universe so narrow and unreflective that it generates its own punishment for its creator. In the Summoner's Tale we see a world where speech and meaning have become capable of limitless expansion. They serve no needs, address no reality beyond private selfishness.

Such selfishness is enacted rather differently in the Pardoner's Tale. Whereas the Friar and the Summoner expose the inadequacies of each other's forms of utterance, the Pardoner shows his own verbal limitations through his insistently autobiographical presence, one which reduces the actual narrative of his Tale to less than half of his total performance. For the rest, we are presented with both a demonstration of his sermonizing skill and his own gleeful insistence on its lack of moral purpose. His preaching, he insists, is 'by rote . . . of nothyng but for covetise' (VI, 433). And yet he contrives to tell a Tale that is exquisitely shaped in its ironies and wholly appropriate to his only theme 'radix malorum est cupiditas'. The conclusion he reaches is that 'though myself bee a ful vicious man, A moral tale yet I yow telle kan' (VI, 459–60). There is, he maintains, no connection between moral assertions and the moral integrity of the teller. This is an assertion that has bothered many critics, some of whom have devoted much ingenuity to trying to prove that the Pardoner is not really a 'ful vicious man'.[7]

But the evidence is not to be found. The Pardoner's self-analysis is demonstrably correct: he is 'a ful vicious man'. Equally, his sermon is a 'moral tale' told with force and narrative economy. But if it is to achieve its purposes, the sermon must not signify to the Pardoner what it must to his audience: 'For mye entente is nat but for to wynne / And nothynge for correctioun of synne' (VI, 403–4). For that 'entente' to be achieved his audience must be conscious of the need for 'correccioun of synne'. And as it succeeds in that purpose it simultaneously demonstrates the ultimate failure of his Pardoner's utterance. For if the words were to have any meaning for him, he could not say them, for if they meant anything to him they would destroy his purpose in saying them. The only way the Pardoner might be a moral man would be if he were to say nothing.

But, of course, like all Chaucer's clerical men he continues to talk. And like nearly all of them he talks too much for his own good – or anyone else's. It is not for this reason that they are obvious foci for satire. But it is this reason that is shown to be the ultimate cause of their moral inadequacy.

When we contrast Chaucer's clerical men with his religious women the point becomes clearer. A number of these do not say too much; indeed, the problem for critics has often been that they do not seem to say nearly enough. One thinks here most immediately of Chaucer's, as it were, non-institutional ladies, Constance and Griselda, who embody most conspicuously such qualities of verbal restraint in the face of extraordinary adversity. They are not medieval Epicoenes. But their responses to such adversity is based on a form of Christian stoicism. In Lydgate's aphorism, they 'see moyche, say lytell and lerne to soffar in tyme'.[8]

Constance manifests this stoicism in its most extreme form. Her silence becomes a way of demonstrating her imperviousnes, her impregnability to the

---

[7] The most famous is G.L. Kittredge's, who places great weight on one passage: 'And lo sires thus I preche / And Jhesu Crist that is oure soules leche / So graunte you his pardoun to receyve, / For that is best: I wol yow nat deceyve' (VI, 915–18). Kittredge describes this as 'an ejaculation profoundly affecting in its reminiscence of the Pardoner's better nature, which he himself thought dead long ago' ('Chaucer's Pardoner', reprinted in *Chaucer: Modern Essays in Criticism*, ed. E. Wagenknecht, New York, 1959), p. 123. But his words, far from being some form of groping recognition of a world higher and better than his own, form an essential part of his total selling strategy. Immediately afterwards he goes on: 'But, sires, o word forgat I in my tale, / I have relikes and pardoun in my male, / As faire as any man in Engelond . . .' (VI, 919–21). The reference to Christ's pardon is clearly a transitional passage to his main theme, his own rather more readily accessible pardon.

[8] See *The Minor Poems of John Lydgate*, ed. H.N. MacCracken, EETS OS 192 (1934), II, 800–1.

adversities that constitute the Christian tragedy – or, more accurately, comedy[9] – of her life in a mutable world. She actually says very little in the Tale.[10] All she does say is designed to demonstrate her trust in God in the midst of her most extreme, most unwarranted sufferings and thereby to demonstrate the force of her initial prayer: 'But Crist that starf for our redempcioun / So yeve me grace his heestes to fulfille,' (II, 283–4). Her final cry is, therefore, particularly striking: 'Now, goode fader, mercy I yow crye! / Sende me namoore unto noon hethenesse, / But thonketh my lord heere of his kyndenesse' (II, 1111–13). This is the first intimation of concern for self in the Tale. Its occurrence at her moment of greatest worldly joy gives an unexpected plangency to her cry. Rather more has perhaps been of Constance's pathos by critics than by Chaucer. Normally the obtrusive presence of the narrator impedes the possibility of emotional engagement at critical moments in the narrative. Her words here give emotional resonance to a figure who would otherwise be largely symbolic, whose silence is generally more powerful than words and whose occasional utterances serve largely to reassure the audience of her trust in her relationship to God.

With Griselde utterance functions rather differently, but to ultimately the same ends. She says a lot more than Constance and says it increasingly in sustained set pieces that are usually additions to or expansions of Petrarch. Whereas Constance's infrequent utterances seem to deflect attention away from her to her consciousness of Divine Mercy, the effect of Griselde's more frequent speeches is to direct attention towards her. They invariably stress the pathos of her situation. And, at the same time, they almost never insist that her sufferings are unjust. Her words affirm Walter's right to behave as he does. Indeed, that she should submit in such an affirmative way has always seemed one of the major critical problems of the Tale. But it is perhaps through the way that Griselde talks to Walter that she becomes intelligible, not in psychological, but in doctrinal terms. For her consciousness of whom she is ultimately addressing seems more significant than what she actually says. Thus, while Walter almost invariably addresses his wife as 'Griseld',[11] she never calls him 'Walter', but always 'lord'.[12] And as her sufferings increase, her uses of the term becomes hedged around with emphatic qualifiers: 'my lord' (IV, 845), 'myn owene lord' (IV, 889), 'myn owene lorde so deere' (IV, 881). The manner of address simultaneously impersonalizes the source of her afflictions and invests it/him with a growing intensity of love, where anger or hate might be expected. Her final speech makes clear the nature of the 'lordship' she ultimately acknowledges:

9 See M.W. Bloomfield, 'The Man of Law's Tale: A Tragedy of Victimization and a Christian Comedy', *PMLA* 87 (1972) 384–90.

10 The most generous account gives her a total of sixty five lines (in a narrative of 1129 lines). Whether all these lines can be confidently attributed to Constance remains moot. I am particularly uncertain about the famous couplet 'Wommen are born to thraldom and penance, / And to been under mannes governance' (II, 286–7), lines which seem more consistent in tone and sentiment with the narrator than with Constance herself.

11 He calls her 'Griseld' ten times: IV, 297, 344, 365, 466, 470, 792, 953, 1030, 1051, 1062 and 'wyf' once (IV, 624).

12 She addresses him fifteen times as 'lord': IV, 523, 568, 570, 575, 579, 581, 652, 814, 845, 858, 881, 889, 967, 1032, 1088. He is only identified as 'Walter' by the narrator: IV, 77, 421, 612, 631, 716, 722, 986, 1044, 1107. He is most commonly referred to as 'a/the/this markys'.

'Grauntmercy lord God, thanke it yow,' quod she,
That ye han saved me my children deere!
Now rekke I nevere to been deed right heere;
Sith I stonde in youre love and in your grace,
No fors of deeth, ne whan my spirit pace!   (IV, 1088–92)[13]

This prayer of thanks provides a moment of spiritual reorientation, affirming a hierarchy of doctrinal priorities that suddenly becomes intelligible in this moment when both social and political hierarchy once more stabilizes. And her utterance triumphantly vindicates her submission, which has enacted the constancy of Christian love, a submission through man to God.

Utterance is rarely employed in this way by Chaucer's virtuous women. But when it is the characters are moved into a different emotional register, one in which feeling intersects with doctrine to inform it with an intensity of experience. Indeed, in both these Tales words become a way of affirming the Word, or articulating doctrine without formal exposition. They dramatize the protagonists's consciousness of their relationship to God, and make their suffering emotionally compelling and doctrinally intelligible, within the structure of Christian faith.

Something of the contrast between Constance and Griselde is represented in the two female religious, the Prioress and the Second Nun. In recent years the Prioress has undergone some critical rehabilitation as her Tale has been seen more in its own terms and less as an extension of her portrait in the General Prologue. Her Tale can be properly seen as a serious attempt to articulate some form of pious utterance. The form of that utterance is one that is set in contradistinction to the spoken word. David Benson has shown clearly that the spoken word in the Tale is often 'incompetent when not actually evil'.[14] The emphasis falls instead on song, replacing reason with feeling. Spoken discourse is to be avoided, the Tale suggests, since it deflects attention from truth.

The Second Nun's Tale is also concerned with the problem of the spoken word, albeit in a rather more complex fashion. The Tale is encapsulated within Cecilia's formal modes of utterance. It begins with song and ends with preaching. The first words Cecilia utters are the praise of God she 'sang' (VIII, 135). Her last are her demonstration of the power of Christian exposition to transcend death as 'she gan to preche' (VIII, 539). These moments, with their strong liturgical associations, remain curiously distanced from the effect of the narrative itself. Emphasis there seems to move from a demonstration of the power of the spoken word to initiate a process of conversion in the first part of the Tale to a demonstration of its failure to do so at the Tale's climax. The dramatic set piece of the narrative is Cecilia's dialogue with her enemy Almachius (VIII, 424–511). Here the effect is to present Cecilia in her own words as an embodiment of Christian constancy. But the demonstration of such constancy derives from the ultimate failure of her words to function in Christian

---

13 As will be apparent, my punctuation of IV, 1088 differs from that of most editions, which read: 'Grauntmercy, lord, God thanke it yow'. This punctuation creates a reading that is, in some ways easier, but which seem ultimately less intelligible, particularly if we credit that Walter is the reason why 'rekke I nevere to been deed right herre' (IV, 1090). The use of 'thank' with the dative of person as an indirect object is attested in Middle English usage in the fourteenth century: *OED*, s.v. 'thank', *v.*4.a.

14 C. David Benson, *Chaucer's Drama of Style* (Chapel Hill, N.C., 1986), p. 137.

terms; they fail to convert. Climatically, what Cecilia says is presented as less important than what she embodies.

This is scarcely surprising, given both traditions of female hagiography and Chaucer's apparent fidelity to his putative source, a version of the *Legenda Aurea*. What may be suggestive, in terms of my present argument, is the actual positioning of the Second Nun's Tale in the final sequence of verse Tales. For the Second Nun's Tale is followed by the Canon's Yeoman's. And it is not necessarily coincidental that Chaucer juxtaposes a tale that celebrates a Christian triumph through the failure of the spoken word to convert with one that dramatizes the failure of wholly material conversion through the alchemical process and the related corruption of those who should speak the word of God, his priests. The exploration of such questions modulates from examination of the limits of the spoken word to the broader issue of the limits of poetry itself.

In the balancing of the Second Nun's Tale with the Canon's Yeoman's we see another, more malign demonstration of the power of conversion by words. In the Prologue we are presented with images of haste and urgency, first in the desire of Canon and Yeoman to join the pilgrimage and then in the precipitate departure of the former. Such images merge into the autobiographical revelations of the Yeoman in the first part of the Tale where the spoken word is shown to generate its own dynamic that controls and impels those committed to the pursuit of alchemy through the elaboration of a terminology that becomes self referential and self justifying providing its own momentum to the further pursuit of folly: 'We faille of that which we wolden have / And in oure madnesse evermore we rave' (VIII, 959–60).

The point is underlined in the switch in narrative modes between Parts I and II of the Tale. We move from a world where we are caught up in the compulsively obfuscatory energy of alchemical jargon to one where all is painfully clear. In Part I we see the impetus to false faith; in Part II we see the spiritual consequences of being swept away by this impetus, as the false canon deludes the foolish priest. It is said of the canon that:

> . . . in his termes he wol hym so wynde
> And speke his wordes in so sly a kynde
> Whanne he commune shal with any wight,
> That he wol make hym doten anonryght,
> But it a feend be, as hymselven is.   (VIII, 980–4)

Faith depends on words to give form to the incorporeal. These 'wordes [of] so sly a kynde' lead to a grotesque dislocation of spiritual language as the priest prays 'for love of God' (VIII, 1351) and 'for Goddes sake' (VIII, 1357) for the key to 'real' wealth. The focus of this part of the Tale remains firmly on the deluded and the consequences of delusion, as faith becomes directed to an illusory quest for the material.

This demonstration of the deluding potential of the spoken word provides an obvious point of contact between the Canon's Yeoman's and the Manciple's Tale, Chaucer final verse one. This is a tale that explicitly preoccupies itself with problems of terminology, with the relationship between naming something and the thing named:

> The wise Plato seith, as ye may rede
> The word moot nede accorde with the dede.

> If men shal telle proprely a thyng,
> The word moot cosyn be to the werkyng. (IX, 207–10)

But the Tale goes on to question whether such a situation actually exists, whether there is a meaningful correspondence between words and truth. The crow is punished for using words that do 'acorde with the dede'. His long reflection on terminology (IX, 211–34) suggests that 'the word' is not typically 'cosyn . . . to the werkyng', that truth is not a fixed thing but defined by the pressure of circumstance. This bitter conclusion leads to the insistence that silence is the only proper course: '. . . be noon auctour newe / Of tidynges whether they been false or trewe' (IX, 359–60).

The positioning of a Tale that embodies such pessimism about the possibility or usefulness of using language to tell the truth is once again suggestive. After the Manciple's Tale Chaucer abandons poetry altogether for the prosaic, didactic clarity of the Parson's Tale and the Retraction. This is a mode of utterance with which Chaucer the pilgrim has aligned himself earlier, after the failure of the 'drasty rymyng' of Sir Thopas, which burlesques not just creaking romance motifs and collocations, but also the creating figure of the poet. And Melibee's prose form parallels that of the Parson's Tale, just as its concluding prayer for 'the blisse that nevere hath ende' (VII, 1888) is echoed in the Retraction, which repudiates much of Chaucer's *oeuvre*.

The poetric incapacities of Chaucer the pilgrim are linked to the difficulties other characters have in the *Canterbury Tales* in establishing whether speech is 'false or trewe'. For words often do not provide insight but some form of limitation that circumscribes characters emotionally, or physically or spiritually. In observing this, Chaucer seems also concerned to distance the figure of the poet/author from the implications of such activities and to range himself with modes of utterance that are usually literal and prosaic, in their affirmation of the promise of 'the word of Jhesu Crist' (X, 1076) with which the *Tales* end.

We see, then, in the *Tales*, a recurrent preoccupation with the nature of utterance, which can itself be seen to mirror a larger concern with the role of the poet as speaker. This larger concern becomes finally a pessimistic one if the evidence of the Retraction is to be properly understood in the light of what has preceded it. Indeed, the Retraction, the greatest critical problem in the *Canterbury Tales*, may perhaps best be read, not as ironical, nor as an extended modesty topos[15] but as a confirmation of what many of the Tales seem to suggest: as, that is, a serious reflection on the responsibility of poetic utterance and on the difficulties in fulfilling those responsibilities.[16]

---

[15] Such views are summarized, and references given in James D. Gordon, 'Chaucer's Retraction: A Review of Opinion', in *Studies in Medieval Literature: In Honor of Professor Albert Croll Baugh*, ed. MacEdward Leach (Philadelphia, 1961), pp. 81–96.

[16] For helpful observation I am indebted to my colleague, Professor Elizabeth Archibald.

CAVE AND WEB: VISION AND POETRY IN CHAUCER'S *LEGEND OF GOOD WOMEN*

PAUL B. TAYLOR

> 'Love weaves its own tapestry, spins
> its own golden thread, with its own sweet
> breath breathes into being its mysteries –
> bucolic, lusty, gently as the eyes of daisies'.
>
> John Hawkes, *The Blood Oranges*, p. 1

In Chaucer's *Legend of Good Women*, Philomene speaks for the first time when she finds herself in a cave, deep in a dark wood, into which Tereus has led her. 'Where is my suster, brother Tereus?' she asks.[1] If the question sounds ingenuously pathetic, it is because Philomene is giving voice to her terror rather than seeking information. Evoking what she does not, but would rather, see, her words bring to a vision of cave an inner image of palace, and attribute to Tereus's open design for sexual treachery a potential kindly love and care. Her language proves poetry's capacity to collocate visible appearances with hidden forms. Her question, then, would metamorphose strange cave into a familiar domestic shape and correct Tereus's intent by displaying that sign to him verbally. Poetry, as such, is orthoscopic. It directs vision to ideas behind substances. Tereus's lust, however, is unmoved by either tears seen or words heard, and he fulfils his foul intent.

Philomene's words fail to mediate her desire because they cannot convert a character earlier misread. The ontological blur between a man's casual appearance and his formal reality is the topic Chaucer announces in the motto which heads the legend (in two of the twelve extant manuscripts) – *Deus dator formarum* – and in the gloss to the motto in the legend's opening lines:

> Thow yevere of the formes that has wrought
> This fayre world and bar it in they thought
> Eternally er thow thy werk began,
> ... Whi sufferest thow that Tereus was bore,
> That is in love so fals and so forswore? (2228–35)

In other than philosophical contexts, *form* designates the visible aspect of a thing, its shape, array or manner; but, in the jargon of the Neoplatonist Scholastics, the word identifies the invisible creative pattern of a thing.[2] In the perfec-

---

1 *Legend of Good Women*, line 2315. The text is Larry D. Benson, ed., *The Riverside Chaucer* (Boston, 1987). All subsequent quotations are identified in parentheses by line number.
2 Robert Worth Frank, Jr., *Chaucer and The Legend of Good Women* (Cambridge, Mass. 1972), p. 144, cites this passage as an 'effort to give some philosophical weight and foundation to the poem, It tells us how to look at Tereus'. The conceit is found in similar terms in Ovid,

tion of God's Creation, the outer form of a thing is a transparent sign of its inner form. In Dante's version of Creation, '*Forma e materia, congiunte e puette / usciro ad esser che con avia fallo*'; Form and matter, joined and simple, came into being with no defect.[3] Ovid describes Philomene as *divitior forma* (*Metamorphoses* 6, 452) 'richer in beauty' than her array. In the *Consolation of Philosophy*, Boethius's Lady Philosophy explains the philosophic sense of the term by distinguishing between the *form* of a man which is contained in Divine thought, and his *figure* which is contained in nature. *Form*, she continues, is difficult to recognize in the figure because the figure signifies a thing, but not the thing which forms it (5, prose 4). The matter that is man, like Tereus, has a natural appetite for form, an innate yearning to achieve its original design as well as a natural need, as matter decays, to take on new shapes and appearances; to renew its life. In the *Legend* Chaucer describes Jason's sexual appetite in these terms:

> As Matter appetiteth forme alwey
> And from forme into forme it passen may,
> Or as a welle that were botomles,
> Ryght so can false Jason have no pes.
> For to desyren thourgh his apetit
> To don with gentil women his delyt,
> This is his lust and his felicite.   (1582–8)

Painting man matter and woman form makes of amatory pursuit a game of body chasing spirit, but in traditional thought man is form and woman matter, and Chaucer's Jason is concerned with the form that is flesh, not idea. Yearning after the body of a woman is not a sin in Christian dogma until reason consents to the desire.[4] The organ of desire is the eye, the same organ which mediates

---

Metamorphoses 1, 1–25, Bernard Silvester's *Cosmographia* 1, 2, 3–23, though Chaucer's immediate source is probably Jean de Meun's *Roman de la Rose* 16731–3:

> Dont il portoit en sa pensee
> La bele forme porpensee
> Touz jors en pardurableté.

Jean's source is Boethius's *De Consolatione Philosophiae* 3, m. 9, which Chaucer translates as 'Thow, that art althir-fayrest, berynge the faire world in thy thought, formedest this world to the lyknesse semblable of that faire world in thy thought' (11–14). *Form* is Aristotle's *eidos*, the formal cause of creation, whose final cause in *physis*, nature, whom Jean personifies as the guardian and continuer of forms (16791–2). *Form* is an element's intelligible structure, its DNA if you will, and its principle of motion. In Latin, *forma* designates 'beauty', 'outer appearance', 'species', 'ideal' and 'figure'. *Figure* is Chaucer's usual term for the appearance which conceals a form. The *OED* defines the philosophical sense of the word with reference to Chaucer's use as 'the essential principle of a thing; that which makes anything (matter) a determinant species or kind of being: the essential creative quality'. In Scholastic dialectics, *form* is *actus* in the world of being, while matter is *possibilitas* in the world of becoming. Andreas de Capellanus defines *love* as an inordinate contemplation of a woman's or man's *form* (*De amore* 1,1).

3   *Paradiso* 29, 22–23. The text is Charles S. Singleton (Princeton, 1970–75). Dante aligns *form* with *puro atto* and matter with *potenza*. Boethius, in *De Trinitate* 2, defines God as *uere forma neque imago* 'pure form without image'.

4   Augustine, *De civitate Dei* 12,6. See also *Peter Abelard's Ethics*, ed. D.F. Luscombe (Oxford, 1971), p. 74. Bernard Silvester's Nature (*Cos.* 1,1, 35–36) explains matter's desire to achieve form. Ibn Gabirol, *Fons Vitae* 3, m. 9, identifies form in search of matter as *intelligentsia universalis*.

insight into the virtuous form beneath flesh to stimulate the act of honest love which serves the general good. Jason and Tereus pursue the less honest felicity of sexual pleasure, and their victims are easy prey, having read too late the lust beneath the figure of the men who pursue them.

The *Legend of Good Women* is a catalogue of examples of the complicity of sight in the tragedy of love. As a whole they belie the theory that words can reveal to the inner eye of understanding the invisible forms behind visible shapes,[5] and they constitute a denial of language's orthoscopic capacity to reveal and tighten the essential bond of love which joins man to God.

One can divide the *Legend* into a three-part epistemological track to prove poetry. The first part is the poet's spring outing which incites the second part, a dream which, in turn informs the third part which is the collection of tales of woman-martyrs to love. This triadic structure is headed by a philosophical exposition of the links between seeing and knowing. As familiar as they are, the lines bear repeating:

> A thousand tymes have I herd men telle
> That ther ys joy in heven and peyne in helle,
> And I acorde wel that it ys so;
> But, natheles, yet wot I also
> That ther nis noon dwellynge in this contree
> That eyther hath in hevene or helle ybe
> Ne may of hit other weyes witen
> But as he hath herd seyd or founde it writen;
> For by assay ther may no man it preve.
> But God forbede but men shulde leve
> Wel more thing then men han seen with ye!
> Men shal not wenen every thing a lye
> But yf hymself yt seeth or elles dooth;
> For, God wot, thing is never the lasse sooth,
> Thogh every wight ne may it nat ysee.
> Bernard the monk ne saugh nat all, pardee!   (1–16)[6]

If this passage appears to be a rather light treatment of the sober issue of the soul's eternal reward, it is because Chaucer has framed his epistemological concerns within a 'lewed' and popular perspective of experience. It would be a neat cavil to complain that 'noon dwellyng in this contree' excludes Christ who performed return journeys from both Heaven and hell, as well as Chaucer's own Alceste who addresses the poet after her return from hell, Hercules who sought her there and Theseus who sought another. Heaven and hell are but

---

5   Philosophy, says William of Conches at the beginning of his *Philosophia Mundi*, is the comprehension of things seen and unseen, and an inderstanding of the coherent order of things. The poet has the capacity to reveal the physical and astronomical wonders of the world, says Manilius. See Brian Stock, *Myth and Science in the Twelfth Century* (Princeton, 1972) p. 73 n. Shakespeare's Theseus, inspired by Chaucer's Theseus of the Knight's Tale, sums up this theory:
>   The poet's eye, in a fine frenzy rolling,
>   Doth glance from heaven to earth, from earth to heaven;
>   And as imagination bodies forth
>   The forms of things inknown, the pet's pen
>   Turns them to shapes.   (*MND* 5,1, 12–16)

6   Unless noted otherwise, I refer exclusively to the F-version.

common examples of things inperceptible to the physical eye and unknowable by human experience. Those examples are pertinent, however, to the strategies of the poet in his legends later, for the moral hell on earth suffered by the women of the legends for their blind steadfastness should qualify them for an ultimate heavenly reward, if, as the god of Love declares to the poet in his dream, no true lover goes to hell.[7] If such a reward for earthly suffering is not doctrinally valid, though popularly anticipated, the gap between the doctrine of authority and the expectations of experience is precisely the epistemological issue with which Chaucer is grappling, and specifically with the gap between the words which describe experience and the words which invent ideas. The passage contains banal examples. God can neither *forbede* not *wot* since ne has neither a tongue for the former not an eye for the latter (*wot*, from Old English *witan* implies a knowing from having *seen*). The *Ysee/pardee* rime nicely links two distinct ontologies, and the *ye/lye* rime puts into question man's ability to apprehend truth through his senses.[8] The syntactical ambiguity of the last line quoted has Bernard both knowing of more things than he has seen and seeing more things than God's gift of insight has allowed him.

Besides its dubious match of topic and style, this passage delineates a clear epistemological hierarchy for sight. At the bottom of the scale is the eye which sees the natural form of things, higher is the eye which perceives things as signs, and highest is the eye of faith, like Bernard's, which understands the invisible forms behind natural things.[9] The hierarchy is conventional but most sources have a four-part scale. Boethius's Philosophy has at the bottom of the scale the eye which sees things as matter, then the imaginative eye which discerns things distinct from matter, the reasoning eye which perceives the species or form a substance represents, and, highest of all, the eye of understanding which grasps *forma simplex*.[10] Similitude of things obtained by physical sight alone, warns Augustine, is the matrix of error.[11] 'Allas,' cries a disconsolate Dido in the

---

[7] Lines 552–3. Donald W. Rowe, *Through Nature to Eternity: Chaucer's 'Legend of Good Women'* (Lincoln, Neb., 1988), p. 17, sees the heaven-hell antithesis as a frame for the whole poem. Lisa J. Kiser, *Chaucer and the 'Legend of Good Women'* (Ithaca, N.Y., 1983), 95–131, surveys the infernal imagery of the poem. It is worth heeding Derek Brewer's observation in *Chaucer: The Poet as Storyteller* (London, 1984) that 'Chaucer was evidently quite prepared to bend or drop a scientific scheme if his overall literary purpose required, and this seems typical of all the intellectual structures he enjoyed and . . . played with' (p. 26).

[8] The knight's false witness in the Man of Law's tale is repaid by the loss of his eyes (*CT* 2, 671).

[9] Chaucer uses the terms *visible* and *invisible* similarly at the close of *Troilus* (5, 1866–7), probably thinking of Augustine, *De civ.* 11,4: *Visibilium omnium maximus mundus est, inuisibilium omnium maximus Deus est. Sed mundum esse conspicimus, Deus esse credimus.* King Alfred's *Meters of Boethius*, 11, 5–7, adds to Boethius's 2, m. 8, a comparison of things seen and things unseen in creation.

[10] *Cons.* 5, prose 4. Chaucer's version is: 'wit ne mai no thing comprehende out of mater ne the ymaginacious ne loketh not the iniversal speces, ne resounne taketh nat the symple forme so as intelligence takith it' (172–5). The Parson of the *Canterbury Tales* has: 'God and resoun, and sensualitee, and the body of man been so ordeyned that everich of thise four thynges sholde have lordshipe over the oother . . .. Whan man synneth, al this ordre or ordinaunce is turned up-so-doun' (*CT* 10, 261–3).

[11] *Soliloquae* 2, 10. Shakespeare's *Troilus and Cressida* 5, 2, 112, echoes: 'Minds sway'd by eyes are full of turpitude'. the blindfold on Synagogue's eyes on the portal of the Cathedral in Strasbourg, D.W. Robertson, Jr. points out, *The Literature of Medieval England* (N.Y., 1970), p. 4, indicates her inability to see the spiritual realities beneath the surfaces of the visible and

House of Fame, 'what harm dothe apparence, / Whan his is fals in existence' (I, 265–6), and the poet adds: 'Loo, how a woman doth amys / To love him that unknowen ys' (269–70).

This philosophical entry into the record of a dream and its consequent text authenticates Chaucer's reading of the daisy in the meadow; and that vision, we are permitted to believe, shapes Alceste of the dream who is a sign of the daisy's ideological form. It would appear at first that Chaucer's account of his disdaining book for daisy, after giving books priority over religious devotion, reverses the epistemological hierarchy of spirit, reason and sense; but this is not necessarily the case if the poet's appreciation is of all three in harmonious accord. Chaucer sees the daisy as a flower, but reads it as a sign of virtue and honour before which the poet, filled with heat of love, takes a courtier's devotional pose (51–9). The poet's imagination, in collaboration with his words, metamorphoses the daisy into a woman adored for an inner virtue joined with an outer beauty. The daisy is, for the poet, a figure of natural, social and moral authority. It is the poet's devotion for the daisy which incites him to rise before daybreak to witness its *resurrection* on the first day of May, the festival of love. Alceste and the daisy conjoin, then, with an idea of Christ, for the date and the poet's feelings join seasonal with eternal love. The poet's etymological exposition of *daisy* as 'ey of day' (184) re-enforces the association. The day's eye figures both the world and the sun.[12] In medieval herbal lore, the daisy is the *consolida media* in a triad of vulneraries which includes comfrey and bugle. The daisy is bruisewort and bonewort, a panacea for wounds, just as Alceste is a comfort for women. The floral sign of the sun is also a sign of the sun's element, gold. The alchemical graph for gold – a circle with a centre dot – is the astrological graph for the sun. Cupid's love-darts are tipped with gold.[13]

Besides seeing in the daisy a conjunction of physical and moral virtues, the poet hears a seasonal and moral celebration in the chirping of the birds. First he hears them sing 'the foweler we deffye' (138), a text which challenges death, and then, as if love of kind is confirmable in gestation, each couple reaffirms its Saint Valentine's Day vows, swearing upon blossoms to be true (157).[14] There is in these songs a foreshadowing of the language of the heroines of the tales to come. It is easy enough to assume that this imaginative thrust of what Coleridge

tangible. The friar of the Summoner's Tale claims that his order can see more of spiritual things than 'burel folk' (*CT* 3, 1872). Ovid's Tereus, when he dwells on Philomela's beauty, sees beneath her array to her naked body (*Metam*. 6, 490–3).

12 In *Troilus* 2, 904–5, Chaucer addresses the sun as 'dayes honour and the hevenes yë'. In *Troy Book* 2, 5592, Lydgate calls Apollo 'daies eye'.

13 *Roman de la Rose* 5245. Before Cupid became blind his love darts corresponded to his eye beams, a secular version of the beam of light in Christian iconography which carries the Holy Spirit from Heaven into Mary's bedchamber. Cupid's eye is carnal and each of his five arrows, *quinque linea amoris*, incites one of the five senses – sight, hearing, touching, kissing and coitus (*factum*) – which Chaucer's Parson calls the five fingers of the Devil's left hand (*CT* 10, 852 ff.).

14 Ivan Illich and Barry Sanders, *The Alphabetization of the Popular Mind* (San Francisco, 1988), 134–8, discuss the process by which the book replaced the ear as witness in the fourteenth century. Though they point to Chaucer's style as evidence of the imposition of literary on human activity (88–9), Chaucer's characters swear on heads and hearts more often than on Scripture. A notable exception is the false pagan knight who swears upon a 'Britoun book' (*CT* 2, 666).

called the powers of the primary and secondary imagination informs the dream in which a Daisy-queen appears before her flower. Falling asleep, he dreams himself doing exactly what he had planned when he set his arbour bed in order to be close to the object of his morning quest. The dream, in its inception, at least, mediates between what is seen and what is read of the daisy.

The dream has no beginning, no act of entry, but opens with a vision of himself lying in devotional wonder before the daisy, as a woman, dressed in green, wearing a white crown with a gold fret, approaches. Though the dreamed figure recognizes the god of love by his appearance, and sees in the figure of his 'queen' the form of the daisy, he does not seem to know *who* she is. The dream sequence turns at once into a wry comedy of mistaken identities worthy of music-hall repartee. One need not know by what signs the poet knows Love, but why should he be ignorant of his lady?[15] When the god demands 'Who kneleth there?' (312), the cury reply 'It am I' (314) exposes him at once as the poet-adversary of love. In defending Geoffrey, Alceste drops her own name and rank as queen of Thrace (432); but, when Love asks later if he knows who his defender is, Chaucer replies: 'Nay . . . . No moore but that I see wel she is good' (505–6), as if sight into moral virtue blurs focus on its figure. Love is equally obtuse. He chides the poet for omitting Alceste from the list of women whose beauty is surpassed by . . . Alceste (537–40). Chaucer, the recollector of the dream, is guilty of complicity in this confusion, for the *balade* is composed *after* the dream in homage to the beauty of Alceste witnessed *in* the dream (247–8).[16] Clearly within the dream the poet muddles the knowledge he has of Alceste before the dream. When Love reminds him that this lady is the Alceste of Chaucer's books who chooses to die in her husband's stead, and who is rescued from hell by Hercules (510–16), the poet recalls excitedly her metamorphosis into a daisy and her stellification (517–26), two details which seem to have no authority outside of the dream.

The formal issue of seeing and knowing is involved in the trial and sentence of the poet for having written so that 'men to wommen lasse triste' (33). As she sets Chaucer's penance, Alceste remarks: 'Thogh the lyke nat a lovere bee, / Speke wel of love' (490–1), as if appearance can belie talent. *Lyke* refers to the poet's physical features, and she implies that one can write of love without having being a lover.[17] In the courts of Chaucer's day, writing love-poetry is tantamount to loving. The *lois d'amor* of the *Academie de jeux floraux*, Larry D. Benson notes, award the title *fin amant* to the winner of a poetic competition.[18] But, true to the epistemological muddle of the dream, Alceste has already denied Chaucer's poetic skills and attributed to his poetry a capacity to attract only 'lewed folk' to love (414–16). How can she expect Chaucer to write better now?

---

15 Chaucer knew Apuleius's *Metamorphosis* which recounts the love of Cupid and Psyche, who loved whom she was not permitted to see. Chaucer need not have known of the etymological sense in Alceste's name: *alki* 'strength, radiance'.

16 In the G-version, the confusion is avoided by having the balade sung by Alceste's attendants as they dance about the daisy (199–227).

17 In *Troilus* 1, 16, Chaucer notes his own *unliklynesse* for love, and in the *Parliament of Fowls* 8–11, he avows to not being a lover, though he knows of love in books.

18 *Morte Darthur* (Cambridge, Mass., 1976), p. 157. Similarly, the minstrels at Theseus's court in the *Knight's Tale* compete in speaking feelingly of love (*CT* 1, 2197–203).

Writing better involves a conception of what love poetry is as well as does. It is clear, however, that Geoffrey and the god of love entertain rival theories.[19] Love would have poetry draw devotion to himself by good examples of love. This is a poetics of respectability. He orders Chaucer to hold up the history of Alceste as a guide for women and an example for men of women's truth (542–50). Since no true lover goes to hell (553), men and women alike can be drawn to the profit of love, whose prime example is the queen. Truth in love, Alceste has already explained, is loving faithfully to the end of one's life (485).[20] The standard is mundane, pertinent to the furniture rather than to the Furnisher of Creation. The theory justifies Love's anger at Chaucer's Criseyde who lost her respectability by allowing her courage to slide and her affections to shift from a high to a lower courtly object. There is a sexual bias here, of course, for the focus on female fidelity excludes Troilus whose steadfastness earns him a fuller sight of both heavenly bliss and worldly woe.

Chaucer's theory of poetics is implicit in his defence of his poetry on the grounds that it serves truth by negative examples (466–7). His intent, he argues, known to God (471), is to convey the meaning, if not the letter of his sources, and to attract his readers to virtue by exposing folly, error and vice (470–4). Chaucer's is a poetics of morality, a theory of poetry as an eye to hidden forms. Chaucer's 'negative' poetics has solid philosophical backing. First of all, Boethius's Philosophy argues in the *Consolation* II, prose 10, that since man lacks the capacity to see God's perfection, he must assume it through observation of the world's inperfection. This is *apophasis*, a denial of man's ability to comprehend or achieve true love, and a denial of poetry's capacity to display or to engender it.[21]

Chaucer's reception of Love's theory and command to practuce, as well as his own defence of a different practice, is experienced in a dream whose images, in keeping with current belief, are transmitted to the sleeping mind by the waking eye. The ability of language to render the similitude of dream is questionable, and a theory of negative poetics is but a fantasy so long as it is trapped within a *somnium*, and there is reason to wonder if it ever escapes in order to prove itself in conscious labour. The theory might be at work in the histories which follow, but Chaucer blurs even the ontological boundary between oneiric

---

19 Robert O. Payne, *The Key of Remembrance* (New Haven, CT, 1963), p. 56, considers the prologue to the *Legend* 'close to being a treatise on the art of poetry' in so far as it establishes a point from which Chaucer synthesizes the past, artists of the past, and his own poem with experience, history and art (p. 63).

20 Malory qualifies Guenevere as a 'trewe lover, and therfor had a goode ende' (*Morte Darthur* 18, 25).

21 Negative Theology, of gnostic origin, is the *via negativa* of John Scot Erigena and Nicholas of Cusa, poetized in Alanus de Insulis' *De Planctu Naturae*. Because God shares no identity with any human concept or knowledge, and because he does not exist within any category of nature, it is easier to say what is not known of God than to assert knowledge of Him. A. Hilary Armstrong, 'Negative Theology', *The Downside Review* 95 (1977), p. 185, calls it a 'critical negation of all affirmations which one can make about God, followed by an equally critical negation of one's negation'. Denis Donahue, *Ferocious Alphabets* (Boston, 1981), 135–7, characterizes Negative Theology simply as misreading and miswriting. A Chaucerian example is the Man of Law's statement that God's purveyance 'ful derk is / To mannes wit' (*CT*, 481–2).

and conscious states of knowing and doing. The god of love's last words advise the poet to keep his examples of true women brief:

> . . .with that word my bokes gan I take,
> And ryght thus on my legend gan I make.   (578–9)

Take and *make* chart a motion from book toward poem, but Chaucer forgets to tells us if a *wake* takes place.[22] Awake or dreaming, however, the poet's reach is baffling. It might seem more credible for the poety to accept Love's sentence within the dream which contains it, though even there the poet expresses neither contrition nor confession before setting out to perform satisfaction for his poetic sins. If still in a dream when he reaches for his sources, then the legends are collected within a dream, and the reader of the *Legend* is drawn into the dream. The dream may not end until the poet awakes just as he is about to pronounce the moral of the tale of Hypermnestra. How can we know? If we take it as a matter of reason that Chaucer must awake before reaching for his books, we have no easier time explaining the occasion for the stories. He set a bed in his arbour in order to devote the next morning to daisy-gazing. Why should he cancel this project to move hastily back into his study to compile out of his books a collection in which he has no vested interest, unless the labour is to drive off a dream spectre? Why should the force of a dream experience reverse the hierarchy of attractions which brought him to the daisy?

In earlier dream poems Chaucer dozes off with a book in hand or a story on his mind, and awakes to make a book of the dream the story informs.[23] In the *Legend* we have a dream informed by sight of a daisy from which the dreamer awakes, not to record the dream – though he does so as a matter of course – but to copy out stories indicated within the dream, and to do so in the spirit of a schoolboy set, for misbehaviour, to repeating twenty times: 'women are true in love'. Assiduity and not invention is the motor of this poetic vehicle. Puzzling too is Chaucer's apparent loss of the perspecacity with which he read Alceste as a figure of Nature, Sun, Love and Christ, as well as his loss of his moral poetics in the pursuit of a poetic enterprise which disdains Charity to uphold a vulgar ideal of love as blind constancy to a physical person.

Notwithstanding the poet's deference to Love's charge, the stories repel rather than attract us to love. They expose waste, pain and destruction of womanhood in the cupidinous exercise of love. The stories continue the wry comedy of sight and reading contained in the prologue, but with tragic rather than comic overtones. They expose faults of sight in selection of lovers and impotence of words to reform the deficiencies of choice. Throughout the stories, sense rules reason, and the vulnerary of language fails to heal the thirl of remembrance of the effects.[24] In short, women read men badly, and write

---

[22] Chaucer is aware of the *aporia*, for the G-version has:
> And with that word, of slep I gan awake,
> And ryght thus on my legende gan I make.   (544–5)

[23] Piero Boitani, 'Old books brought to life in dreams: the *Book of the Duchess*, the *House of Fame*, the *Parliament of Fowls*', in *The Cambridge Chaucer Companion*, eds. Piero Boitani and Jill Mann (Cambridge, 1986), pp. 39–57, exposes the process by which the books diffused and blended in dreams are given new life.

[24] In *Confessions* 11, 26, Augustine says that memory apprehends the presence of the past, sight the presence of the present, and expectation the presence of things future. Chaucer's martyrs

futilely of the fault which they understand too late; and yet, they would make virtue of constancy of error. The women of the *Legend* earn no reward for their truth, despite Love's promise of exemption from hell. Rather, they suffer much of 'the hell / That suffreth Anelida the quene' (*Anelida*, 166–7) for her mischosen love. The women of the *Legend* shadow Chaucer's dream experience, for as he errs in his depiction of Criseyde, according to Love, and is set to redeem himself with words, the women of his stories err in their reading of men and set themselves to retrieve love with words.

Chaucer's tales subvert Love's design, nonetheless, by taking the negative way of tracing defects and ill effects of love. They ignore Love's promise of reward by eliminating the consolation for suffering that is found in Chaucer's sources. Four women kill themselves in despair over lost love. Cleopatra, the first, consigns her last words to a text of her truth:

> . . .That shal be wel sene,
> Was nevere unto his love a trewer queene. (694–7)

Thisbe loves what she has never seen but what she imagines in her mind's eye from words heard through a cracked wall. She sees Pyramus dead after he kills himself believing the blood on the wimple is hers. She, to be constant, kills herself to make of her corpse testimony to true love (910–11). Dido falls in love with Aeneas's fair form and words (1066–71). When he deserts her in order to pursue the noble idea of Rome, she writes him a bitter reproach and kills herself. Phyllis falls in love with Demophon because she 'liketh wel his port and manere' (2453), but fails to perceive, the poet reminds us, the falsity in his blood-strain (2394–400). When he deserts her she laments the faith she placed in the public fame of his lineage and in the charms of his fair tongue (2526) before she hangs herself.[25]

Other women fall into the same fault without killing themselves. Hypsipyle falls in love with Jason through Hercules's report, and Medea is seduced by Jason's leonine looks and good speech, which she later regrets:

> Whi likede me thy yelwe her to se
> More than the boundes of myn honeste?
> Why lykede me thy youthe and thy fayrnesse,
> And of thy tonge, the infynyt graciousnesse? (1672–5)

This makes it quite clear that she had chosen respectability of appearance over morality. Ariadne's love is moved by her infatuation with the title 'Duchess' (2127) that she imagines as her reward for saving Theseus's life, though she had not yet even seen him. In return for a promise of marriage, she gives him a 'clew of twyne' (2016) which guides him out of the maze and into her arms. After he leaves her for her sister Phaedra, the future mother of the false Demophon (an indication that a woman's blood can infect progeny as well as a man's), she makes a lament to her empty bed.[26] Hypermnestra is immune to the pernicious

---

to love like Anelida suffer wounds of remembrance (*Anelida* 201) which words fail to convert into expectation of good.

[25] In the *Roman* 13173–274, La Vieille points to Dido, Phyllis and Medea as examples of the folly of loving only one man. Chaucer must have known the continuations of the story which recount Demophon's return after Phyllis had been transformed into an almond tree.

[26] In the continuation which Chaucer skips, Ariadne is rescued from the island by Dionysios, to whom she bears a son Thoas, future father of Hypsipyle.

character of her blood, and chooses to save a husband she does not love rather than serve a father who professes to love her. Thus, she places her 'wifly honeste' (2701) over a father's perfidy. The virtue of her act is reduced by Chaucer's chastizing of her husband's negligence of his wife's slowness of foot in her escape with him, but the pains of her slow-footedness in filial disobedience are not recounted. By her self-sacrifice, though not exercised in the name of love, Hypermnestra is the only heroine of the *Legend* who emulates Alceste's example.

Neither Lucrece nor Philomene are married to or love the men who sexually aggress them. Their tragedies are not in seeing badly, but in being seen. Tarquinius's lust is ignited by Lucrece's beauty and gestures of virtue. After being raped, her final gesture of fidelity to her husband is suicide in remorse for having spoiled his good name (1845).[27] The rape of Philomene is incited by her beauty, and her mutilation by fear of her accusing words. In both tales, the men responsible for protecting the women, husband and father, are guilty of exposing the victims to their rapists, and guilty of not reading the intentions of the men to whom they expose women.

I have explained these stories very narrowly as examples of the malefic role of physical sight in blurring insight, and as examples of the impotence of words to either repair or retrieve lost love. I have done this to emphasize Chaucer's 'negative' poetics, but Chaucer counters Love's intentions in another way, and that by turning his poetic eye more unto men as examples of falsity than upon women as examples of truth. In some of these stories men's exploitation of women serves worthy ends. Aeneas's love affair with Dido serves the continuation of his quest to found Rome. Theseus's desire to save his own skin lends some reason to his false words, but his escape from Minos has public consequences in Athens. Jason's amatory intrigues advance his quest for the Golden Fleece, and Lyno, whether or not he neglects his wife, is innocent of any charge of 'using' her for his own ends. Neither Antony nor Pyramus act from motives lower than those of the women they love. Demophon, Tarquinius and Tereus, however, display no motives other than personal pleasure for their violence.

Aside from Antony and Pyramus, both of whom die before the women they love, the stories of men in the *Legend* comprise a book of wicked men. Where women would possess a man in order to love, these men love in order to possess. Aeneas and Theseus contribute to a general good at the expense of specific women, but no woman produces a profit from her love. No woman is shown rewarded or consoled for her constancy in love. No man is morally uplifted by woman's love, as Troilus is raised to superlative heights by his love for Criseyde. Criseyde herself is elevated in love by Antigone's song in the garden which praises the security of love (*Troilus* II, 827–75). Chaucer's *Legend* reveals a reverse side of love, its harms and harmers rather than its balms. The poetic strategy, true to his defense before Love in the dream, is repulsion, but

---

27 One's 'good name' is the fiction of public form and word. The irony of Lucrece's fate, as R. Howard Bloch argues, 'Chaucer's Maiden's Head: "The Physician's Tale" and the Poetics of Virginity', *Representations* 28 (1989), p. 124, is that Collatinus, in the game of praise of wives, prefers to display rather than to praise his wife. Tarquinius sees and hears her, and his intent to rape is born.

there is no hint of the existence of the truer charitable love which re-enacts God's Creation or Christ's sacrifice.[28]

Nowhere in the *Legend* is the issue of a woman's frailty of sense and man's exploitation of a woman's body made more of than in the tale of Philomene; and yet, paradoxically, it is the only story which concludes in a triumph of sight and word in retrieval of love. It is clear that Chaucer invents to make this particular story serve his strategic ends. To begin with, neither by Love's design for the book nor by its narrative structure does Philomene's story pertain to the collection. All the other eight stories feature heroines who are mentioned in the *balade* which praises Alceste, but Philomene is not there. She is not among the nineteen attendants of Alceste whom Love indicates as topics for the poem (554–7).[29] Only Philomene, among the women of the *Legend*, loves *no* man. Her sister, who does not love a husband to the end of her life, is relegated to a minor role in Chaucer's version. The tale of Philomene is not of a woman's love, but of unwanted loving.

Chaucer makes Philomene an exceptional case by making essential changes in his sources to focus particularly on the process of her suffering and of her redemption. He invents the detail of the cave as the locus of violation in order to increase the terror of the moment as well as the unfit setting for love. Ovid locates the rape in a *stabulum* in a *Silva obscura* (*Metam.* 6, 521). Chrétien's 'et de la hupe . . .' in *Ovide Moralisé* does not mention a place for the rape, but describes Philomene's prison as a *maison gaste*, a deserted or ruined house.[30] Chaucer's Tereus 'kepte hire to his usage and his store' in a castle keep (2335–7). In both Ovid and Chrétien, as well as in Gower's *Confessio Amantis* (5, 5715), the fearful question 'Where is my suster?' is not Philomene's, but Progne's to Tereus when he returns alone from Athens.

Chaucer reduces Philomene's speech to this single line and to her outcry to sister, father and God as she is assaulted (2328–9). Ovid has her cry first to her father, and Gower adds her mother.[31] Chaucer's order – from potential help close by, to distant help left behind, and to the invisible Guardian of souls – traces a verbal vector of desperation. The scolding of Tereus for marital infidelity is absent in Chaucer's text. He has Tereus cut out her tongue without waiting to hear an accusation. Chaucer makes a good deal, however of what she does *not* say. He describes her in prison with all the food, drink and clothing she needs, as well as with a loom upon which she can practice her familiar and feminine skill in weaving. Further,

> She coude eek rede and wel ynow endyte,
> But with a pen coude she nat wryte.   (2356–7)

For a brief tale, this is abundant pointing of detail, but its purpose is elusive. Does Chaucer mean that Philomene did not know *how* to write, though she

---

28 Frank, *Chaucer and The Legend*, p. 133, sees the poem as a whole as an abandoning of the courtly code without an offering of anything to take its place. As such, the *Legend* is an escape from idealized love.

29 Neither Cleopatra nor Philomene are mentioned in the Man of Law's list of Chaucer's works (*CT* 2, 63–185).

30 *Ovide Moralisé*, ed. C. de Boer (Vaduz, 1984), vol 4, 2217–3684.

31 Lucrece, facing rape, 'no word she spak. . . . What shal she seyn?' (1796–7), but immediately 'she axeth grace and seyth al that she can' (1804).

knew how to endite? Or, did she lack writing materials like pen and ink? Or was she afraid of watchful guardians or the eye of Tereus? She could weave, however, and she weaves the story of her voyage from Athens on a *radevore* (2352). She 'waf it wel, and wrote the storye. . . / How she was served for hire systers love' (2364–5). Perhaps fearing unwanted readers, she wove a text in cryptographs which her sister could decode. Ovid has her weave purple letters on a white background. Chrétien says she *escrit an la cortine* 'wrote on the curtain' (either a bed curtain or a wall hanging). Gower says her message combined 'letres and ymagerie'. By gestures she directs a knave to deliver the tissue, adding a ring to authenticate its source. Textile, gesture and ring mediate a desire to which her mouth could give no voice. There is no other purpose for her web except to have it serve the achievement of her journey from father's care to sister's bosom. Progne reads it well, feigns a pilgrimage, itself a voyage to a shrine of love, and rescues her dumb sister.

Despite violation and mutilation of her body, voiceless and unable to write, Philomene succeeds in reknitting a broken bond of affection. Her weaving, passing a shuttle through threads is, as A. Hillis Miller has pointed out, a sort of sexual inversion of penetration.[32] By means of the tool of feminine domestic security she achieves an authority over her male aggressor.[33] Ovid opens his sixth book of *Metamorphoses* with an account of the weaving match between Arachne and Minerva in which Arachne, picturing on her web sexual assaults of gods upon women, wins, but is transformed to a spider for her audacity and skill. Hyphology, the study of webs, is an apt term for a theory of orthoscopic poetry.[34] Philomene invents a language to mediate her love, but despite her accomplishment, she is inimitable for the women Love would have the tales guide. Hers is a quest to escape the torturous constraints of a sexual cage by inventing a language of escape. She figures the poet himself who would escape the constrining poetic prescriptions of Love by inventing a text.

If Philomene's web depicts the story of how she was sexually served, Chaucer shapes the moral of his tale not to praise the resiliency of his heroine but to warn against her mutilator:

> Ye may be war of men, yif that ye liste.
> For al be it that he wol nat, for shame,
> Don as Tereus, to lese his name,
> Ne serve yow as a morderour or a knave,
> Ful lytel while shal ye trewe hym have –
> That wol I seyn, al were he now my brother –
> But it be so that he may have non other.   (2387–93)[35]

---

32 'Ariachne's Broken Woof', *Georgia Review* 31 (1977) 36–48.

33 Nancy K. Miller, 'Arachnologies: The Woman, the Text, and the Critic', in *The Poetics of Gender*, ed. Nancy K. Miller (N.Y., 1986), pp. 270–95, coins the word 'arachnology' to refer to the text as texture, and cites Patricia Joplin's argument that Philomela elevates weaving into a means of resistance (p. 282).

34 This is Roland Barthes's term, from *hyphos* 'web', in *The Pleasures of the Text* (N.Y., 1973), p. 64.

35 Chrétien's moral to the tale identifies Pandion as *diex, rois d'immortalité*, Progne as *l'ame* in His image, Tereus *cors* pursuing 'Philomene, qui signifie / Amour decevable et faillie'. In Ovid's account, Procne would avenge herself by cutting out Tereus's tongue, eyes, and penis. The name *Philomela* means 'love of song', though *melos* also designates a bodily member.

As an address to the previous heroines of the *Legend*, this retrospective warning is tragically late. It is entirely irrelevant to Philomene who neither wanted nor had Tereus true. It ignores the men in Chaucer's audience who would be attracted to examples of good women; besides, neither Philomene nor Progne are true to men. The moral simply exposes all men as false in love, *except* those who 'may have non other'. Who may have no other woman, unless he is imprisoned like Tereus in the web of Philomene's *radevore* or like Theseus at the end of Ariadne's string? The limitation of men liable to be true is strategic, for it narrows the circle of steadfast men out of the orbits of experience inward toward the centre of art. The moral Chaucer gives the tale of Phyllis, which follows, tightens the circle:

> Be war, ye wemen, of youre subtyl fo,
> Syn yet this day men may ensaumple se;
> And trusteth, as in love, no man but me.   (2559–61)

The circle has collapsed to a centre point where only the poet stands. His authority, though no experience were in this world, is enough to validate the truth in love. The moral is long in coming. The tales of Cleopatra and Thisbe close remarking on the rarity of men true in love. The tales of Dido and Hypsipyle close with reproaches to false men, and the ending of Lucrece's story warns women against the brittle trust of men. After the moral of the tale of Phyllis, there is no place left on the map of Chaucer's *Legend* for true men. The poet has replied to Alceste's charge to tell of true women and false men by removing from the game all men worthy of being loved at all.[36]

An easy conclusion to be drawn from these observations is that the *Legend* is not so much concerned with the truth in women's love that attracts men to virtue as it is with wicked men whose examples both deny the profit of feminine love and turn women away from love altogether. The tactic of repulsion involves not only potential lovers, but all readers of love stories. The opening lines of Chaucer's tale of Philomene impugns itself:

> Whi sufferest thow that Tereus was bore,
> That is in love so fals and so forswore,
> That fro this world up to the firste hevene
> Corrumpeth whan that folk his name nevene?
> And, as to me, so grisely was his dede
> That, whan that I his foule storye rede,
> Myne eyen wexe foule and sore also.
> Yit laste the venym of so longe ago,
> That it enfecteth hym that wol beholde
> The storye of Tereus, of which I tolde.   (2234–43)

Poetry violates its readers to the measure false lovers abuse the women who populate its verses. Chaucer makes the pollution he rails against, and the effect reaches up past the Temple of Fame right up to the Creator's porch. Do not read

---

Chrétien may have gotten his form of the name, which mens 'well-loved', from Alanus's *De Planctu* 5, but I cannot find which work was composed first.

[36] In this respect, the *Legend* has a closure. Rowe, pp. 118–22, considers the work finished for other reasons.

of love, Chaucer implies, or you will only infect those to whom you recount your story. Trust me, but avoid my tales. Foul poetry fouls wits.

A harder conclusion is that a theory of poetry as an attraction of man away from *amor folie* toward *amor pur* by sensitizing a moral repulsion to physical love is denied both by examples of vacuous women with iniquitous men and examples of infectious poetry. The existence of a pure and enduring love is put into question by the absence in the *Legend* of any quest for and mention of a spiritual or philosophic dimension to love.[37] The *Legend's* prefatory theoretical premise that there is authority that directs man beyond the epistemic limits of his own experience toward the invisible society of ideas is denied by the practice of the tales. This denial, even if only viewed as a comic subversion of a dream god's design, involves the poet's own status as lover.

The *Legend*, like Demophon's blood, is infected by a genealogical stain, those ancient and authoritative texts of love which venerate womanhood. Like his own Hypermnestra, Chaucer would deny the tyranny of fathers, and free his poetry from the restraints of dictators. Hypermnestra saves her husband by waking him softly (2708) to danger so that he can leap from the window and save his skin. Chaucer's recollection of female martyrs to love is itself a mosaic nightmare, an oneiric aperient to cleanse his art of vapid conventions of love-poetry. With Lyno he awakes, and he leaves Alceste behind.

Coda

'In dreams begins responsibility', goes an old saying.[38] I do not for a moment believe that Chaucer would have his dream of Alceste and Love invalidate the anthology it informs. With purpose he muddles both the account of his dream and the thematic organization of the texts the dream spectre of Love sets him to. This is a strategy of destabilization which challenges reading of writing. What the example of Philomene finally argues, in the context of the whole book, is where the descriptive style of speech and writing fail love, an *inscriptive* textual style can succeed. The story of Philomene sends both the poet and his audience to a retracing of the language of experience that recounts dream, and the language of authority which translates old authorities. The *Legend*, in this respect, mediates between distant literary fathers, recent dream poetry and the poetry to be born in the *Canterbury Tales*.[39] Chaucer's denial of love and its poetry, like the spiritual reward of penitence in pilgrimage, is but punctual and tentative.

---

37 At the close of *Troilus* Chaucer turns from his initial task to 'don gladnesse / To any lovere, and his cause availee' (1, 19–20) to persuade his audience to forsake worldly love 'and loveth [Christ] . . . / For he nyl falsen no wight' (5, 1842–5).

38 W.B. Yeats, *Responsibilities* (London, 1914). The title is taken from the saying, which is the book's motto.

39 I apologize for a use of the term 'mediation' distinct from R. Allen Shoaf's in 'Dante's *Commedia* and Chaucer's Theory of Mediation: A Preliminary Sketch', in *New Perspectives in Chaucer Criticism*, ed. Donald M. Rose (Norman, Okla., 1981), pp. 83–103. Shoaf's mediation concerns the referentiality of words, like coins, to mediate value. I use the term more along the lines of Frederic Jameson in *The Political Unconscious* (London, 1981), p. 225, where mediation is explained as 'invention of an analytic terminology or code which can be applied equally to two or more structurally distinct objects or sectors of being'.

GENERIC VARIATIONS ON THE THEME OF POETIC AND CIVIL AUTHORITY

HELEN COOPER

The Fourth Tractate of Dante's *Convivio* takes as its subject the nature of true nobility. In the course of it, Dante discusses what constitutes authority, and he does so under two heads: the authority of the Emperor, and the authority of the philosophers. He defines the word by its root, as the act of an author:

> È dunque da sapere che 'autoritade' non è altro che 'atto d'autore';[1]

and he offers two etymologies for it. One derivation is from the Greek 'autentin', 'degno di fede e d'obedienza':

> E così 'autore', quinci derivato, si prende per ogni persona degna d'essere creduta e obedita. E da questo viene questo vocabulo del quale al presente si tratta, cioè 'autoritade'; per che si può vedere che 'autoritade' vale tanto quanto 'atto degno di fede e d'obedienza'.   (IV.vi.5; p. 248)

The faith and obedience demanded by civil and philosophical authority should ideally reinforce each other: 'l'una con l'altra congiunta utilissime e pienissime sono d'ogni vigore' (IV.vi. 17, p. 251). The second, rather more elaborate, etymology he gives is for *autore* in the sense of 'poet'. Poets, he adds, are not his immediate subject; but the passage none the less serves to remind the reader of his own authoritative role in the work. The theme of the whole tractate is the exposition of a poem of which he is himself the author; and when he goes on to analyse the differences, and affirm the connections, between imperial and philosophic authority, he does so with the authority deriving from his own standing as poet – as author.

It is this set of collocations – of secular authority, of philosophic or moral authority, and of the authority of the poet – that is the subject of this paper. It is potentially a subject of the same size as the entire corpus of world literature; so I shall concentrate on one small area, of Chaucerian and post-Chaucerian English literature, where the issues raised by the various sorts of authority run particularly close to the surface and raise particular problems. My basic premise is a simple one: that in late medieval narrative, stories that endorse orthodox order are likely to cite their sources, to claim poetic authority; conversely, stories that disrupt or invert patterns of secular authority are given no claims to literary authority. The two approaches are most clearly exemplified in historical or pseudo-historical romances, especially in dynastic ór ancestral romances that have a role to play in legitimating political authority, and in fabliaux. Fabliaux do not cite sources:[2] they present themselves simply as something that happened, and what does happen is likely to undermine established order. They are

---

[1]   *Dante Alighieri: Convivio* ed. Piero Cudini (2nd edn., Milan, 1987), IV.vi.3 (p. 247).
[2]   It is difficult to document a negative of this sort, but it is pervasively evidenced by the six

not necessarily anti-authoritarian, but they carry no generic expectation that official authority, especially male authority, will be maintained; those rulers of the hearth and the parish, husbands and priests, frequently come off particularly badly. Ancestral romances, by contrast, endorse established power structures; and they also assemble ranks of poetic and historical authorities, whether they were actually used by the poet, or indeed existed, or not.

There is one obvious counter-argument to such an equation between the two sorts of authority, the poetic and the political: that the citation of sources depends not on the endorsement of civil power structures but simply on the truth value of the narrative. One major scheme for generic analysis in the Middle Ages, derived from Isidore, divided poetry on this basis, into *historia*, *argumentum* and *fabula*, corresponding to the true, the fictional but possible, and the downright impossible.[3] To say that source citation tends to accompany *historia* would then be to recognize the same phenomenon as that history textbooks cite sources and novels do not. In practice, however, things are not so straightforward. The other categories, *argumentum* and *fabula*, do not show any sliding scale of source citation. Fabliaux, with their absence of sources, are generally examples of the middle category, *argumentum*; and at least one type of totally implausible story, the beast-fable, an acknowledged subsection of *fabula*, shows an increasing tendency in post-Chaucerian Britain to claim sources. Moreover, implausible stories are sometimes buttressed by poetic authority when it is politically useful to do so, so that *fabula* is metamorphosed into *historia*, and source citation becomes a way of endorsing an otherwise unconvincing piece of propaganda.

What this suggests is a shift from truth interpreted as verifiable fact towards ideology. Ancestral romances show some tendency to emphasize their sources in *inverse* proportion to their credibility. The implausible and impossible beast-fable may contain moral truth under its fictional cover, but as this moral truth becomes less a matter of pragmatic wisdom, as it is in Aesop and Avianus and their early medieval redactors, and more a matter of theological principles, as happens in Lydgate and Henryson, so the authority of the source is given a new prominence. Poetic authority, in other words, increases in importance as the 'truth' expressed in a work comes closer, not so much to factual or historical *res gestae*, but to the ideologies that support the hierarchies of Church and State: that serve to legitimate received structures of power. And the bearers of such authority, whether political, moral or poetic, are assumed to be male – a point that will be of importance later.

Like all conventions, this equation between poetic and political authority is

volumes of *Recueil général et complet des fabliaux des XIII et XIVe siècles* ed. A. de Montaiglon and G. Raynaud (Paris, 1872–90).

3 Isidore, *Etymologiae* (*PL* LXXXII cols. 74–728) I.xliv.5: 'Inter historiam, et argumentum, et fabulam interest. Nam historiae sunt res verae, quae factae sunt. Argumenta sunt quae, etsi facta non sunt, fieri tamen possunt. Fabulae vero sunt quae nec facta sunt, nec fieri possunt, quia contra naturam sunt' (col. 124). There is a fuller discussion of the issue in *The Parisiana Poetria of John of Garland* ed. and trans. Traugott Lawler (New Haven and London, 1974) V.315–9, 321–2, 327–8 (p. 100): 'Narratio . . . tres habet species siue partes, scilicet Fabulam, Hystoriam, Argumentum. *De Fabula* Fabula est que nec res ueras nec uerisimiles continet; vnde si contingit narrationem esse fabulosam, ne sit uiciosa, mentiri debet probabiliter. . . *De Hystoria* Hystoria est res gesta ab etatis nostre memoria remota. . . *De Argumento* Argumentum est res ficta que tamen fieri potuit, ut contingit in comediis.'

one that relies for its effect on its familiarity to both author and audience, both for the resonance of the basic theme and for the impact of the unexpected variations. Its familiarity can best be demonstrated by its appearances in writers who work at both extremes of the generic spectrum – in Chaucer, for instance, or Hoccleve or Caxton. Chaucer makes the basic model clear in the opening tales of the *Canterbury Tales*, the pseudo-historical 'noble storie' told by the Knight and the Miller's 'cherles tale'.[4] The first lines of the two tales at first glance look almost identical:

> Whilom, as olde stories tellen us,
> Ther was a duc that highte Theseus, (I,859–60)

against

> Whilom ther was dwellynge at Oxenford
> A riche gnof, that geestes heeld to bord. (I,3187–8)

Each couplet introduces the character who should be the authority figure of the story; but the difference is crucial. The Knight's Tale, despite the chances of fate and fortune, endorses the control of Theseus, and confirms his authority by reference to 'olde stories' (not true, of course – the model is a rather recent story, Boccaccio's *Teseida* – but the formulation Chaucer chooses adds the authority of antiquity). The implication of the opening of the Miller's Tale, as with all fabliaux, is that it is just something that happened; and it shows the head of its household fooled, cuckolded, and taking a very literal fall. Hoccleve's series of linked poems that opens with his *Complaint* contains two contrasting inset stories from the *Gesta Romanorum*.[5] The first is about a chaste and virtuous Roman empress, who repeatedly suffers from the machinations of intending rapists and is finally restored to her husband and her proper status; the second, 'fabula de quadam muliere mala', is about a youngest son, a student named Jonathas, who is stripped by a whore of the three magic gifts bequeathed him by his father. Although he, like the empress, manages to get back what he has lost, there is none of the same sense of rightful order being restored, and the story still has a great deal of the fabliau about it. Hoccleve names his source twice for the story of the empress (XXI,820, XXII,1); for the second, although he mentions in the frame being lent the book that contains the story (XXIV,78–9), he never cites any source by name.

A similar pattern emerges in Caxton, through the prologues describing his sources, or the lack of such prologues, that he provides for his narrative publications and translations. His historical or pseudo-historical works are given prefaces that endorse both their historiographical and moral authority (they have sources, and are of value to the reader): *Godeffroy of Boloyne* and the *Morte Darthur* are notable examples, the *Morte* not least in that it ranges written

---

[4] *The Riverside Chaucer*, general ed. Larry D. Benson (Boston, 1987), *Canterbury Tales* I,3111, 3169. All references to Chaucer are to this edition.

[5] *Hoccleve's Works: The Minor Poems* ed. F.J. Furnivall and I. Gollancz, revised by Jerome Mitchell and A.I. Doyle (EETS ES 61, 73, 1892, 1925, revised repr. 1970), pp. 140–78, 219–42. The source stories are in *Gesta Romanorum* ed. Hermann Oesterley (Berlin, 1872) nos. 249 (the accused empress, pp. 648–54) and 120 (Jonathas, pp. 466–70); see also *The Early English Versions of the Gesta Romanorum* ed. Sidney J.H. Herrtage (EETS ES 33, 1879) pp. 311–22, 180–96.

authorities against the accusation that the Arthurian stories are 'but fayned and fables',[6] two crucial words that threaten to turn the work from being worthy *historia* to valueless *fabula*. In his translations of Raoul Le Fevre's histories of Troy and of Jason, Caxton not only cites their immediate sources in their prologues, but also adds epilogues that bring further authority to the works: for *Troy* he provides the traditional exposition of the various sources for the Trojan War; the *Jason* epilogue adds supplementary references to Boccaccio's *De Genealogia Deorum* and Statius.[7] By contrast with this serious treatment of authority in the pseudo-historical works, his *History of Reynard the Fox* starts straight in on its narrative of 'iapes and bourdes' with no justificatory prologue; and it is perhaps worth mentioning that Chaucer uses 'jape' as an effective synonym for 'fabliau'.[8]

It is notoriously difficult to square medieval generic theory, with its classically-derived categories, with actual poetic practice, and the concept of *historia* is one of the most problematic. It appears to translate into the French *histoire*, but that means, in modern terms, both 'history' and 'story', and in medieval terms also the middle ground between the two for which we frequently use the word 'romance'. And 'romance' itself is a weasel word in the Middle Ages; it changes historically from describing the language of a text to describing something about its content or structure, and even contemporary writers will use the term in markedly varied ways that often do not square with our own usages. Discussions of Chaucer's romances in the *Canterbury Tales*, for instance, tend to overlook the fact that he only uses the word once in the whole work, and that is to describe Sir Thopas's light entertainment – the

> . . . romances that been roiales
> Of popes and of cardinales
> And eek of love-likynge   (VII,849–900)

that his *mynstrales* and *geestours* sing to him, and that include those of Horn, Bevis and Guy of Warwick, the last two at least being ancestral romances that should – and in other hands sometimes do – carry an ideological charge and appropriate authorities,[9] but that Chaucer clearly thinks of as both ahistorical and implausible. *Sir Thopas* itself, incidentally, claims no source – no written authority.

The tendency of romance to move into legendary history is widely recognized, but arguments that historical romance and the overtly fictional kind are separate genres will not altogether work either, for there seems to have been no consensus as to where any dividing line should be drawn, or whether it should be drawn at all.[10] There is a nice example in the story of Melusine, the sup-

[6] *The Works of Sir Thomas Malory* ed. Eugene Vinaver (3 vols, 2nd edn, Oxford, 1973) I,cxliii–vi (quotation p. cxliv). See also *Godeffroy of Boloyne* ed. Mary Noyes Colvin (EETS ES 64, 1893) pp. 1–5, esp. p. 2.

[7] *The Recuyell of the Historyes of Troye* ed. H. Oskar Sommer (2 vols, London, 1894), pp. 701–2 (350r–v); *The History of Jason* ed. John Munro (EETS ES 111, 1913 for 1912), pp. 198–9.

[8] *The History of Reynard the Fox* ed. N.F. Blake (EETS 263, 1970); see p. 112. Caxton does give a very brief mention at the end of the work's being a translation from Dutch. For Chaucer's use of 'jape', see *CT* I,4343.

[9] On *Guy*, see e.g. p. 96 below.

[10] This does not mean that there was no sense that division was possible: see Paul Strohm,

posedly historical foundress of the house of Lusignan, who was made the subject of two dynastic romances (one in prose, by Jean d'Arras, and one in octosyllabics, by La Couldrette) at the end of the fourteenth century, when there was a renewed vogue for genealogical works of this kind. Both were translated into English a century later.[11] As ancestral romances, they potentially carry considerable ideological weight; but the story itself has to the uninstructed ear a great deal more of the *fabula* than the *historia* about it, and the authors are at pains to put their audiences in a receptive frame of mind.

Melusine's distinctive feature was to turn every Saturday into a serpent from the waist down; when her husband discovers this and eventually reproaches her for it, she turns completely into a serpent and flies off from a window of the castle. It is not the most promising raw material for historical treatment, but the authors do their best. Jean d'Arras repeats over and over again that his sources are in 'vrayes croniques', given him, moreover, by those figures of political authority Jean duc de Berry and the earl of Salisbury; he backs up his written authorities with eyewitness claims about the flying serpent's continuing reappearances, and supports those with appeals to the philosophic and religious *auctores* Aristotle and St Paul as to the importance of believing the evidence of one's eyes; and he discourses on the evidence for fairies as given him by one Gervaise, who, the English translator adds, is 'a man worshipfull and of credence' (p. 4) – a reliable authority, in other words. There is even physical evidence for the truth of the story: 'on the basse stone of the wyndowe apereth at this day themprynte of her foote serpentous' (p. 320). At this point, even if one admits the possibility of recognizing a serpent's footprint, one may feel that the writer is protesting too much, and to rather less effect than Caxton's reminder to his readers of the existence of King Arthur's Round Table at Winchester; but the protestations continue to the very end:

> I haue putte my self to myn vtermost power to rede & loke ouer the Cronykles & many bokes of auncyent hystoryes, to thende that I might knowe the trouth of the forsaid matere. Therfore yf I haue wryton or shewed ony thing that to som semeth neyther possible to be nor credible, I besuche them to pardonne me. For as I fele & vnderstand by the Auctours of gramaire & phylosophye they repute and hold this present hystorye for a true Cronykle.[12]

The rhymed version is yet more meticulous in detailing its sources in French and Latin, and in stipulating how important it is that great men should know their pedigrees. Moreover, it cites Aristotle, whom Dante describes in the *Convivio* as the ultimate authority, most worthy of trust (IV.vi), in its very first line. The English translator endorses the seriousness of the work by turning its octosyllabics into rhyme royal, the stanza of Chaucer's *Troilus* or Lydgate's *Fall of Princes*.

'*Storie, Spelle, Geste, Romance, Tragedie*: Generic Distinctions in the Middle English Troy Narratives', *Speculum* XLVI (1971) 348–58.

[11] *Jean d'Arras: Melusine* ed. Louis Stouff (Dijon, 1932, repr. 1974); the English translation is ed. A.K. Donald, *Melusine* (EETS ES 68, 1895). La Couldrette's octosyllabic version is ed. Francisque Michel, *Mellusine* (Niort, 1854); it was translated as *The Romans of Partenay*, ed. W.W. Skeat (EETS OS 22, 1866, revised 1899).

[12] Ed. Donald, p. 370. Jean d'Arras adds a further reference to Gervaise at this point (ed. Stouff, p. 310).

The Troy books present similar problems, for all their claims to historical truth. They, like *Melusine*, carry a celebratory function for contemporary secular power, since both Britain and France, like Rome, were supposedly founded by the fleeing Trojans or their descendants. Guido delle Colonne inserts an account of their dispersal across Europe at the head of his *Historia destructionis Troiae*, and is at some pains to refute the association of Sicily, seat of the Emperor Frederick, with Greece.[13] It is Guido too who turns the debate on the comparative veracity of the authorities for the Troy story into a set piece. Joseph of Exeter had condemned Homer and Virgil for writing *fabula*;[14] Dares and Dictys by contrast were regarded as reliable eyewitnesses – Dares especially so in the West, as he backed the ideologically correct side, the Trojans, while the Greek Dictys was favoured in the Byzantine world.[15] Guido's elaboration of the theme in his account of his own sources transmits the idea to the later Middle Ages, persuasively enough for his own name regularly to be added to the list as the definitive authority.[16] His own claims of historical authenticity are however consistently undermined by his use as his main source of the one work he does not mention, Benoit's *Roman* (or, more correctly, *Ystoire*) *de Troie*: a work with overtly romance-style emphases on the inner (and therefore unverifiable) world of love, and on the marvellous (and therefore implausible). His successors' attempts to convince their audience of their trustworthiness can go astray through other kinds of mixing of the fabulous with the historical. The author of the Laud *Troy Book* supplements the source discussion in his prologue with a long list of all the romance heroes who were not quite so great as Hector: a list that includes Tristram, Gawain, Havelok and Wade, and three from Sir Thopas's list, Bevis, Horn and Guy of Warwick.

> Here dedis ben in remembrance
> In many fair Romaunce,[17]

the poet tells us, so it is only proper that those of Hector should be recorded for posterity as well. This poet, at least, makes no generic distinction between Trojan history, the more overtly fictional end of the Arthurian stories, ancestral romances of greater or less plausibility, and the downright mythological. Factual authenticity again comes a poor second to the authoritative endorsement of dynastic legend.

---

[13] *Guido de Columnis: Historia Destructionis Troiae* ed. Nathaniel Edward Griffin (Medieval Academy of America, Cambridge, Mass, 1936; repr. New York, 1970) Lib. II, pp. 11–12. Mary Elizabeth Meek discusses the Sicilian dimension of the work in the introduction to her translation of the *Historia* (Bloomington and London, 1974), pp. xxv, xxix–xxx. Meek also gives a good account of the development of the Troy story in post-classical times, and of Guido's use of sources.

[14] *Frigii Daretis Yliados Libri Sex* 24–9, in *Jospeh Iscanus: Werke und Briefe* ed. Ludwig Gompf (Mittellateinische Studien und Texte 4, Leiden and Cologne, 1970). The more common title, 'De bello Troiano', first appears in the printed editions (Gompf p. 10).

[15] See Gildas Roberts's introduction to his translation, *Joseph of Exeter: the Iliad of Dares Phrygius* (Cape Town, 1970), p. ix.

[16] He is mentioned in the prologues to the three Middle English Troy books derived directly from him, the *Gest Hystoriale of the Destruction of Troy*, the Laud *Troy Book*, and Lydgate's *Troy Book* (which makes frequent further reference to him in the course of the work); and in Chaucer's *House of Fame*.

[17] *The Laud Troy Book* ed. J. Ernst Wulfing (EETS OS 121, 122, 1902–3), ll. 25–6. The poem dates from c. 1400.

When Chaucer turns to the Troy story, he shows a much more sophisticated alertness to the kinds of problems it raises. He treats aspects of the history of Troy three times: in *Troilus and Criseyde*; in the Legend of Dido, in the *Legend of Good Women*; and in his retelling of the *Aeneid* in the first part of the *House of Fame*. In both the last two he makes poetic running out of the conflict of named authorities, Virgil, the master-poet of literary tradition, who had written to extol Rome and Britain's ancestor Aeneas, and Ovid, whose Epistle of Dido in the *Heroides* had presented Aeneas not as hero but as cad.[18] In the third section of the *House of Fame*, with the presentation of the poets and historiographers in Fame's palace, he destabilizes the whole idea of their authority still more radically, in a passage that presents itself at first glance as that *locus classicus* of historical, 'authorized' writing, the comparative reliability of the authorities for the story of Troy. Chaucer's list, however, differs significantly from the usual run of Dares, Dictys, Homer, Virgil and Guido delle Colonne. He adds in 'Lollius' (1468), and, whether or not he thought when he wrote this poem that Lollius was an expert on the Trojan War, it is quite clear that by the time he was writing *Troilus and Criseyde* he was using him as a pseudo-author, as a cover for doing the most inauthentic things, such as having Troilus sing a Petrarch sonnet.[19] Chaucer also includes in his list Geoffrey of Monmouth, 'Englyssh Gaufride' (1470), who, with Guido, brings the history of Troy down to the point where it opens into the history of Britain. It is at this juncture that Chaucer mentions the disagreements between the various authorities, in particular the accusation that Homer 'made lyes. . . feynynge. . . fable' (1478–80), a run of all the words *opposed* to the authorized or historical – though it is worth noting too that the basis of the charge of fabulousness is ideological, in that he 'was to Grekes favorable' (1479). Virgil, supporting the 'fame of pius Eneas' (1485), is the last in the list; but this fame, as Chaucer has already insinuated by his mingling of Ovid with Virgil in the first part of the poem, is itself an untruth, for Eneas's *pietas*, his 'godlyhed', is simply a hypocritical cover for vice (274–5; compare 263–7, 330–1, and *Legend* 1285–6). In addition to all this, the entire collection of authorities, whether they are supporting the fame of Aeneas or Troy or Thebes or Rome, are in the hall of Fame herself, and the whole argument of the poem is that reputation, and therefore historiography, is a matter of chance. Fame is arbitrary: a signifier that bears no necessary relationship with what it appears to signify. Poetic authority and both factual and exemplary truth are therefore distinct, and coincide only randomly.

It is a commonplace of criticism that Chaucer delegates his poetic authority onto a series of surrogate narrators or non-existent sources: dreamers or pilgrims or old books or Lollius. The one kind of authority he will claim for himself is that of poet, of maker. The one time he names himself in his poetry occurs in the *House of Fame* (729), the poem in which he defines himself as the *auctor* with whom the work begins and ends: for by casting it as a dream poem, a *secular* dream poem with no claim to being a window on an ultimate truth, he shifts its sources to lying entirely within his own mind and imagination, his

---

[18] See especially *Legend* 924–9, 1002, 1352, 1367; *HF* 143–50, 265–75, 375–80, 427–32, 1484–5.

[19] *Troilus* I,394, the first place where Lollius is mentioned by name. The only other reference to him (V,1653) comes at a point where Chaucer is inventing.

'Thought, that wrot al that I mette' (523). When he writes his most substantial contribution to the story of Troy, in *Troilus and Criseyde*, his playing with these ideas of unverifiable authority and fictionality is built into the whole structure and texture of the poem. Far from insisting on the authenticity of his version, as Guido and the rest do, he claims to be at the mercy of what his 'auctors' say or fail to say. Behind the disclaimers, he seems to have done some serious research, reading what he almost certainly thought was the original Dares in Joseph of Exeter's version;[20] but he is also happy to invent variations on an original that he never names[21] and that he must have recognized as being fictional in all but the bare outline. He names accepted authorities at two points. At the beginning he refers his audience to Homer, Dares and Dictys, for the larger story he is not going to write (I,145–7). At the end, rather more prominently, he lists Virgil, Ovid, Homer, Lucan and Statius; and he cites them, not as sources, but as models of 'alle poesye' (V,1790).[22] He looks to them as authorities, not for what they say about what happened, but for how they say it.

It is hard to overestimate the importance in the history of English poetry of that moment when Chaucer humbly but decisively attaches himself to the line of acknowledged poetic authorities. It was effectively that that created an awareness of an English tradition of poetry, of the fact that English poetry did itself participate in a tradition. It meant that later generations of poets in their turn could look to their sources – in the sense of their springs of inspiration, their roots – and continue the tradition that Chaucer had brought to perception. With Chaucer, English poetry becomes self-conscious.[23]

There were, however, enormous problems in defining the tradition.[24] It was easy to regard Chaucer as a model of *poesie*, as he sees Virgil and the rest, and poet after poet, in his own lifetime and throughout the fifteenth and sixteenth centuries, speaks of him in those terms: Deschamps, Gower, the authors of the *Court of Sapience* and the *Kingis Quair*, John Walton, John Lydgate, Osbern Bokenham, George Ashby, Henryson, Dunbar, Gavin Douglas, Hawes, Skelton, Lindsay and so on.[25] All these, however, limit Chaucer to being a model of

[20] See R.K. Root, 'Chaucer's Dares', *MP* XV (1917) 1–22.

[21] The reasons for Chaucer's never mentioning Boccaccio have been much debated, but no conclusion is possible. It is conceivable that the Boccaccio manuscripts he had seen carried no attribution; but the number of different works on which he draws makes the argument unlikely. Both his modernity and his writing in the vernacular may have made him seem less than convincing as an authority, and his name may not have been familiar in England at this date; the situation with Petrarch seems to have been rather different – see p. 94 below.

[22] Chaucer was following authoritative convention in naming himself as the sixth poet of six: see David Wallace, *Chaucer and the Early Writings of Boccaccio* (Chaucer Studies 12, Woodbridge and Dover, N.H., 1985), pp. 46–53, for a discussion of the motif in Jean de Meun, Dante's *Commedia*, and the *Filocolo* of Boccaccio.

[23] On the lack of an awareness of English tradition before Chaucer see N.F. Blake, *The English Language in Medieval Literature* (London, 1978), pp. 21–33.

[24] A.C. Spearing discusses the problematic nature of the fifteenth-century assimilation of Chaucer in his *Medieval to Renaissance in English Poetry* (Cambridge, 1985), pp. 88–110, though he ascribes it to somewhat different causes from those I put forward here. For the nature of Chaucer's influence, see Spearing, chapter 3; Alice S. Miskimin, *The Renaissance Chaucer* (New Haven and London, 1975); and *Chaucer Traditions*, eds. Ruth Morse and Barry Windeatt (Cambridge, 1990).

[25] See Caroline Spurgeon, *Five Hundred Years of Chaucer Criticism and Allusion* (Chaucer Soc., 1914–25) for a comprehensive listing. Fuller extracts covering the more significant

rhetoric; they do not treat him as an authority, either of source material or of *sententiae*, even when they are in fact using him as such.[26] His own resolute avoidance of claims to authority is reflected in their discomfort at treating him as *auctor*. Two of the more self-aware of these poets, Henryson and Gavin Douglas, tackle the problem explicitly, again with the focus on the Troy story. Henryson, who seems to have had no sources for his sequel to the story of Criseyde except Chaucer's poetic example and his own imagination, starts by questioning Chaucer's authority – or to be more specific, by using Chaucer's *lack* of authority as justification for his own:

> Quha wait gif all that Chauceir wrait was trew?
> Nor I wait nocht gif this narratioun
> Be authoreist, or fenȝeit of the new
> Be sum poeit.[27]

The contrast between what is 'authorized' and what is 'feigned' is explicit, and Chaucer is left in as uncertain a position as he had left all the historiographers in the *House of Fame*, as a poet whose credentials are unverifiable. Gavin Douglas has no such problem of authoritative source, for he is translating the *Aeneid*; but he does, gently, take Chaucer, his acknowledged poetic master, to task for challenging Virgil's authority, and when he looks for reasons as to why he might have done so, he finds his answer in the story of Dido. Chaucer was 'evir (God wait) all womanis frend':[28] a friendship so strong as to have blurred his recognition of the authority of Virgil and the political and moral weight of Aeneas.

In a system of patriarchal authority, women are, by definition, the main threat. For Chaucer to be 'womanis frend' is to recognize an element of potential subversiveness in almost everything he wrote, for there are few of his works that do not give women a significant role. The *Canterbury Tales* goes some way towards justifying this reading of him as subversive; but only some way, for most often the tales in which the women do emerge triumphant are those that lay no claim to poetic authority anyway. Chaucer furthermore explicitly writes himself out of the first of such stories, the Miller's, since 'the Miller is a cherl' and the blame for the story is none of his (I,3182–5). I mentioned the Knight's and Miller's Tales as exemplifying the equation between social and poetic authority, and the fact that they head the collection sets them up as normative: this is how the pattern of authority should be. All the Tales follow the same model of narrative structure in that they open with the character who ought to be the authority figure, just as Theseus is mentioned in the opening couplet of the Knight's Tale; but those who enter without any endorsement from a written source rarely remain in authority. The husbands of the four fabliaux, the Oxford carpenter, the miller of Trumpington, the merchant of St Denis and January are

---

allusions are given by Derek Brewer in *Chaucer: The Critical Heritage* (London and Boston, 1978), vol. I.

[26] Egregious examples occur in Lydgate's *Troy Book* 4677–718, where Lydgate interrupts his description of Criseyde to praise Chaucer's art, insists that he has to follow Guido, and then borrows generously from the *Troilus* (ed. Henry Bergen, Part I, EETS ES 97, 1906); and in Henryson's retelling of the Nun's Priest's Tale.

[27] *The Poems of Robert Henryson* ed. Denton Fox (Oxford, 1981), *Testament of Cresseid* 64–7 (p. 113).

[28] The relevant extracts are in Brewer, p. 86; I,448 quoted.

all cuckolded. The fifth cuckold of the *Tales* does enter with an endorsement from 'olde bookes' (IX,106), but he is not dislodged from his position of authority within the household: he is the Phebus of the Manciple's Tale, and he kills his adulterous wife. Another potential cuckold, Arveragus, the knight who opens the Franklin's Tale and of whom 'thise olde gentil Britouns . . . maden layes' (V,709–10), does maintain his authority over his wife, despite having granted her equal rights at the start of the story, and even though he uses his authority against his own apparent interests (V,1459–92). The Physician's Tale provides an even stronger instance of both poetic and domestic authority, for in that,

> . . . as telleth Titus Livius,
> A knyght that called was Virginius   (VI,1–2)

exercises his patriarchal right in the most extreme form, by killing his own daughter. In both these last instances, Chaucer falsifies his actual sources in order to enhance the authority and antiquity of his narratives: the Franklin's Tale is loosely based on a story twice told by Boccaccio, whom Chaucer never cites by name, possibly because his modernity or his obscurity at this date in England made him less than convincing as an authority; and while Livy is the grandfather to the Physician's Tale, the immediate parent of the story of Apius and Virginia is the *Roman de la rose*, another comparatively recent work in a European vernacular, and an overtly fictional poem that lacks the claim to historical truth and the Classical authority of Livy.

It should be strong corroboration for this equation of domestic or political and poetic authority that the Wife of Bath's Tale, in which King Arthur hands over the execution of justice to his queen, and his knight accords sovereignty to his wife, is given no source, either by Chaucer here or in its two closest analogues, the metrical romance of the *Wedding of Sir Gawain* and Gower's Tale of Florent in the *Confessio Amantis*.[29] Their models were in fact fairly certainly vernacular, perhaps even a folktale in oral circulation, such as would have carried no significant authority anyway; but Chaucer could easily have introduced a reference to 'olde bookes' or some similarly all-purpose written original if he had wished, for he is notoriously a poet more concerned with rhetorically appropriate moments for citing authorities than with the accuracy of his citations.

---

[29] For *The Weddynge of Sir Gawen and Dame Ragnell* see *Sources and Analogues of Chaucer's Canterbury Tales* ed. W.F. Bryan and Germaine Dempster (1945; repr. Atlantic Highlands, N.J., 1968), pp. 242–64. For the Tale of Florent, see *The English Works of John Gower* ed. G.C. Macaulay (EETS ES 81–2, 1900–01), *Confessio* I,1403–06 and textual variants. Gower does eventually add a reference to 'a Cronique', but only in the third recension. The earlier versions contain the single couplet,
> And in ensample of þis matiere
> A tale I fynde, as þou schalt hiere.
The third recension substitutes
> Wherof (i.e. about Obedience) if that the list to wite
> In a Cronique as it is write,
> A gret ensaumple thou myht fynde,
> Which now is come to my mynde.
The formulation is still odd, in its failure to make finally clear the relationship of the 'Cronique' on the topic of Obedience and the 'ensáumple' in Genius's mind.

Clearly, this tale, with its intolerance of orthodox structures of authority, did not appear appropriate.

In the Wife's Tale, however, things are not so simple, for Chaucer – or the Wife, or, to be exact, the loathly lady – does give prominent mention to one authority; and that is 'the wise poete of Florence / That highte Dant' (III,1125–6). It is not uncommon in the *Canterbury Tales* for speakers to name the sources of their *sententiae*, but this particular instance is rendered unusual both by the detail of the naming, and by the narrative implausibility of the footnote: not only is the loathly lady in bed, on her wedding night; she is also quite possibly a fairy;[30] and she certainly belongs to 'th'olde dayes of the Kyng Arthour' (III,857). Chaucer does not commit such anachronisms lightly,[31] and the reasons here are significant. The passage to which Chaucer and the hag are referring is precisely that Fourth Tractate of the *Convivio* with which I opened this paper – or, specifically, its opening *canzone* on which the rest is an extended commentary: that

> ... God, of his goodnesse,
> Wol that of hym we clayme oure gentillesse. (III,1129–30)

Nobility – the inherited quality that conferred the right to political power – is here, as in Dante, redefined as being individual virtue derived directly from God. It is an idea to which Chaucer returns on numerous occasions, always with seriousness; and the Fourth Tractate throws the whole weight of moral and poetic authority behind the idea. Chaucer is not so conciliatory at this point to political authority, however: he has nothing resembling Dante's digression on the divinely sanctioned foundation of the Roman Empire, a sanction which, incidentally, takes the form of its foundation by the Trojan Aeneas coinciding with the founding of the lineage of the Virgin Mary in David (IV.v). Dante also assumes that the various kinds of authority of which he speaks, and even apparently virtue itself,[32] are male prerogatives, and that assumption too is undermined by the context of Chaucer's use of the passage, narrated as it is by the Wife of Bath, and spoken within the fiction by the woman who knows that what all women most desire is their will, and who is about to claim the *maistrie* for herself. Chaucer is using Dante, in fact, for purposes beyond what Dante actually authorizes: both promote a system of values based not on imperial-political authority, but on virtue derived from God; Chaucer extends that liberation to cover male authority too.

The story in the *Canterbury Tales* that appears to put this principle most fully into practice is the Clerk's Tale of patient Griselda. It does not, however, present itself in quite this way; it looks indeed like the positive proof of the equation of poetic and civil authority, in a way that should confirm its role as the dramatic antonym of the Wife's Tale. The story puts absolute power into the hands of the

---

30 See III,859–61, 990–8. In contrast to all the analogues of the Tale, Chaucer's hag appears to have control over her shape, and not to be the victim of enchantment.

31 In his stories with pagan settings, for instance, the characters may refer to episodes that Chaucer got from Ovid or to *sententiae* from Boethius, but they never themselves cite such later authors.

32 'E noi in donna e in età novella / vedem questa salute, / in quanto vergognose son tenute, / ch'è da vertù diverso' (Canzone Terza 105–8, p. 226); and see also Dante's commentary on the passage, IV.xix.8–10 (pp. 302–3).

man who opens the tale, who is both ruler and husband; and it is the work where Chaucer specifies his source with unique accuracy and detail, both at the beginning and the end. Its *auctor*, who provides authorization for the narrative, is Petrarch:

> Fraunceys Petrak, the lauriat poete,
> Highte this clerk, whos rethorike sweete
> Enlumyned al Ytaille of poetrie.   (IV,31–3)

And at the close, he cites Petrarch again as authority for the moral, of steadfastness in adversity (IV,1147–8). It is appropriate for a clerk to footnote his sources; Chaucer's readiness to do so accurately must reflect the early recognition of Petrarch's *auctoritas*, particularly in his Latin works.

In strong contrast to Boccaccio's anti-authoritarian conclusion to his version of the story in the *Decameron*, Petrarch's reworking, in the *Epistolae Seniles*,[33] finally reads the husband, Gualterius, as a figure for God, Griseldis for the human soul. The figure works in the other direction too, bearing a strong implication both that husbands have godlike rights over their wives (Gualterius suffers nothing in return for his cruelty), and that wives ought to obey their husbands as submissively as they would God, however incapable (as Petrarch notes) they might in practice be of doing so. Petrarch himself offers two ways of reading his work, by means of the device of presenting two friends who are listening to it. One takes it as *historia*, as something that actually happened, and weeps; the other takes it as *fabula*, as an exemplary but impossible fiction, and remains unmoved. Moral truth, it seems, does not elicit the same empathy as fact.

If Chaucer's treatment of the story were as complacently patriarchal as Petrarch's, there would be no problem: in contrast to the 'unauthorized' tales of the Miller or the Wife of Bath, it would be a strongly authorized *exemplum* of male dominance. But Chaucer is seldom straightforward in his relationship with literary authority, and the Clerk's Tale is not, I think, so easy. The narrator rarely enters the mind of either Walter or Grisilde, but the story is told predominantly from her point of view – certainly in sympathy with her. Chaucer condemns Walter's actions strongly and repeatedly; and the epithets and phrases he associates with husband and wife increasingly run against the equation of Walter with God to suggest rather the association of Walter with an unstable Fortune, Grisilde with the steadfastness of Christ.[34] Given this radical shift of emphasis, Chaucer's calling on Petrarch for authoritative endorsement of both the story

---

[33] *Epistolae seniles* xvii.3. The tale of Griseldis and the French version Chaucer also used (but does not mention) are given in *Sources and Analogues* pp. 296–331; the full text of the letter, including the reception accorded the story by Petrarch's friends, is given in *Originals and Analogues of some of Chaucer's Canterbury Tales* ed. F.J. Furnivall, Edmond Brock and W.A. Clouston (Chaucer Soc., 1872–7), pp. 151–72. The ultimate source may have been in folktale: see William Edwin Bettridge and Francis Lee Utley, 'New Light on the Origin of the Griselda Story', *Texas Studies in Language and Literature* 13 (1971–2), 153–208. Boccaccio's version (*Decameron* 10,10) is the most overtly anti-authoritarian of all the treatments; he gives no source for the story, but that is true of most of the tales in the *Decameron*, whether they endorse orthodox authority or not.

[34] See Jill Mann, 'Satisfaction and Payment in Middle English Literature', *Studies in the Age of Chaucer* 5 (1983), 17–48, and Helen Cooper, *The Oxford Guides to Chaucer: The Canterbury Tales* (Oxford, 1989), pp. 190–201.

and the moral looks increasingly subversive. Grisilde is the primary instance in the *Tales* of true *gentillesse* derived not from ancestry but from God, such as the loathly lady advocates on the authority of Dante. Her association with Christ and, on other occasions, the Virgin suggests a kind of divine endorsement for her, as when her wisdom and 'juggementz of so greet equitee' exercised in her husband's absence – exercised, that is, when she assumes his political authority – lead to her being regarded as 'from hevene sent',

> Peple to save and every wrong t'amende.   (IV,441)

But if Grisilde's is a rightful authority based on God-given virtue, then Walter's right to abuse his wife, whether exercised as marquis or as husband, is left in shreds. The authority of Petrarch, to put it another way, is called on, not, as one would expect, to legitimate male power, but to lull the readers into a sense of false security, to predispose them to accept a story that is in point of fact potentially explosive.

Grisilde's endorsement by God does, however, suggest a parallel reading in which the story can be subsumed back into the orthodox order, for the authority of God overrides the authority of men as justly as the authority of men overrides that of women. There was one genre in which women were allowed dominance without causing any *frisson*, and that is the lives of women saints. As with other literary kinds, there was an increasing tendency as the Middle Ages progressed to cite sources for saints' lives, and here the poetic authority is used to endorse, not political power, with which a saint is likely to be in conflict, nor male power, with which a female saint is inevitably in conflict, but the power of God. There was a further reason for emphasizing the authority of saints' lives in that, as with ancestral romances, it drew them closer to *historia*, authentic fact, than to the *fabula* that some of their contents threatened to suggest. Essentially, source citation in the saint's life continued to serve its function of authenticating belief, of endorsing an ideology. In the case of women saints, paradoxically, their very powerlessness within the secular order becomes a way of affirming God's might. God's strength is made perfect in weakness precisely because weakness has no strength of its own. Chaucer's Life of St Cecilia, told by the Second Nun, illustrates the process. It is Cecilia, not the prefect, the pope, or even her husband, who is mentioned in the very first line, and who is the dominant source of authority within the tale. By right of her special position before God, she can boss the men of her family as energetically as the Wife of Bath, and she likewise rejects the authority of the state, the 'power and auctoritee' of princes (VIII,471). Like the Clerk's Tale, but without its potential subversiveness, the Second Nun's Tale not only claims to follow a written source but actually does so:

> For bothe have I the wordes and sentence
> Of hym that at the seintes reverence
> The storie wroot, and folwen hire legende.   (VIII,81–3)

Compared with the casualness or misleadingness of most of Chaucer's other source references, the precision here is striking. The upsetting of the earthly order, it seems, requires the authority both of God, within the narrative, and of written sources for the story itself.

Post-Chaucerian saints' lives follow a similar model. Lydgate cites the languages of the sources of his saints' lives, and goes into increasing detail on his authorities as the authenticity of the legends gets thinner (what one might call the *Melusine* phenomenon): *Guy of Warwick*, which one might have thought had received its *coup de grace* in *Sir Thopas*, even has the chapter number of its 'auctoritee' specified.[35] Osbern Bokenham repeatedly refers back to Jacobus de Voragine, as 'Ianuence', and the *Legenda Aurea* in his *Legendys of Hooly Wummen*.[36] He is one of the writers who pays poetic homage to Chaucer (1403–4, 4058), and his use of rhyme royal for many of his legends suggests Chaucerian influence; but his own Life of St Cecilia is translated into something between octosyllabics and riding rhyme, and shows a resolute avoidance of any direct use of Chaucer in either form or content. The fact that his subjects are women again makes the endorsement of their authority of especial importance, and it seems that Chaucer does not carry appropriate legitimation for even covert use.

Women who had the backing of God and the recognition of the Church for taking authority into their own hands were sanitized: they presented no threat to a patriarchal order. Secular women who exercised unofficial power, and especially wives who bossed their husbands without the authority of God, were a very different matter. Narratives that show wicked wives getting away with it are usually fabliaux, and cite no authorities. But if Chaucer treats the idea of authority seriously in the life of St Cecilia, he certainly does not do so in his life of the Wife of Bath. Her Prologue is at once her autobiography, her *vita*, and a counter-ideology to justify her resistance to established moral and domestic order; and it contains an abundance of approved, and male, *auctores*, Jerome and St Paul high among them. She cites them, however, precisely in order to challenge them, to undermine their authority and the patriarchal hierarchy they support; and she sets up her own arguments and her own experience as a rival, female, authority. It is appropriate therefore that as that double contradiction in terms, an authority who is both fictional and female, she should herself become the ultimate authority for that most subversive of aspirants to power, the wife who wears the boots: a pseudo-authority to back an unauthorizable claim to domination. Chaucer himself starts the process, when Justinus in the Merchant's Tale refers January to her as the supreme expositor of marriage (IV,1685–7); and in his *Envoy to Bukton*, the advice against marriage is subtended by a non-quotation from Christ at the beginning and the citation of the Wife as recommended reading on the subject at the end. Hoccleve follows Chaucer's example, using the Wife as *auctrice* – a specifically female *auctor*, in other words, and perhaps the 'other word' he uses does indeed negate its primary meaning:

---

[35] *The Minor Poems of John Lydgate* ed. H.N. MacCracken (EETS ES 107, 192, 1911, 1934) Part I: Legends of St Giles (no. 36, line 31); St Margaret (37.72); St Austin at Compton (38.404–5, as an oral legend of general credence). For Guy of Warwick, see Part II, 22.569–79. The source references are confined to narrative *vitae*, and are not found in other forms such as prayers or pageant devices.

[36] Ed. Mary S. Serjeantson (EETS OS 206, 1938 for 1936): lines 3144, 5320, 5734, 5748, 6320, 8268, 8284, 8544, 8947, 9456, 10392, 10524; Bokenham also goes into some detail on his translation practice with regard to St Ambrose, his source for his life of St Agnes (4037, 4099, 4711–28).

> The wyf of Bathe, take I for auctrice
> Þat wommen han no ioie ne deyntee
> Þat men sholde vp-on hem putte any vice.[37]

The wives of Lydgate's *Mumming at Hertford* similarly take the Wife as their authority for claiming *maystrye*:

> And for oure party þe worthy Wyff of Bathe
> Cane shewe statutes moo þan six or seven
> Howe wyves make hir housbandes wynne heven.[38]

When plain antifeminism is at issue, by contrast – when, that is, the rebellious-ness of women is being described from the point of view of patriarchal disap-proval – then the authority of Chaucer as moral *auctor* could be called on, as happens in a series of misogynist poems in the Bannatyne Manuscript that have 'quod chauseir' appended to them.[39]

It is ironic that here, and at other points where Chaucer was acknowledged as moral authority, the works in question should not actually be his at all. The sixteenth century indeed became almost schizophrenic in its attitude to Chaucer, with the works he had actually written, notably *Troilus* and the *Canterbury Tales*, being regarded by one group of religious writers as at the furthest con-ceivable extreme from such morally and spiritually uplifting reading as the Bible,[40] while the ascription to him of a large number of works he had not written – Usk's *Testament of Love*, the anonymous *Jack Upland* and *Plowman's Tale* – led to his being accorded an honourable place in the history of pre-Refor-mation Protestantism.[41] A new church that was looking for legitimation found Chaucer's authority useful, and the more demanding editorial questions that were already being asked by literary historians were best not raised in this different context.

Such a representation of Chaucer brings him nicely into line with all three kinds of authority that Dante speaks of in the Fourth Tractate: he is a famous

---

[37] *Dialogus cum amico* 694–7 (*Hoccleve's Works*, p. 135).

[38] *Minor Poems of Lydgate* II no. 42.168–70. The specific allusion is to the Wife's hope that her giving her husbands purgatory on earth is sufficient to win them heaven (III,489–90).

[39] *The Bannatyne Manuscript writtin in Tyme of Pest, 1568*, ed. W. Tod Ritchie (4 vols, STS) IV, pp. 23, 24–6, 34–5, 35–6 (MS pp. 572–3, 579–81). It is impossible to know whether the attributions are Bannatyne's own, and therefore mid-sixteenth century, or whether he found them in his copy. It is only fair to add that whatever scribe was responsible for them recognized that Chaucer argued on both sides: two further poems in praise of women are also ascribed to him (IV, pp. 49–64, in fact Hoccleve's *Letter of Cupid*, and 64–70, MS pp. 593–608).

[40] William Tyndale, Preface to *The Obedience of a Christian Man* (1528), excerpted in Brewer, p. 87; Sir Thomas Elyot, *Pasquill the Playne* (1533), Brewer, p. 90; Edmund Becke's 1549 Preface to the Bible, Brewer p. 102. In this last instance, Becke's condemnation of 'Canter-bury tales' could be a specific reference to Chaucer's work, or could perhaps be a more general reference to trifling or fabulous works: by the mid-century, preachers such as Cranmer and Latimer seem to have been using the term in that sense (see Spurgeon, pp. 88–9). Such a linguistic equation of the Canterbury tale with the fabulous is in its way more telling than specific attacks on the original work.

[41] John Foxe printed the full text of *Jack Upland* under Chaucer's name in his *Ecclesiasticall History*, and noted, with reference to the *Testament* and the *Plowman's Tale*, that some people 'by readyng of Chausers workes . . . were brought to the true knowledge of Religion': see Brewer, pp. 106–9.

poet whose works give moral and philosophical authority to a state institution, the Church of England being, of course, set up by Act of Parliament with the monarch at its head. Where his actual example rather than his spurious reputation was concerned, however, things were not so easy. His readiness to write in such anti-authoritarian forms as fabliaux or the Wife's Prologue seems to have been as big an obstacle to his being recognized as an *auctor* in his own right as was his refusal to claim authenticity for his narratives. There is only one work that claims Chaucer as its authority in the fullest sense, as its poetic and philosophical model that authorizes its message, and that work, interestingly, has the same theme as the loathly lady's speech or the last *canzone* of Dante's *Convivio*: Henry Scogan's *Moral Balade*, written only shortly after Chaucer's death. This poem is a kind of extended commentary on his *balade* of *Gentillesse*, which it quotes in full;[42] Scogan, in effect, does for *Gentillesse* what the rest of the Fourth Tractate does for its opening poem. He writes it, moreover, for the sons of Henry IV, to whom he was tutor: its message will only be complete when it is received into the political world.

Gentillesse has no 'story': it is a poem *about* a moral, so is not problematic in the way that Chaucer's narratives are. But even acknowledged fictions can contain moral truth, and one of the most fabulous of genres, the beast-fable, exists for precisely that purpose. I mentioned earlier that Lydgate and Henryson add the citation of source authorities to match the new religious emphasis they give to the moralities of their fables, but the source they cite is always Aesop, even though both poets also borrow from Chaucer, Henryson to the extent of rewriting the Nun's Priest's Tale as his fable of the Cock and the Fox.[43] Henryson even has Aesop put in an appearance as authority figure within a dream vision, in the Prologue to the fable of the Lion and the Mouse, which is put into Aesop's own mouth. The following fable, of the Preaching of the Swallow, suggests that 'feinȝeit fables' are not in fact the opposite of 'haly preiching', as Aesop himself had suggested (1389–90), but two different ways of doing the same thing. Even within a genre that offers a way of combining truth with fable,

---

42 In *Chaucerian and Other Pieces*, ed. W.W. Skeat (*The Complete Works of Geoffrey Chaucer* vol. VII, Oxford, 1897), pp. 237–44, especially lines 65–128. See also the discussion in Paul Strohm, *Social Chaucer* (Cambridge, Mass., 1989), pp. 76–8, 107–8.

43 See Henryson, *Fables* III, and Lydgate's 'Tale of the Cok' that opens his *Isopes Fabules* (*Minor Poems of Lydgate* II, pp. 568–74), e.g. lines 66–7, 73–5, 93–4, 99–100 ('He ys of poettis callyd Chaunceleer') etc. Lydgate's collection is based on the fable compilation of Walter the Englishman, chaplain to Henry II (text in *Recueil général des Isopets*, ed. Julia Bastin (2 vols, SATF, Paris, 1929–30) II, pp. 7–66), or on some later version of it (see Derek Pearsall, *John Lydgate* (London, 1970), p. 193). Aesop is never named within Walter's text, though he may figure in manuscript headings. Henryson draws seven of his fables, directly or indirectly, from Walter (I, II, VI, VII, VIII, XII and XIII), and gives all but one of these (XII) an Aesop attribution; in addition he cites Aesop for X (from the *Disciplina Clericalis*) and XI (possibly from Baldo's *Novus Aesopus*) – see Fox's notes on the *Fables*. Fox further argues that the fables derived from Walter-Aesop are deliberately arranged so as to give a grouping of two at each end and three in the middle, with the central fable introduced by Aesop himself (pp. lxxvi–viii); and his views are given a strong numerological elaboration by Spearing (pp. 195–9). While I would not dispute that Aesop is central to the collection in both senses, Henryson's confusion over source citation does disrupt the larger symmetry Fox suggests: no reader, that is, could perceive such a pattern from Henryson's text, where the references suggest not the symmetrical 2-(3)-3-(3)-2 arrangement of Aesopic fables (with the others in parentheses), but rather 2-(3)-3-(1)-2-(1)-1.

it seems, Chaucer will not serve either as a moral authority or as an authenticating source.[44]

The culmination of this deep ambivalence towards Chaucer's authority comes with the Elizabethan poetic Renaissance, when the question of his status took on a new urgency. I shall summarize the variety of answers to the question reached by four writers: George Gascoigne; the anonymous author of a collection of prose tales called *The Cobbler of Canterbury*; Robert Greene, who was accused of having written it; and England's own new Virgil, Edmund Spenser.

Gascoigne's line on Chaucer is one that does not deny the scurrility for which the moralists damned him, but overrides it: the best thing about Chaucer – and this is a unique argument – is that he retracted and wrote the Parson's Tale. All writers should

> followe the trace of that worthy and famous Knight Sir Geffrey Chaucer, and after many pretie devises spent in youth, for the obtayning a worthles victorie, might consume and consummate his age in discribing the right pathway to perfect felicitie.

This is from the introductory epistle to the first edition of his *Hundred Sundry Flowers*;[45] by the time the volume reached its second edition, as *Posies*, Gascoigne had reneged on the idea by dropping the epistle and adding a 'generall advertisement' that is itself an elaboration on Chaucer's Retractions, but that reaches the opposite conclusion.[46] It starts with the quotation from Romans 15, 'All that is written is written for our instruction', used by (among others) Chaucer and Caxton on Malory, but, like Caxton and unlike Chaucer, he then goes on to justify the book on those grounds:

> So coulde I never yet reade fable so ridiculous but that therein some morallitie might be gathered . . . I pray thee to smell unto these Posies, as Floures to comfort, Herbes to cure, and Weedes to be avoyded.

Where Chaucer rejects his 'enditynges of worldly vanitees' (X,1085),

---

44 It is also true that the *moralitas* of the Cock and the Fox, in contrast to most of Henryson's, offers no model of authority: the cock represents vainglory, the fox flattery, and both should be rejected. There is less of a shift towards a theological reading compared with its original than in the fables derived from Walter.

45 *George Gascoigne's 'A Hundreth Sundrie Flowres'*, ed. C.T. Prouty (University of Missouri Studies XVII.2, Columbia, Missouri, 1942), p. 50. The work dates from the early or mid 1570s. The description of the 'right pathway to perfect felicitie' sounds as if it must refer to the Parson's 'righte wey of Jerusalem celestial' (X,80), but Gascoigne goes on to discuss whether it is 'over grave a subject to be handled in stile metrical', which does not sound like a reference to a prose work. Either he is generalizing about Chaucer's works (which seems unlikely); or his acquaintance with them is less than perfect (which was true of many of the authors who referred to them, perhaps most devastatingly in the hash Lydgate makes of describing the Canterbury pilgrims in the prologue to his *Siege of Thebes*); or else he has in mind one of the pseudo-Chaucerian works such as the *Plowmans Tale*, though the description would not fit it very well.

46 *The Complete Works of George Gascoigne* ed. John W. Cunliffe (1907; repr. Anglistica and Americana 82, Hildesheim and New York, 1974) Vol. I, pp. 15–17. A further complication in the nature of the allusion here is that while the Retractions had appeared in the earliest printed editions of Chaucer, they were dropped in Thynne's 1532 edition and later sixteenth- and seventeenth-century printings. The similarities to Chaucer might therefore be coincidental; but it would seem unlikely to be mere chance that would lead Gascoigne to replace a reference to Chaucer's change of heart with an echo of the Retractions.

Gascoigne justifies his; he uses the Chaucerian model to authorize precisely the kind of story that moral authority would reject.

The *Cobbler of Canterbury* does not treat Chaucer as problematic at all, and is content to take him in effect as *im*moral authority. It tells of a group of passengers on a barge travelling from Billingsgate to Gravesend, who decide to tell each other tales on the model of 'old father Chaucer'.[47] The nature of that model emerges from the fact that five of the six tales are fabliaux. Greene's response to the accusation of authorship focuses on the question that the *Cobbler* never asks, of what kind of authority can be claimed by Chaucer when he writes stories of this kind. In *Greene's Vision*, he imagines Chaucer and Gower – 'moral Gower', possibly the only thing Greene knew about him – appearing to him in a dream, and arguing whether a scurrilous or mirthful story can be as effective in teaching as one that is more overtly didactic. Gower comments that 'Men honor [Chaucer's poetry] more for the antiquity of the verse, the english and prose, than for any deepe loue to the matter':[48] eloquence and morality are now explicitly at odds, with antiquity lending a spurious authority. The two poets agree to a miniature story competition in which each will tell a tale 'for the suppressing of iealousie', to see which style, the merry or the moral, is the more effective. Chaucer tells one very much on the *Cobbler* model (as Gower points out), about how the wife of a wheelwright from Grant-chester arranges for her jealous husband to see her sitting on a student's knee, then for him to be drugged and returned to his own bed where he is assured that everything he has seen was his own delusion. The tale is a kind of cross between the Oxbridge fabliaux of the Miller and Reeve, and the Merchant's story of January's willingness to be deceived – except that in this tale, the wife is presented as innocent. It is, none the less, a fabliau in which the woman wins out: in which the authority of the husband is destroyed. Gower responds with a tale about a gentleman who turns his wife out of the house on suspicion of her unfaithfulness, and only after returning in disguise to test her and finding her loyal and chaste does he take her back. As in Petrarch's version of the story of Griselda, husbands, even bad ones, are given absolute rights, and the most virtuous woman is the one who accepts such patriarchy with the greatest sub-missiveness. The antifeminist bias of the piece surfaces most explicitly at the end, when Gower urges Greene to leave love and Venus, 'or els, if thou wilt needs Poetically have her a Woman, accept her an infamous strumpet' (p. 69): women, by this reading, are either utterly obedient, and therefore men's play-things, or utterly depraved, and therefore men's playthings. Either way, male authority wins. The point is driven home by the appearance of Solomon, the ultimate authority on wisdom and learning (and, for the Middle Ages, on women too), who confirms Gower's triumph over Chaucer; and the work is framed by the warning that the authors of 'wanton bookes' are rightly banished

---

[47] *The Cobler of Caunterburie and Tarltons Newes out of Purgatorie*, ed. Geoffrey Creigh and Jane Belfield (Medieval and Renaissance Texts 3, Leiden, 1987), p. 23.

[48] *An Edition of Greenes Vision and A Maidens Dreame by Robert Greene*, ed. Mary Evelyn McMillan (Ph.D., University of Alabama, 1960; University Microfilms), p. 23 (a more comprehensive study than in A.B. Grosart's *Life and Complete Works of Robert Greene* Vol. XII (London, 1886)). Greene had apparently not read any Gower, and bases his assessment of him solely on the epithet 'moral' attached to him ever since the end of *Troilus and Criseyde* – thereby paying unwitting homage to Chaucer's authority.

by the civil powers, as Augustus banished Ovid (pp. 7–8, 69). Imperial authority can assume the role of moral arbiter if the poets fail to endorse orthodox ideology.

Chaucer was none the less the master poet of the English tradition; and for a poet such as Spenser, whose aim was to create a national literature in English such as would bear comparison with that of Rome or Italy, the authority of Chaucer becomes a crucial issue. He never acknowledges just how problematic that authority had become, but his particular ways of handling the matter suggest that he was aware of it.

The issue surfaces first in the February eclogue of the *Shepheardes Calender*, where Chaucer is cast as Tityrus, the shepherd-poet who was assumed to be a figure for Virgil himself in the *Bucolics*. Spenser's old shepherd asks,

> ... Shall I tel thee a tale of truth,
> Which I cond of Tityrus in my youth,
> Keeping his sheepe on the hils of Kent? (91–3)

His young interlocutor answers,

> To nought more Thenot, my mind is bent,
> Then to heare nouells of his deuise:
> They bene so well thewed, and so wise,
> What euer that good old man bespake. (94–7)

The tale of the Oak and the Briar which follows is, however, as E.K. notes in his commentary, 'cleane in another kind [from Chaucer], and rather like to Aesopes fables'. The slide away from a more overtly Chaucerian kind of story is, I think, intentional. Spenser above all Renaissance poets believes in the didactic function of poetry; his fable is eminently instructive – 'none fitter then this to applie' (100). The fictional end of Chaucer's work, *argumentum* or *fabula*, can be rendered safe by its transference into the mode where fable carries the same authority as preaching.

The *Faerie Queene* raises a different set of problems, not least in its claims to being ancestral romance. It has one outstanding advantage over *Melusine*, however, in that it is allegorical, therefore overtly fictional. The fact that as narrative history it is not authorized ceases to matter when the fiction itself is a fabular cover for moral truth. It therefore does not need to claim historicity: it is at one and the same time the English equivalent of the *Aeneid* and of its moralizing commentaries. This has advantages when the dynasty it celebrates is of somewhat dubious legitimacy. But Spenser does not overlook the fact that a dynasty must have an authorized history, and in Alma's house, in the chamber of Memory – the faculty in which poets deal to preserve the deeds of ancestral heroes – Spenser has his own two heroes find two volumes that record the deeds of the past. The fictional fairy hero of this part of the poem, Guyon, finds a book entitled 'Antiquitie of Faerie lond'; the pseudo-historical hero of the whole work, Arthur, finds one called 'Briton moniments' (II.ix.59–60).[50] Spenser summarizes the contents of both. Arthur's covers the legendary history of Britain

---

[49] *The Poetical Works of Edmund Spenser*, eds. J.C. Smith and E. de Selincourt (London, 1912), pp. 423–7.

[50] A.C. Hamilton's edition (*The Faerie Queene*, London and New York, 1977) discusses the actual sources of Spenser's history.

from the Trojans down to the reign of Uther Pendragon, the time when the poem is set. Guyon's gives the history of Faerie land, which eventually turns into an account of the Tudor genealogy and so gives it a spurious appearance of antiquity (II.x.75–6). Fiction the poem may be, but it is fiction that integrates and correlates with the historical world, and that can adopt the authenticity of history as part of its ideological programme of the celebration of Elizabeth and her parvenu dynasty.

The *House of Fame* had made explicit Chaucer's refusal to join in such a pretence of historical authority; but if Spenser is to make the *Faerie Queene* the English equivalent of the *Aeneid*, with Virgil and Chaucer, the master poets of the Latin and English traditions, as his joint models,[51] Chaucer cannot be left out of account altogether, however problematic his authority had become. Two examples will illustrate Spenser's ways of dealing with the problem.

The first and most extensive passage is in Book IV, where Spenser calls on 'Dan Chaucer, well of English vndefyled' as the original teller of the story of Cambello and Canacee (IV.ii.32). The subject of the book, Friendship, and the opening line of the story,

> Whylome as antique stories tellen vs,

both recall Chaucer's serious narrative, the Knight's Tale. The story itself, however, is from the rather more fabulous, and unfinished, Squire's Tale; and Spenser does not in fact rework Chaucerian material, but rather supplies the ending that is now 'no where to be found'. Chaucer again turns out to be not a source authority, but a rhetorical model of how to write poetry in English.

The final example I want to take from Spenser, from the last book of the *Faerie Queene*, also brings this paper full circle.

> True is, as whilome that good Poet sayd,
> The gentle minde by gentle deeds is knowne.   (VI.iii.1)

The 'good poet' is Chaucer; and the passage to which Spenser is referring is the loathly lady's speech, with its insistence that the most *gentil* person is the one who

> ... moost entendeth ay
> To do the gentil dedes that he kan;
> Taak hym for the grettest gentil man.   (*Tales* III.1114–6)

It is the same principle that Chaucer in his turn refers to 'the wise poete of Florence / That highte Dant'. But there is a crucial difference between what Dante and Chaucer are saying, and how Spenser interprets them. He goes on,

> For a man by nothing is so well bewrayd,
> As by his manners, in which plaine is showne
> Of what degree and what race he is growne.
> ...
> Gentle bloud will gentle manners breed.   (VI.iii.1–2)

Dante and Chaucer use the concept of *gentillesse* to liberate virtue from birth; Spenser uses it to glue the two together again. It may not be possible for him to

---

[51] His principal model in practice is a different poet altogether, Ariosto, whom, like Chaucer with Boccaccio, he does not mention.

use Chaucer to endorse his view of the dynasty of Britain, but he will at least misuse him to endorse a political system that locates, not just power, but also virtue – and therefore, necessarily rightful power – in the gentleman. The authority of the father of English poetry is used to invent a moral justification for the civil power. It may shock our sense of Spenser's own authority that he makes such a move, whether it happened through a deliberate bending of his original or through an ideological predisposition that prevented him from seeing what Chaucer was actually saying. It is finally more interesting, though, that he should have felt the need to make the connection, to bring together those three authorities of Dante's, the political, the moral and the poetic, so that they could speak with a single voice, and to have made that voice Chaucer's.

LIFE AND FICTION IN THE *CANTERBURY TALES*:
A NEW PERSPECTIVE

PAULE MERTENS-FONCK

In his illuminating volume entitled *Chaucer and the Imagery of Narrative*, Van Kolve examines 'several groups of images in relation to the opening sequence of tales . . . not in search of some "reciprocal illumination of the arts" but simply in order to join the part of Chaucer's audience that knew these traditions from many other places, for whom such knowledge was part of the essential literacy they brought to his narrative art.'[1]

My approach in the first part of this essay will be similar to Van Kolve's and greatly indebted to it, for I will attempt to bring out an image with which we are no longer familiar but which was part of the literary culture of the poet and which, almost certainly, was shared by his audience. But the image I shall deal with is a purely mental one, it has no iconographic support: it is conveyed by a literary tradition handed down in several Latin, French and Anglo-Norman poems, a few copies of which have come down to us.[2]

The image in question is called up in the first place by the crystalline name of the Prioress in line 121 of the *General Prologue*: Eglentyne. Within a few lines, the image is confirmed by the associations suggested by Chaucer's reference to her convent, St Leonard's at 'Stratford atte Bowe'. That nunnery was well-known among the English aristocracy in the second half of the fourteenth century: for many years, it had sheltered, together with other ladies of the nobility, Queen Philippa's sister, Elizabeth of Hainaut, who died there in 1375. Her will, by which she bequeathed her personal belongings to a dozen people, one of them a member of the royal family and several others members of the aristocracy, was translated by J.M. Manly in *Some New Light on Chaucer* because it contained interesting details.[3] Indeed, the late queen's sister's will cannot have escaped our poet's notice for he knew some, if not all, of the legatees; they belonged to the social circles in which he moved, or had moved. Eglentyne seems to have inherited some of Elizabeth's jewels: 'a pair of beads', her green 'gauds', which might refer to Elizabeth's emeralds, and her gold brooch. Two of the noble nuns to whom Elizabeth bequeathed jewels were

---

[1] V.A. Kolve, *Chaucer and the Imagery of Narrative. The First Five Canterbury Tales* (London, 1984), p. 359.

[2] The poems are now known collectively as 'the Clerk-Knight Debates'. There are three Latin versions of them: *Altercatio Phyllidis et Florae, Concilium in Monte Romarici* and Song 55 of *Carmina Burana*; several French versions: *Le Jugement d'Amour ou Florance et Blancheflor*, and reworkings of the same, among which *Hueline et Aiglantine* (also spelt Eglentine); and two Anglo-Norman versions: *Blancheflour et Florence* and *Melior et Ydoine*. There are also a Franco-Italian and a Spanish version. Most of them were edited by Charles Oulmont in *Les Débats du Clerc et du Chevalier dans la littérature poétique du Moyen-Âge* (Paris, 1911) and *Le Jugement d'Amour* was later re-edited by Maurice Delbouille (Paris, 1936).

[3] J.M. Manly, *Some New Light on Chaucer* (Gloucester, Mass., 1959), pp. 206–8.

called Madame Argentyn and Madame Ydoine. The similarity between the name of Madame Argentyn, a real nun, and Eglentyne, a fictitious prioress, was pointed out by Manly.[4] However, Madame Ydoine also deserves some attention.

As an historical name, Ydoine, which means 'fit', 'suitable', 'becoming', is extremely rare; like Eglentyne, it is a literary name. Ydoine and Eglentyne belong to the same tradition: both appear in the titles of French and Anglo-Norman verse debates, *Hueline et Aiglantine* and *Melior et Ydoine*, composed between 1150 and 1250. These poems belong to a group of six debates in the vernacular probably derived from a Latin poem: *Altercatio Phyllidis et Florae*.

The relationships between the different versions have been studied by Edmond Faral, a well-known French literary historian, whose conclusions, published in 1913, are summarized in a stemma.[5] It is extremely significant that Faral, whose deductions have never been questioned, should have discovered such similarities between the French *Hueline et Aiglantine* and the Anglo-Norman *Melior et Ydoine* that he regards the latter as having been derived from the former. *Melior et Ydoine* was composed in Anglo-Norman and, like another version, also in Anglo-Norman, *Blancheflour et Florance*, was almost certainly written in England. If, as Faral claims, the author of *Melior et Ydoine* was acquainted with *Hueline et Aiglantine*, it means that a version of the latter was probably available in England and may, consequently, have been known to Chaucer and to some of his better read contemporaries.

On the other hand, the author or adaptor of the second Anglo-Norman debate, who calls himself Brykhulle, declares that he is translating into French from the English of a certain Banastre.[6] Though the English original has long been lost, its existence can hardly be doubted and it seems reasonable to assume that one version of the poem was probably available to people who knew only English.

According to Faral, all debates on love in a vernacular language derive from one and the same prototype, the *Jugement d'Amour*, the earliest of the series of debates in French and English. Consequently, the variety of French in which it was written may be of some importance: providing there was no lost earlier version, it may point to the area in which the vernacular versions originated.

---

4 Manly, *New Light on Chaucer*, pp. 210–12.
5 Edmond Faral, 'Les Débats du Clerc et du Chevalier', in *Recherches sur les Sources latines des Contes et Romans courtois du Moyen Âge* (Paris, 1913), p. 248:

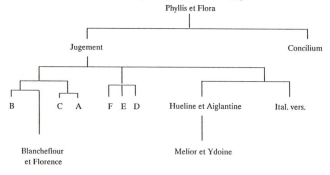

6 The last stanza of the poem begins with the following lines: 'Banastre en englois le fist / E Brykulle cest escrit / En franceois translata'.

Faral draws attention to a number of distinctive Picard characteristics. If he is right, this means that the model on which all later versions were made was written in Picardy, or in the south of Hainaut, where Picard was and still is spoken; Philippa, her sister Elizabeth and their attendants, among whom, perhaps, we may number Chaucer's father-in-law, came from Hainaut. The members of England's court and of the aristocracy might have taken a special interest in that particular genre, feeling it to be a product of Philippa's homeland or of a neighbouring area, Picardy.

The subject of these poems is invariably a debate between two young ladies on the respective merits of clerks and knights as lovers. In his study of the group of poems, which he entitles 'Les Débats du Clerc et du Chevalier', Faral emphasizes the part played in the *Jugement* by courtesy. The terms 'courtois' and 'courtoisie' are used repeatedly, whereas the Latin model of the *Jugement, Altercartio Phyllidis et Florae*, only refers to the strength, the beauty and the wealth of the suitors.[7] Obviously, the author of the *Jugement* was adapting his model to the requirements of courtly love literature, which was becoming fashionable. The discussion usually begins in an extremely traditional setting, an orchard or a meadow in April or May, when nature is in its prime, and it continues when the ladies decide to ride to the paradise of love, or to the court of the God of Love, the arbiter. On the way, they meet two 'bachelors' who offer to guide them. The ladies' horses are usually beautiful mounts, whose valuable ornaments are described in detail.

This is only a sample of the factual information we need in order to imagine some of the associations which might be called up in a reader's mind by a single name. It is some of the context that will turn the 'signal' contained in Eglentyne's name into 'communication'.

When, in the *General Prologue*, Chaucer says that the Prioress is called Eglentyne, he knows her name will evoke the image of Aiglantine and her friend Hueline, prancing along on fine horses and debating whether a clerk or a knight is to be preferred as a lover. By the time the name is mentioned, several other elements have already been introduced: the season of the year and the state of burgeoning nature, for example, are given in the first lines of the *General Prologue*. These elements, which are traditional and multivalent, acquire a specific quality when the name of Eglentyne is uttered. Eglentyne inserts herself into an environment which, though it belongs to a polyvalent context, suddenly appears to have been created specially for her, for a knight and his attendants are already waiting for her. Suspense mounts: will there be another lady? Will there be a clerk? Once summoned, the image will linger at the back of the mind, leaving an impression which will guide and influence the reader's response and understanding.

Chaucer's nearest analogues for the framing device of the *Canterbury Tales* are Boccaccio and Sercambi, both of whom exploit the idea of a journey undertaken by a group of people, but neither of whom refers to horse-riding as the means of travelling. As is usually assumed, Chaucer probably drew the idea of a pilgrimage on horseback from his observation of life, but he may have been influenced in his creation of the female pilgrims by the recurring image of the

---

7   E. Faral, 'Les Débats', pp. 225–6.

disputants in the Clerk-Knight Debates: Phyllis and Flora, Florance and Blancheflor, Melior and Ydoine, Hueline and Aiglantine. The name of the Prioress would connect her instantly with that literary tradition and, through it, with courtly literature in general, for the ladies who debate the choice of a lover have much in common, indeed, can be easily equated with the lady who holds in her hands her courtly lover's fate.

The only other woman described in the *General Prologue*, the Wife of Bath, does not seem, at first sight, to have any of the characteristics of the ladies of the debates or of the heroines of courtly love. But a close examination of the portrait of her in the *General Prologue* reveals a number of elements whose primary meaning belongs to the semantic field of knighthood, the world in which courtly love developed. Her hat is said to be as broad as a buckler or a shield; she is the only pilgrim whose spurs are mentioned, and they are sharp, that is to say, in working order; her stockings are as tightly stretched as those of the Green Knight,[8] she is presented as being as worthy as the pilgrim-knight himself[9] and her wanderings seem to parallel those of a knight-errant. The image of a mock-knight that emerges from this scattering of clues has often been recognized and, in an earlier study, I explained how it functions within the portrait of the Wife of Bath.[10] The answer is to be found at the end of the Wife's *Prologue*, when Alice-knight does what a knight is supposed to do: she fights. Her opponent is her fifth husband, a clerk, who enjoys reading and commenting on anti-feminist stories. But the real objects of her struggle are, on the one hand, literary anti-feminism, handed down by books such as Jankyn's, and, on the other hand, the stereotypes that restrict women, who feel they must conform to them. Those stereotypes, which prevent women from being themselves and deprive them of identity, are embodied in the portrait of the Wife of Bath by the images of the Virtuous Woman and of the Adulterous Woman. The latter image is the only one available to women who refuse to conform to the former. The physical struggle between Alice, a mock-knight, and Jankyn, a real clerk, is a burlesque comment on the clerk-knight rivalry, which both conceals and illustrates a deeper human truth: the difficulty confronting a medieval woman who wants to preserve her identity in a world dominated, on the one hand, by men and their anti-feminist prejudices, and, on the other, by stereotypes.

Alice of Bath is, in fact, more closely connected with the Clerk-Knight Debates than this tragi-comic anecdote suggests: in her oral performance, which falls into two parts, a prologue and a tale, she offers an answer to the question underlying the debates. Her *Prologue* shows that a woman can be happy with a clerk if she can persuade him to abandon his anti-feminist prejudices. Her *Tale* demonstrates that a woman can find happiness with a knight providing she succeeds in making him forget his bias towards youth, beauty, wealth and high rank. One cannot say more plainly that the question which the debates try to

---

8   Cf. lines 157–8 of *Sir Gawain and the Green Knight*.

9   See lines 43, 47, 50, 64 and 68 of the *General Prologue*. Quotations from Chaucer are taken from *The Complete Poetry and Prose of Geoffrey Chaucer*, edited by John H. Fisher (New York, 1977).

10 Paule Mertens-Fonck, 'Tradition and Feminism in Middle English Literature', in *Multiple Worlds, Multiple Words. Essays in Honour of Irène Simon*, ed. by Hena Maes-Jelinek, Pierre Michel and Paulette Michel-Michot (Liège, 1988), pp. 175–92.

answer is a silly one: what matters is not the professional category of a prospective husband or the advantages directly connected with it, but a husband's capacity to make his wife happy by accepting her as she is, in the same way as women, who were seldom consulted about their partners, had to accept them as they were. In other words, the Wife of Bath converts a problem which is part of the conventions of courtly love, a debate about the choice of a lover, into an eternal and universal problem: the choice of a partner with whom one can be happy. She converts a fictional, literary debate into a serious examination of one of the major problems of life. Alice has, indeed, a claim to being considered one of the women who have something to say in a debate about love. For, while Eglentyne's claim lies chiefly in her name, Alice's lies in her experience and the permanent validity, the humanism, of her ideas.

However, the image of the two ladies of the French debates reflected in the mirror of the *General Prologue* is completely distorted. The reader of *Hueline et Aiglantine* is made to feel that the two 'puceles' of the French poem are young and beautiful, but their portraits are very sketchy: six lines are devoted to Aiglantine, four to Hueline. On the other hand, the description of the mule ridden by Aiglantine takes thirty lines. The English poet reverses in favour of human characterization the respective lengths of the descriptions: Eglentyne's portrait takes forty-five lines, the Wife of Bath's thirty-two, and horses are only briefly referred to. As might be expected, the significant difference in length of description goes hand in hand with a significant difference in tone and meaning. In the French debates, the brief and vague descriptions of the ladies result in vague, unprecise images. Chaucer's portraits, on the contrary, are long, full of details and individualized, so much so that readers are taken in by the realism of his descriptions and some critics even feel that the portraits might have been painted from life. As Jill Mann's indispensable book on *Chaucer and Medieval Estates Satire* has shown, the portraits were put together out of bits and pieces echoing literary works satirizing medieval estates.[11] Chaucer's purpose in developing the descriptions of women he found in the debates was not merely to imitate and adapt those poems. Compared to the 'puceles', 'avenanz et beles', who meet 'en un vergier', the incongruous pair formed by Eglentyne and Alice of Bath, a distinguished nun and an exuberant commoner, who meet in an inn, of all places, can only be undertood as a parody of the debate figures. I hinted at Chaucer's critical attitude to those poems in my discussion of the burlesque episode of the clerk-knight rivalry at the end of the *Wife's Prologue* and in my analysis of the answer given by Alice to the conventional question underlying the debates: 'Who is the best lover, the clerk or the knight?' By parodying the unrealistic group formed by Hueline and Aiglantine or Melior and Ydoine, Chaucer brings out the fictional character of his models and creates a lifelike pair: Eglentyne could be, like Ydoine, an historical nun from Stratford atte Bowe and Alice, the flesh and blood wife of a guildsman. Out of the dreamlike vision of two ladies parading on sumptuous mounts, Chaucer creates realistic portraits, which parody the original pair.

But, while Chaucer's source of inspiration for the figures of Eglentyne and Alice of Bath may be the image of the two ladies riding to the palace of the God

---

[11] Jill Mann, *Chaucer and Medieval Estates Satire* (Cambridge, 1973).

of Love, what is the origin of the male pilgrims? The first three are knights, or men at arms; so are also the Franklin ('Ful ofte tyme he was knyght of the shire', 356), the 'worthy' Merchant-Adventurer (who deals with 'sheeldes', 278), the Miller, who only thinks of fighting and wears a sword and a buckler (558), the Shipman, who has a funny 'daggere hangynge on a laas . . . aboute his nekke' (392–3) and the Summoner, a mock-knight like most of the others, who has made himself a buckler with a cake. Many of the other pilgrims might be called clerks if one includes in this category men with higher or university education, such as the Clerk, the Man of Law and the Physician, as well as ecclesiastics like the Monk, the Friar, the Parson, and such a 'noble ecclesiaste' as the Pardoner. With only a few exceptions, which can all be accounted for, all the men who accompany the Prioress and the Wife of Bath fall, as real knights and clerks or as mock-knights and mock-clerks, into one of the two categories that are the subject of Hueline and Aiglantine's debate.

As very aptly noted by Van Kolve: 'Not only were medieval readers and listeners asked . . . to "see" what they heard described – but the art of literary composition itself was often represented as an act of visual imagining: the author at his desk sees the subject of his work, often a personified idea, standing before him'.[12] Van Kolve's chapter on Audience and Image, from which this quotation is taken, has illustrations with the following captions or comments: 'a man reading a book and simultaneously "seeing" in his mind's eye the knights in armor that he reads about', 'Boccaccio (at his desk) writes about Lady Fortune (who stands before him)', and 'Boethius with his book before him seated in a library, viewing himself and Lady Philosophy in a large picture that hangs from a golden chain on the opposite wall.'[13] Chaucer seems to have viewed himself, like the figure in the third illustration, with the pilgrims he describes. From the point of view of his creation of the male pilgrims, the most interesting illustration provided by Kolve shows 'a Christian and a Jew discussing their respective religious faiths'. This is the subject of the second story of the First Day in Boccaccio's *Decameron*. The respective faiths are personified by Jesus and Moses, painted on the wall behind the disputants.[14] The literary creation of the pilgrims who surround the two ladies is a striking illustration of the process described by Van Kolve: Chaucer at his desk does not only see the two ladies, but he also imagines the subject of their debate, the respective qualities and defects of clerks and knights, whom he visualizes and represents standing or riding before him personifying the qualities attributed to them. These include not only knightly worthiness, knightly accomplishment, knightly perfection of equipment, clerkly disinterestedness, clerkly astuteness, but also clerkly lechery and clerkly greed.

Of course, Chaucer's description of the Knight, who personifies worthiness, cannot correspond to a truthful human portrait. The poet knows, and wants to show, that human nature is more varied, less predictable, in a word, different from such stereotyped descriptions. As a result, he parodies both the medieval practice of representing abstract ideas in human forms and the related practice of presenting human characters as embodying qualities or defects. In fact, he shifts

---

[12] Kolve, *Chaucer and the Imagery of Narrative*, p. 32.
[13] Ibid., respectively pp. 10, 34 and 38–9.
[14] Ibid., pp. 35–6.

from the former practice, the description of personified 'knightly worthiness', to the latter, in creating what can be called 'the worthy knight' or 'the ideal knight', and in the process comes nearer to a truthful human portrait. However, the latter practice is hardly more satisfactory for it relies either on traditional lists of achievements (battles, in the Knight's case), of accomplishments (as in the Squire's portrait), or on stereotypes (as in the portrait of the Friar and of many other pilgrims). The parody, or parodic effect, intended by the poet in order to express his criticism of those literary practices springs from his manipulation of medieval literary conventions. For instance, he exaggerates the number of battles fought by the Knight, all of them in remote parts of Europe and extending over an extremely long period. The detail that leaves no doubt about Chaucer's intention is the extraordinary number of *mortal* battles which the Knight has survived – fifteen! Obviously, Chaucer is boldly mocking traditional literature, of which there were many examples in the fourteenth century, which overemphasized the prowesses of a knight who was the poet's patron or friend.

Chaucer's object is truth, or a truthful representation of life, and demolishing fiction by showing why it is fiction is one way of getting at the truth. Another method consists of telling a truth which the audience can recognize as such. This is what the poet does in the last two lines of his portrait of the Knight:

> For he was late ycome from his viage
> And wente for to doon his pilgrymage. (77–8)

These lines, which are in keeping with St Bernard's conception of the knightly role described by Jill Mann,[15] do not seem to echo any traditional description of knightly behaviour. However, they describe what a knight like Edward, the Black Prince, whose piety was proverbial, might have done when he returned from one of his famous campaigns in France: he might have gone to Canterbury to thank God and St Thomas for preserving his life and giving him the victory.[16]

In the Squire's portrait, one of the most striking parodic touches is the incredible number of accomplishments credited to a very young man who looks more like a courtly lover than like a warrior. As noted by Jill Mann, 'he resembles in this the lover of the *Roman de la Rose*', to whom 'Amour suggests . . . that he should cultivate *one* of those accomplishments.'[17] Similarly, the well accoutred Yeoman is parodied by the number of weapons he carries with him to take part in the most peaceful activity one can imagine: on his pilgrimage, he takes a mighty bow, a sheaf of arrows, a sword, a buckler and a dagger, all of them in perfect condition. Chaucer's portrait of the Prioress parodies satiric literature at the expense of frivolous and worldly nuns who try to imitate the aristocracy. In the penultimate line of the description, we read that the Prioress has a brooch engraved with an 'A', the initial of Aiglantine spelt as in the title of the French debate, surmounted by a crown: a sign that she is probably of royal birth. It is not surprising, then, if her manners are refined, because she was born into the aristocracy and brought up at court. The Monk's portrait is the personification of the worldly prelate and, like the description of the Friar, is composed of traditional features. However, by having the Monk speak and express his

---

15 J. Mann, *Medieval Estates Satire*, p. 108.
16 On the Black Prince's piety, see, a.o., *Life of the Black Prince* by the Herald of Sir John Chandos, ed. by Mildred K. Pope and Eleanor C. Lodge (Oxford, 1910).
17 J. Mann, *Medieval Estates Satire*, p. 120.

contempt of the Benedictine rule, Chaucer suggests that, in this case, estates satire has hit the mark and that such a prelate really exists.

These last two examples, the Prioress and the Monk, indicate that, behind the parody of conventional literature and the satire in the foreground of each portrait, there is an individual who, like the Prioress, is completely different from what traditional estates satire suggests, or, like the Monk, is in keeping with it. Behind the parody of personified worthiness, there is a responsible and pious knight, perhaps the Black Prince himself, who, after a battle, thinks in the first place of giving thanks. Behind the young Squire, whom courtly literature presents as hardly concerned with his future career, is a serious young man, respectful of his duties, who

> Curteis . . . was, lowely, and servysable,
> And carf biforn his fader at the table.   (99–100)

Behind the perfect gear of the Yeoman, there is only emptiness, nothing, no one and this is probably one of the reasons why he does not have a tale to tell.

> Nu wol I turne to another tale.

In other words I will leave for another occasion my analysis of the other portraits. They all spring from the same source and are composed in a similar way, except for the group of guildsmen, which requires a long, separate discussion.

The debate theme, which seems to have been the source of inspiration for the 'creative image' of the *General Prologue*, the image out of which Chaucer created the characters in his introduction, is also present in the tales: it runs like a guiding thread unrolling from a ball, a clew, through the whole collection. It also functions in the narrative part of the *Canterbury Tales* as a yardstick by which Chaucer invites the reader to measure the degree of truthfulness of the courtly literature it represents by contrasting it with a situation which bears the stamp of historical authenticity. More simply, it distinguishes traditional fiction from what Chaucer considers as a truthful representation of life.

It would be easy, and highly desirable, to illustrate Chaucer's practice in more than one tale, but the *Knight's Tale* will take up all the allotted space. However, it is the first story in the collection, it is pregnant with all that the poet intends to say, and, it sets the tone. It is, as Helen Cooper writes, 'a dynamic introduction to the story-telling: it leads in many directions and opens out on to many of the problems and perspectives explored later in the work.'[18] Furthermore, it is about Theseus, whose first heroic achievement is embroidered in gold on his pennon:

> And by his baner born is his penoun
> Of gold ful riche, in which ther was ybete
> The Mynotaur, which that he slough in Crete.   (978–80)

Theseus's victory over the Minotaur calls to mind the trick devised by Ariadne and her sister to help the prince of Athens kill the monster. The story is told by Chaucer in *The Legend of Good Women*, and the poet could assume that it was known to his readers. With the complicity of the monster's jailer, Ariadne and her sister provided Theseus with a weapon to kill the monster and with a

---

[18] *The Structure of the Canterbury Tales* (London, 1983), p. 91.

clew, a ball of thread, he could unwind on his way to meet the Minotaur at the centre of the maze. He could then use the thread in order to find his way back out of the maze after killing the beast.[19] By referring to Theseus's pennon, which is not mentioned in Boccaccio's *Teseida*,[20] Chaucer reminds us that Theseus holds a device that helped him through a maze and in 1976, Donald Howard aptly compared Chaucer's masterpiece to a medieval cathedral labyrinth.[21] The reference to the Minotaur right at the beginning of the *Knight's Tale* reinforces the view that the idea of a maze may very well underlie the collection and at the same time hints at the existence of a clue, in the etymological as well as in the modern sense of the word, which is in Theseus's possession.

The subject of the *Knight's Tale* can be briefly summarized. Two knightly cousins, Palamon and Arcite, who are held prisoners by Theseus in a tower, fall in love with the queen's sister, Emily, whom they see in the garden under their prison cell. Arcite is released on condition that he will not remain in the country. He departs, but is so unhappy at being separated from the lady he loves that he returns in disguise and becomes a servant in Emily's household. Some time later, Palamon escapes. By chance, the two cousins meet in the forest. Still rivals for Emily's love, they decide to obtain weapons and fight. Theseus, who has had a sudden wish to hunt the hart in early May (1674–5), rides into the forest with his wife, Hippolyte, with Emily and with their attendants, and, by chance, they come to the very place where the two knights are fighting. The king intervenes and asks the men who they are. Palamon tells him and ackowledges that he and his cousin both deserve to die. Theseus agrees and condemns them to death. But Hippolyte, Emily and all the ladies in the company begin to weep and their tears move the king to pity. At this point of the narrative, it is difficult to deny that the two noble ladies, pleading in favour of two rivals, recall the central scene of the Clerk-Knight Debates. In case the debate pattern might have escaped his readers' notice, the poet adds the following comment on the cousins:

> For gentil men they were of greet estaat
> And no thyng but for love was this debaat.   (1753–4)

There are, however, a few differences which become significant once the debate pattern has been juxtaposed to the Knight's narrative. To begin with, the two rivals in the *Knight's Tale* are not a clerk and a knight, but two knights. The balance held in the debates between the two categories seems to be broken; but this agrees with the Wife of Bath's conclusion, expressing one of the poet's recurring themes, that categories do not matter. Moreover, the balance is comically restored by the Miller, whose 'heroes' are two clerks, and it is disrupted again, in favour of clerks, this time, in the *Reeve's Tale*. These alternations can only denote Chaucer's jocular attitude to the debate pattern and its unnatural categories.

Another difference is more significant: instead of debating, like Hueline and Aiglantine, the merits of their respective lovers, the queen and her sister plead to save the lives of two men whom they scarcely know. After summoning the image of the debating ladies, the poet represents the queen and her sister falling on their knees, ready to kiss the king's feet:

19 *The Legend of Ariadne*, lines 2012–18 and 2148–9.
20 *The Riverside Chaucer*, 3rd ed. (Oxford, 1989), p. 829, note 980.
21 *The Idea of the Canterbury Tales* (Berkeley and Los Angeles, 1976), p. 327 ff.

And on hir bare knees adoun they falle
And wolde have kist his feet ther as he stood.   (1758–9)

The second image, which takes the place of the first one, calls to mind the memory of a similar scene, performed by real people who were known to everyone. In 1346, after his victory at Crécy, the King of England laid siege to Calais; after nearly a year, the people of Calais agreed to surrender; the King insisted that six burghers in shirts and with cords round their necks, should hand the keys of the city to him. When the representatives of the burghers came before him, he ordered that they should be beheaded. Queen Philippa, who was pregnant, flung herself at his feet, weeping, and begging him to spare the burghers. Moved to pity, the King handed the burghers over to his wife, who ordered them to be given suitable clothes and released. The episode, which took place in 1347, is told by a Liège chronicler, Jehan le Bel, and retold by Froissart, who copied it from le Bel.[22] Chaucer was a child when the episode took place, and he was probably struck by it. It certainly remained for some time in the memory of his contemporaries and is still familiar to some modern Hainaulters.[23]

It is important to note, as Piero Boitani observed, that Chaucer's 'scene of the women begging for mercy for the lovers has no parallel' in his main source for this tale, Boccaccio's *Teseida*.[24] We may assume that Chaucer's addition of it to his source points to a conscious poetic creation. He aimed at bringing to life in his readers' minds a scene which would be recognized as true because it was part of the experience, it was in the memory, of his contemporaries and it had been told in some detail by at least two chroniclers.

The scene of the meeting in the forest as described by the Knight presents two contradictory images in quick succession. On the one hand, it shows us the image of two ladies on royal mounts pleading for two lovers in a romantic setting, which associates it with the Clerk-Knight Debates and, on the other hand, it describes the same ladies flinging themselves at the king's feet in a scene which, through its associations with history, bore the stamp of truth. The latter scene gave the ladies a role which was very different from the one they were supposed to play in the debates and in courtly literature. Instead of standing on a pedestal and holding their lovers' fates in their hands, they are begging for the king's mercy for men they have never seen before. In other words, reality, as represented by the second image is very different from courtly literature. Reality does not lie in what poets write, but in what the readers can recognize as real.

Like Edward III, who spared the burghers, Theseus spares the knights, but from this point onwards, their behaviour differs significantly. Edward adopted a reasonable course: he handed the burghers over to his wife, whereas Theseus falls back onto the conventional course of action dictated by the literary tradition, agreeing that one of the knights can marry Emily. The King devises an

---

[22] *Les Vrayes Chroniques de Messire Jehan le Bel*, ed. by M.L. Polain (Brussels, 1863), II, pp. 138–9. Jean le Bel was born in Liège in the last years of the thirteenth century. He died over eighty years old in about 1370.

[23] The Burghers, memorably rendered in bronze by Auguste Rodin, haunt near the Houses of Parliament, a few steps from Westminster Abbey, where their benefactress lies in her tomb made by Hennequin of Liège.

[24] *Chaucer and Boccaccio*, Medium Ævum Monographs, New Series VIII (Oxford, 1977), p. 124; see also p. 130, 8).

elaborate 'tourney' or battle, to take place exactly fifty weeks later, which will decide who will marry Emily. It does not occur to him that Emily's opinion could be a relevant factor, which might save a lot of trouble and money, for Theseus will have an arena built at great cost for the occasion. The *Knight's Tale* parodies the lengthy descriptions of the elaborate preparations, and the very idea of the preparations, made to choose Emily's husband. Piero Boitani has rightly noted that the period over which the action extends in the *Teseida* is lengthened in Chaucer's version.[25] In the long run, the time elapsing between the beginning of the story and the final decision amounts to about ten years. The Trojan War is definitely lurking in the background, as also suggested by the name Chaucer gives to the country of the Amazons, conquered by Theseus, Feminye, which is that used in the *Roman de Troie* by Benoît de Sainte Maure.[26] That Chaucer parodies traditional chivalric romances inspired by Ancient Greece and that Theseus should have asked Emily's opinion become clearly apparent when the reader discovers, on the morning of the fight, that Emily does not want to get married at all. And after the fight, when the winner is known, a sudden accident reduces to nothing all the efforts made by Theseus and hundreds of other people. It is obvious that a conversation between Theseus, Emily and her sister, a human, friendly debate, could have solved the problem with less cost, less pain and less time.

This brief discussion does not claim to take into account, even superficially, all the aspects of what Helen Cooper calls, with good reason, the 'open-ended exploration contained in a brilliantly controlled narrative and rhetorical structure'[27] or all the artistic, philosophical and theological implications which, as Van Kolve has shown, transcend the action. I simply hope to have suggested that the little scene inserted by Chaucer in the *Knight's Tale* functions like a flash of light that illuminates a hitherto unnoticed perspective and reveals Chaucer's method of showing his readers how to distinguish fiction from the truthful representation of life. It works backwards to emphasize that the substance of the debates about love, and of courtly literature in general, is in contradiction with reality since, at the first opportunity, the ladies leave their pedestal and kneel at the king's feet. And it works forwards to stamp Theseus's behaviour as irrational when, in order to follow the course prescribed by the literary tradition, it deviates from Edward III's pragmatic solution. The scene also suggests that we are justified in looking for close links between tale and narrator. If I am right in assuming that the last two lines of the Knight's portrait might refer to the Black Prince, then the moving story of Philippa's intercession for the lives of the burghers of Calais and of Edward's merciful gesture would have been told by their own son.

In the other *Canterbury Tales*, the reader, alerted by his experience of the *Knight's Tale*, will get into the habit of looking for the clue that will reveal the real meaning of the tale. He will find that it is always associated with the debate theme and that Theseus provides a thread which the diligent adventurer can follow from the heart of the maze of stories into the clear light of day.[28]

25 Boitani, *Chaucer and Boccaccio*, p. 128.
26 See *The Riverside Chaucer*, 3rd ed. (Oxford, 1989), p. 828, note 866.
27 Cooper, *The Structure of the Canterbury Tales*, p. 91.
28 I wish to thank James Gibbs for reading my text and making useful suggestions.

WRITING THE TYRANT'S DEATH: CHAUCER, BERNABÒ VISCONTI AND RICHARD II

DAVID WALLACE

In the *Prologue* to the *Legend of Good Women*, the Chaucer poet-*persona* falls under the gaze of an absolute power, the god of Love:

> For sternely on me he gan byholde,
> So that his loking dooth myn herte colde.   (F 239–40)

The Chaucer figure is plainly unnerved by such stern *loking* and seems ominously ill-equipped to defend himself and his *makyng* when called upon. Happily, however, he is saved by the queen, Alceste, who defends him as a guileless translator and then confronts her spouse with negative exempla, images of what he would not wish to be. The *Legend of Good Women*, as Paul B. Taylor reminds us elsewhere in this volume, is also a book of wicked men.[1] Its *Prologue* warns us that such men may be found in the historical present as well as in the fictional past:

> This shoolde a ryghtwis lord have in his thoght,
> And nat be lyk tirauntz of Lumbardye,
> That han no reward but at tyrannye.
> For he that kynge or lord ys naturel,
> Hym oghte nat be tiraunt ne crewel
> As is a fermour, to doon the harm he kan.
> He moste thinke yt is his lige man,
> And is his tresour and his gold in cofre.

Alceste's speech is a brilliant *tour de force* of political rhetoric that repays the closest attention, particularly for its use of judicial and parliamentary terms. Her master trope might be described as negative or ventriloquized *occupatio*: she insists on Chaucer's right to speak, but she insists at such length that the god of Love recovers his poise and Chaucer is kept from speaking (and so destroying himself). Her discourse is the first sustained attempt in English to represent the delicate art of addressing a lord who is imagined to embody (or imagines himself as embodying) absolute power. Such art is more commonly associated with the Tudors: but the need for such a rhetoric was felt with increasing urgency under Richard II, a famously foul-tempered monarch. In 1385, to cite just one early example, Richard became so incensed with the Archbishop of Canterbury that he drew his sword; the men who restrained him from killing the Archbishop were so terrified by the 'rex iratus' that they leapt from the royal barge into the Archbishop's boat. The Archbishop was subsequently obliged to kneel before the King and sue for his pardon.[2]

---

[1] Paul B. Taylor, 'Cave and Web: Vision and Poetry in Chaucer's *Legend of Good Women*', pp. 69–82.

[2] *The Westminster Chronicle, 1381–1394*, eds. and tr. L.C. Hector and Barbara F. Harvey

The later years of Richard II are commonly described as a tyranny.[3] Queen Anne, a moderating influence on Richard, had died; in the rewritten *Prologue* to the *Legend of Good Women* the active role accorded to Alceste in F is much diminished. By 1398 the gaze of Richard II had hardened into something close to madness: according to the continuator of the monastic *Eulogium Historiarum*, he was accustomed, on state occasions, to sit in silence on a throne in his chamber all afternoon and stare at the company.[4] Anyone who crossed his line of sight, whatever their rank, was forced to genuflect. In 1399 Richard was deposed; the circumstances of his death are mysterious and obscure.

Chaucer, throughout his career, may be seen worrying out the delicate art of addressing men of high degree at moments of intense emotion: this effort runs from the dialogue with the black knight in the *Book of the Duchess* to the *Melibee* to the *Legend of Good Women*. He also studies the effects of such personal emotion spilling out into the greater public domain. In medieval political theory, this triumph of individual will and pleasure over the common good marks the shift from kingship or legitimate rule to tyranny.[5] Chaucer develops a powerful spatial metaphor for this tyrannical state of mind: he calls it 'Lumbardye'. This is most famously exemplified, of course, by the *Clerk's Tale*, but other aspects are explored in the *Merchant's Tale*, the *Prologue* to the *Legend of Good Women*, and by a single stanza of the *Monk's Tale*. Each of these exemplifications is pitched at an uncharted borderland between fiction and history. In Chaucerian texts, 'Lumbardye' is both a real foreign territory and an imaginary place close to home. In the lines from the *Legend's Prologue* quoted above, Chaucer speaks of plural 'tirauntz of Lumbardye'; he knows that (until 1385) more than one tyrant ruled this Italian territory at any one time. Yet he also has Alceste urge her spouse not to act like a tyrannical tax-gatherer and to recognize his subjects as his true wealth and treasure, his 'gold in cofre'. Nothing could speak more directly to English concerns during the reign of Richard II.

Chaucer himself, of course, had direct personal experience of Lombardy and the tyrants who ruled there. His earliest images of Lombardy were mediated by geographical distance and by various forms of political, literary and cultural myth-making.[6] In 1378, however, Chaucer was able to judge Lombard polity for

---

(Oxford, 1982), pp. 116–17, 138–9. The Monk of Westminster, author of this *Chronicle*, was plainly disturbed by the political implications of this incident: 'the truth is that with due regard always to the paths of righteousness and justice he [the Archbishop] would never have bent head or knee in that fashion to anybody, when according to the canonical rule it is rather the necks of kings and princes which should be bowed in submission at the feet of pontiffs' (p. 139).

3   See Caroline Barron, 'The Tyranny of Richard II', *Bulletin of the Institute of Historical Research* 41 (1968), 1–18; May McKisack, *The Fourteenth Century. 1307–1399* (Oxford, 1959), pp. 488–91.

4   See *Eulogium Historiarum sive Temporis: Chronicon ab Orbe condito usque ad Annum Domini MCCCLXVI*, ed. F.S. Haydon, 3 vols (London, Rolls Series, 1858–63), III, 378; Antonia Gransden, *Historical Writing in England, II. c. 1307 to the Early Sixteenth Century* (Ithaca, 1982), p. 183.

5   For the relevant references to Thomas Aquinas, Henry Bracton, Brunetto Latini, Nicholas Oresme and Aegidius Romanus, see David Wallace, ' "Whan she translated was": a Chaucerian Critique of the Petrarchan Academy', in *Literary Practice and Social Change in Britain, 1380–1530*, ed. Lee Patterson (Berkeley, 1990), pp. 156–215 (pp. 188–9). This essay examines the representation of Lombard tyranny in the *Clerk's Tale* and *Merchant's Tale*.

6   Chaucer's first master, Lionel, Duke of Clarence, travelled to Lombardy to marry a Visconti

himself: he was sent 'ad partes . . . Lumbardie versus Barnabo dominum de Mellan',[7] briefed to seek the assistance of Bernabò Visconti and his son-in-law Sir John Hawkwood in England's war with France.[5] But this opportunity did not mean that Chaucer was finally able to separate the Bernabò of fiction and legend from the 'truth' of a historical personage: for what he experienced in Lombardy was the cultivation of fiction and legend as an instrument of state. In what follows, we will first see how this legend served Visconti absolutism and then note how the moment of Bernabò's death caused the legend to be rewritten. We will then consider how, and to what effect, this discursive complex – the fall of Bernabò, the greatest tyrant of the age – reaches into Chaucer's *Canterbury Tales*. We end with the death of Richard II, another unlocatable moment which mocks our habit of seeking clean distinctions between medieval fiction and medieval history.

Bernabò's political position was exceptionally strong at the time of Chaucer's visit to Milan. His brother Galeazzo died at Pavia on 4 August; Galeazzo's successor, Gian Galeazzo, was only twenty-seven years old and had an undistinguished track-record as politician and soldier.[9] Bernabò, it seemed, was set fair to unify the Visconti state under his personal authority at Milan. This process of making himself the sole and absolute embodiment of power within his own expanding territories had been underway for many years. So, too, had the process of finding dramatic forms of representation for this absolutism. In 1360, for example, Bernabò required all the citizens of Parma (from all social classes) to kneel in the street and render homage to him as he rode through the city; failure to comply brought capital punishment.[10] In 1369, an archbishop who refused to follow Bernabò's orders to ordain a certain monk was forced to kneel at Bernabò's feet and endure a pointed lecture, or interrogation:

> Nescis, pultrone, quod ego sum Papa et Imperator ac Dominus in omnibus terris meis et nec Deus posset in terris meis facere nisi, quod vellem, nec intendo, quod faciat?
> (Don't you know, moron, that I am Pope and Emperor and Lord in all my territories, and that not even God can do anything in my territories unless I want and intend that he should do it?)[11]

This anecdote, which is preserved as part of an attack on Bernabò by Pope Urban V, recalls a *novella* by the Florentine Franco Sacchetti which confirms

---

princess in 1368; he died soon after the wedding. During his visit to Florence on a trade mission in 1373, Chaucer would have heard the Visconti spoken of as the tyrants who posed the gravest long-term threat to the *libertas* of the Florentine Republic. In 1374 Chaucer was appointed controller of the wool custom and wool subsidy in the port of London, a position which brought him into frequent contact with dozens of Italians from various cities (most of them Tuscan).

7 See *Chaucer Life-Records*, eds. M.M. Crow and C.C. Olson (Austin, 1966), p. 58.
8 Hawkwood was one of the many mercenary captains whom Bernabò attempted to bind to the Visconti state through marriage to an illegitimate daughter.
9 See E.R. Chamberlin, *The Count of Virtue. Giangaleazzo Visconti, Duke of Milan* (London, 1965), pp. 62–63. Chamberlin notes that at the moment of Gian Galeazzo's accession to power at Pavia, 'two military humiliations and a piece of political trickery were his sole claim to notice' (p. 63).
10 See *Storia di Milano*, 16 vols (Milan, Fondazione Treccani degli Alfieri), VI, p. 537.
11 *Storia di Milano*, VI, p. 537.

Bernabò's determination to command both sacred and secular authorities. In this *novella*, the first of six in the *Trecentonovelle* featuring Bernabò as protagonist, Bernabò finds a miller that he considers more learned than an abbot he is interrogating. He promptly decrees that they should exchange jobs: the miller becomes an abbot, and the abbot a miller. This fictional abbot first attracted Bernabò's attention, and aroused his displeasure, by neglecting to feed two of his hunting dogs adequately.[12] The passion of the historical Bernabò for hunting was legendary. In 1372, having conquered Reggio, Bernabò declared that every city official should send him a certain number of well-bred dogs every year. Anyone caught hunting at Reggio in the area Bernabò had reserved to himself would have their eyes put out. Anyone who informed on illegal hunters would be awarded 50 gold florins.[13]

It is, we have noted, impossible to make clear distinctions between the legendary Bernabò of *novella*, poem, and anecdote and the historical figure: some of the best anecdotes are, in any case, supplied by official annals, records, and decrees. This blurring of the historical and the imaginary to create a figure of terrifying, enigmatic potency was an essential element of Bernabò's statecraft: if all authority was to reside in one person, that person needed to be larger than life and omnipresent: present through decrees, *novelle*, and images if absent in person. The most famous such image of Bernabò is the equestrian statue by Bonino da Campione that stood in the Milanese church of San Giovanni in Conca (and is now in the Castello Sforzesco, Milan).[14] This is generally described as a funeral monument, but the statue was in place long before Bernabò's death in 1385. The chronicler Pietro Azario, who had completed his *Liber Gestorum in Lombardia* by 1364, was clearly unnerved to discover that Bernabò had had this image of himself – armed, helmeted, and mounted on a war horse – placed on the church's main altar.[15] A contemporary Frenchman, visiting Milan, recoiled with shock on seeing this same 'abominable idol' surmounting the altar of a church.[16] His reaction can be fully understood not by viewing photographs of the statue, but by standing beneath it. Looking up from the ground, little can be seen of the barbaric figure of Bernabò, standing stiffly in his stirrups as he gazes to the far horizon. The viewer sees more of the virginal female figures of Justice and Fortitude, fashioned on a smaller scale on either side of the horse, and the gigantic equine penis that hangs between them.

This image of Bernabò and a giant marble penis bestriding a church altar neatly emblematizes Bernabò's policy of strengthening the state by marrying off the progeny generated by his own formidable virility. At one count Bernabò was credited with thirty-six living children and with eighteen women in various stages of pregnancy. His official consort, Regina della Scala, bore him five sons

---

[12] *Il Trecentonovelle*, ed. Antonio Lanza (Florence, 1984), IV, p. 4. Sacchetti was born some time between 1332 and 1334 and died in August 1400, probably from the plague.

[13] *Storia di Milano*, VI, pp. 535–6.

[14] See *Storia di Milano*, V, pp. 538, 808–12; John White, *Art and Architecture in Italy 1250–1400*, second edition (Harmondsworth, 1987), pp. 610–12; Boitani, ed., *Chaucer and the Italian Trecento*, xi–xii and back jacket; W.R. Valentiner, 'Notes on Giovanni Balducci and Trecento Sculpture in Northern Italy', *The Art Quarterly* 10 (1947) 40–60 (pp. 53–54).

[15] See the edition by Francesco Cognasso in the series Rerum Italicarum Scriptores, vol. XVI, Part IV (Bologna, 1939), pp. 133–4. Azario is anxious to emphasize that the statue is actually standing on the altar: 'super quo altari, dico in superficie ipsius altaris'.

[16] See *Storia di Milano*, VI, p. 537.

and ten daughters. Legitimate offspring were employed to further the extensive networking of the Visconti through Europe, especially northern Europe: Bernabò's legitimate daughters were married to a Duke of Austria, two Dukes of Bavaria, a Count of Württemberg, a King of Cyprus, and to Lionel, Duke of Clarence, Chaucer's first master.[17] His daughter Caterina married his nephew (her cousin) Gian Galeazzo Visconti. Legitimate sons and daughters sometimes shared a complicated wedding day, as on 12 August 1367, when his daughter Taddea married Stephen, son of Duke Stephen of Bavaria, and his son Marco married Isabella, sister of Duke Stephen and daughter of Duke Frederick of Bavaria.[18] Illegitimate daughters married *condottieri* from outside the state, such as Sir John Hawkwood, and illegitimate sons became *condottieri* in the service of the state.

For Bernabò, the development of absolutist polity entailed not the denial of the worst excesses traditionally attributed to despots – unbridled sexual appetite, extreme and violent anger, cruelty, wilfulness, sudden and arbitrary changes of mind – but the cultivation of them.[19] If all authority was to be derived from the mind and person of the prince, all attention must habitually turn to the prince and away from law, custom, and conventional expectations. This lesson is understood by the first *novella* in a manuscript section entirely devoted to Bernabò stories.[20] In riding between Pavia and Milan, Bernabò comes to a wooden bridge over a river. The bridge is blocked by a peasant and his heavily-laden ass. Bernabò's sergeants shout at him: 'Turn back, for the Lord is here'. The peasant immediately heaves his ass into the river to clear the way and do honour to his Lord. Bernabò summons the peasant and asks him to account for his actions. The peasant complies, and Bernabò orders *him* to be thrown into the river. Bernabò explains: it would not have bothered him, he says, if the peasant had behaved like a peasant, but he could not be allowed to boast (*vantare*) of having thrown his ass into the river to honour the Lord. 'And,' the *novella* concludes, 'the peasant struggled to drag himself away, half-dead and totally broken in body; his ass he lost.'

The performance and report of such violent and arbitrary acts formed part of the long and painful educative process through which *cives* were transformed into *subditi Domini*.[21] Subjects were forbidden from speaking of a Guelf or Ghibelline lord, but should speak only of one lord: 'ipse dominus vivat'.[22] Such relentless insistence upon the term *dominus* did not pass without notice: the

---

17 See Geoffrey Trease, *The Condottieri. Soldiers of Fortune* (New York, 1971), p. 76; Michael Mallett, *Mercenaries and their Masters* (London, 1974), p. 49; *Storia di Milano*, V, p. 494.

18 See *Storia di Milano*, V, p. 429.

19 In a letter written to Gian Galeazzo in 1383, Bernabò embellishes his own legend by claiming to have killed one of his uncle's doctors when he was a schoolboy of seventeen. He was, in fact, twenty-three years old in 1346, the year of his exile. See *Storia di Milano*, V, pp. 324–5.

20 See *Novelle inedite intorno a Bernabò Visconti*, ed. Piero Ginori Conti (Florence, Fondazione Ginori Conti, 1940), pp. 39–40. These nine *novelle* appear in a fifteenth-century manuscript (owned by Ginori Conti) that opens with Goro Dati's *Storia di Firenze* and contains other political material, including a piece in *terza rima* by a Florentine merchant that lists history's greatest traitors. This runs from the beginning of the world to Iacopo da Piano's murder of the *signore* of Pisa under the tutelage of Gian Galeazzo Visconti. The eighth of the Bernabò *novelle* is a much longer version of the miller and the abbot story told by Sacchetti.

21 On this process, see *Storia di Milano*, VI, p. 475.

22 See Gianluigi Barni, 'La formazione interna dello Stato Visconteo', *Archivio Storico Lombardo*, new series, 6 (1941), 3–66 (p. 38), referring to a document dated 21 September 1382.

humanist Gabrio de' Zamorei observed that 'these tyrants no longer wish to be called "Lord Peter", "Lord Martin", but simply "the Lord": "the Lord wishes" and "the Lord ordains" '.[23] The aim, of course, was to suggest the god-like qualities of the ruler by merging fear of the Lord with fear of the despot. The Visconti were frequently accused of heresy and blasphemy by the Pope: in 1371, for example, Bernabò was declared a heretic and made the target of a papal crusade; the whole of Europe was canvassed for money.[24] But the Visconti were anxious to dramatize their own zeal for piety: on 10 June 1378, Gian Galeazzo decreed that blasphemers against the saints should stand naked in a public place and be doused with three buckets of water; those who blasphemed God and the Virgin would lose their tongues.[25] The suggestion, again, is that an act of impiety directed at the godhead will be punished as if it were an insult to the prince.

Insults, threats, and conspiracies against the laws which emanated from the Visconti prince were similarly punished as if they represented a physical assault on the prince's person. The rationale for this has been neatly summarized by Foucault in his survey of the spectacle of torture and public execution staged by the absolutist regimes of Renaissance Europe: 'Besides its immediate victim, the crime attacks the sovereign: it attacks him personally, since the law represents the will of the sovereign; it attacks him physically, since the force of the law is the force of the prince'.[26] The ensuing 'liturgy of punishment' must be seen as 'a spectacle not of measure, but of imbalance and excess . . . an emphatic affirmation of power and of its intrinsic superiority'. (p. 49) The longest such spectacle of atrocious and terminal torture to be found in *Discipline and Punish* is eighteen days (p. 54). Foucault terms this 'an infinity of vengeance', but it lasted less than half as long as the infamous 'Lenten observance of Galeazzo'. (Galeazzo Visconti, we should recall, was Petrarch's chief patron during his years in Visconti service.) The 'liturgy of punishment' envisaged by this savage *quaresima* was to last forty days and forty nights. This might seem more than any human body could withstand, but the survival of the condemned was ensured by alternating each day of torment with a 'day of repose'.

According to the chronicler Azarius, Galeazzo devised and published his 'Lenten observance' by way of terrifying (*perterrere*) prospective traitors.[27] Detailed, day-by-day instructions are laid out in the document Galeazzo sent to his rectors in cities that might anticipate acts of rebellion. Tortures are to be administered little by little ('paulatim'): floggings and repose for the first week, then the drinking of water, vinegar, and slaked lime, then the loosening of limbs on various machines of torture. Dismemberment begins on the twenty-third day with the removal of one eye from the head ('unus oculus de capite'). The second eye is not to be removed: it is important in such spectacles that the

---

[23] Translated from text in *Storia di Milano*, VI, p. 537; see also *Storia di Milano*, V, p. 361. For more on the life and works of Gabrio de' Zamorei, see Marco Vattasso, *Del Petrarca e alcuni suoi amici*, Studi e Testi, 14 (Rome, 1904), pp. 35–63.

[24] See Gene A. Brucker, *Florentine Politics and Society 1343–1378* (Princeton, 1962), p. 271; *Storia di Milano*, V, pp. 467–73.

[25] See *Storia di Milano*, VI, p. 523.

[26] Michel Foucault, *Discipline and Punish*, tr. Alan Sheridan (New York, 1979), p. 47.

[27] See *Liber Gestorum*, p. 161, in which Azarius quotes from and comments upon the document sent by Galeazzo 'rectoribus suis'.

victim be able to observe his own physical disintegration.[28] On day twenty-five the nose is cut off; hands, feet, and testicles are then removed, one at a time; and on day thirty-nine the sexual organ ('membrum') is cut off. Day forty is a day of repose; the next day the victim is hanged from a cart and then put on a wheel. Azarius follows his long quotation from the document by observing that many people were subjected to this treatment in 1362 and 1363.[29] In a document dated 1 February 1364 Bernabò prescribes a similar course of treatment, but with two-day intervals between amputations.[30]

The prison in the castle at Pavia was known as 'La lunga dimora', 'the long stay'; Bernabò's infamous Milanese prison was called the Malastalla. Bernabò freed prisoners whenever his wife gave birth. On learning that some prisoners were being released before the appointed time, Bernabò wrote to the *podestà* of Milan instructing him that the prison's custodians were to incur the same penalties as those they had released.[31] The citizens of the conquered comune of Como were informed by a decree inserted into their statutes by Galeazzo on 9 October 1370 that those who plotted against the state would be suspended by one leg until they were dead, 'so that others may be terrified by this example'.[32] One political rationale for such a culture of terror was that it promoted social cohesion and equality: all subjects are united in their fear of the Lord and by their subjugation to the princely *arbitrium*. This principle is neatly exemplified in a Bernabò story that Pietro Azario folds into his *Liber Gestorum* (pp. 143–5).

Bernabò is out hunting one day, and in his furious and headlong pursuit of his quarry he becomes detached from all his noble followers. He wanders through a dark and marshy wood of dead trees until he comes upon a poor, ill-dressed rustic whom he greets with the works 'Ave frater'. The laborer says he is in dire need of God's aid, because he has lost estate ('perdidi estatem'). Bernabò gets down from his horse and asks his *amicus* to explain. The rustic complains of having a devil for a Lord ('diabolum pro Domino') who has driven him to ruin through the ruthless expropriation of his wealth. To this 'dominus Bernabos' replies: 'Certe talis dominus male facit' ('certainly such a lord did wrong').

Bernabò and the rustic then negotiate the price to be paid for leading Bernabò out of the wood. The rustic asks for one Milanese groat ('unum grossum de Mediolano') to recompense his loss of labour; he demands payment in advance, since the officials of the aforesaid devil, his master, are wont to cheat him. Bernabò cuts off one of his silver trappings and hands it to him. He persuades him to climb up onto the horse, arguing that he has eaten so little that his weight is negligible. As they ride along, Bernabò engages him in conversation:

[28] In the public execution of traitors as described by William Blackstone, *Commentaries on the Laws of England* (1766), it is specified that the belly of the condemned man is to be ripped open fast enough for him to see, with his own eyes, his own entrails being thrown onto the fire (see Foucault, *Discipline and Punish*, p. 12). See also the account of the public torture and execution of the regicide Damiens on 2 March 1757 as reported by the *Gazette d'Amsterdam*, which twice emphasizes how Damiens raised his head to observe the state of his own body (Foucault, p. 4).

[29] Cognasso's edition of the Latin text reads 'Executio quorum facta fuit in personas multorum MCCCLXII et MCCCLXII'; I take the second MCCCLXII to be an editor's error for MCCCLXIII.

[30] See Cognasso, ed., *Liber Gestorum in Lombardia*, pp. 161–2 (note 3).

[31] See *Storia di Milano*, VI, p. 521, which refers to a document dated 3 May 1369.

[32] *Storia di Milano*, VI, p. 475.

'Brother, you have told me bad things about your Lord. What then is said in your brotherhood of your Lord who is at Milan?'

The rustic replied: 'He is spoken of better, since although he may be savage ('ferus') he keeps the peace, and if he did not I and other poor men would not dare to enter the remote parts of the dead wood in order to work. And he preserves good justice and that which he promises he holds himself to; this other Lord does just the opposite.'

Bernabò continues interrogating the rustic until they emerge from the wood and approach a fortress, where they encounter a huge search party. On discovering the identity of his interlocutor, the rustic is frightened to death ('ad mortem timuit'); he wishes himself dead, and as they enter the fortress he expects to be put to death ('poni in exterminio'). Bernabò laughingly tells his knights and rectors of his adventures with the rustic ('gesta cum rustico'); the terrified rustic is accorded royal treatment. The next day Bernabò commands that he be presented with a groat and promises to fulfil any petition he may care to put. The rustic asks for his life and, on further prompting, for the restoration of his plots of land. Letters are sent to the offending *castellanus*, the rustic regains all his property and lives in peace.

This narrative of a self-revealing dialogue with a mysterious stranger encountered in a deserted place draws from folkloric origins that are also tapped by Chaucer's *Friar's Tale*. Bernabò, like Chaucer's yeoman, is dressed for hunting. Bernabò wears black, and the rustic at first fears that he may be an impure spirit ('spiritus immundus.') This image of Bernabò as a devil, who may be encountered by any of his subjects in any part of his *dominio*, however obscure, is as useful to the purposes of Visconti propaganda as the association between the Visconti Lord and the Lord of the Christian religion. Other motifs of Visconti propaganda are active within the tale. Bernabò's cruelty is justified as a necessary instrument of distributive and retributive justice. The Lord of Milan is shown to be a powerful ally of the simple labouring man in his struggles with the iniquities of local feudal arrangements. But the most convincing feature of the tale is the abject terror of the *rusticus* before Bernabò: he is evidently more terrified when Bernabò is fêting him in his fortress than he is when speaking to a mysterious, devil-like knight in a dark wood.

In the *Liber Gestorum in Lombardia*, the legend of Bernabò is already well-developed, and Bernabò was to live for more than twenty years after this date. It is not known how much personal contact Chaucer had with Bernabò in 1378: he may (just conceivably) have achieved some degree of intimacy through shared bookish interests, as Donald Howard suggests,[33] or he may have dealt exclusively with ministers and notaries and have had no direct contact with him at all. But it is evident that Chaucer must have experienced the legend and power of Bernabò on every street-corner, as manifested through anecdotes, statutes, sites of punishment, ceremony and display, and above all by the specific configurations assumed by courtiers, administrators and subjects around the centre, visible or invisible, of the princely *arbitrium*.[34] During his

---

[33] *Chaucer: His Life, His Works, His World* (New York, 1987), p. 229.
[34] See the photographic essay of John Baldessari, 'Crowds with Shape of Reason Missing', *Zone* 1/2 (1986) 32–39.

visit to Lombardy, in short, Chaucer observed and experienced the art of living within the ambit of absolute power.

On 6 May 1385 Gian Galeazzo Visconti rode into Milan with Iacopo dal Verme and some of his German mercenaries, having apparently persuaded his uncle and father-in-law Bernabò that he wished to pay him a courtesy call en route to a pilgrimage site at Varese. Bernabò was surrounded and imprisoned and was dead and buried by the end of December.[35] His imprisonment and death is recorded by almost every chronicler in Italy, by chroniclers in England and France, by *canterini*, sonneteers, *novellatori*, by Visconti and Florentine propagandists, by religious moralists, and by Chaucer's Monk. But the fall of Bernabò was an event so momentous and exemplary for medieval Europe that the event itself almost disappears beneath heavy-layered determinations of political rationalization, religious moralization, and genre.

The three *cantari* of Milanese (or north Italian) provenance that narrate Bernabò's end (presumably to a large popular audience soon after the event) sacrifice all sense of historical detail or plausibility to the expectations of the genres they are working through. Matteo da Milano's sixty-two *ottave*, preserved within a holograph manuscript of Giovanni Sercambi's *Cronica*, have Bernabò mugging a pious friar who has come to visit him and sneaking out of the prison in disguise; he is recognized by a small boy and reincarcerated. Matteo does, however, have Bernabò address himself in an *ubi sunt* lament. The other two *cantari* are written almost exclusively within this neo-Boethian theme *de diversitate Fortunae*: each begins with a *vanto*, which exalts the virtues and magnificence of Bernabò; each ends with a *lamento* of his fall, his lost riches and lost honours, and with a confession of his guilt.[36]

An anonymous Florentine chronicler, writing at the time of Bernabò's death, is quick to assert that Bernabò was punished for his manifold sins by 'God, the just avenger'. Coluccio Salutati, Chancellor of Florence, soon after argued that Gian Galeazzo had acted rightly in deposing a confirmed tyrant like Bernabò.[37] But Goro Dati, who began his account of the years 1380–1405 around 1409, represents Bernabò as a victim of treachery and murder who was, none the less, allowed a decent interval by the will of God to free himself from material possessions and repent and atone for his sins.[38] This shift in emphasis is already evident in the curious sentence with which Sacchetti prefaces the first of his Bernabò *novelle*:

> Questo signore ne' suoi tempi fu ridottato da più <più> che altro signore; e come che fosse crudele, pur nelle sue crudeltà avea gran parte di iustizia.
>
> (IV, 3)
>
> (This lord was, in his time, more feared than any other lord; and although he may have been cruel, there was nonetheless in his cruelty a great deal of justice.)

[35] See Chamberlin, *Count of Virtue*, pp. 75–83.

[36] See *Storia di Milano*, V, pp. 620–24.

[37] See Chamberlin, *Count of Virtue*, pp. 81–2.

[38] See Louis Green, *Chronicle into History. An Essay on the Interpretation of History in Florentine Fourteenth-Century Chronicles* (Cambridge, 1972), pp. 112, 123–4; *L' 'Istoria di Firenze' di Goro Dati dal 1380 al 1405*, ed. Luigi Pratesi (Norcia, 1902), pp. 7–16.

This justification of Bernabò's cruelty as an instrument of justice recalls the words of the rustic in Azario's *Liber Gestorum*. But Sacchetti and Dati are interested in commemorating the justice and piety of Bernabò only by way of discrediting the man who displaced him: once Bernabò is dead, the Visconti threat to Florence is embodied by Gian Galeazzo. According to Dati, Bernabò died in prison not as a fallen tyrant but as a repentant sinner: by murdering his own kin in his lust for earthly power, Gian Galeazzo pledged himself to the devil.[39]

News of Bernabò's death came to Chaucer from out of this complex network of shifting political imperatives. How then does Chaucer construct the meaning of this event?

De Barnabo de Lumbardia

> Off Melan grete Barnabo Viscounte,
> God of delit and scourge of Lumbardye,
> Why sholde I nat thyn infortune acounte,
> Sith in estaat thow cloumbe were so hye?
> Thy brother sone, that was thy double allye,
> For he thy nevew was and sone-in-lawe,
> Withinne his prisoun made thee to dye –
> But why ne how noot I that thou were slawe.   (VII, 2399–406)

Donald Howard argues that 'when Chaucer called Bernabò Visconti "god of delit and scourge of Lombardie" he was not necessarily calling him a tyrant'.[40] But that is exactly what he was doing. One of the defining characteristics of tyranny for medieval political thought was the pursuit of pleasurable (*delectabile*) good rather than the cultivation of *bonum commune*. 'Scourge' suggests not so much 'chastisement or reform'[41] as it does wholesale destruction of the kind practised by Attilla the Hun, *flagellum dei*. And the name of 'Lumbardye' is so strongly associated with 'tyrannye' elsewhere in Chaucer that throughout the stanza we half-expect it to show up in a rhyming position. There is little in this stanza, then, to further the search for signs of personal regret at the demise of a former acquaintance that Howard's biographism commits him to. But perhaps it is only post-Romantic illusion that leads us to assume that the search for subjective emotional experience must take us outside of or behind the boundaries of genre, that feeling precedes (and is hence more authentic than) generic expression. Here, in a letter dated 10 February 1386, we find Franco Sacchetti experiencing the fall of Bernabò within the generic bounds of *de diversitate Fortunae* even as he recalls his last face-to-face encounter with the dead man:

---

[39] See *Istoria*, ed. Pratesi, p. 9. In Dati's account, Bernabò comes to sound Christ-like in his championing of the poor and of women who seek his help: ' "Venite a me e non temete voi, che siete imponenti, che i ricchi e i grandi hanno i loro avvocati i quali sono pagati da loro e io sono l'avvocato vostro ..." ' (p. 12). Even the old stories of Bernabò's atrocities are now enveloped in a glow of sentimental affection. A monk has his penis cut off by a barber because Bernabò (en route to visit one of his concubines) believes that he is too young and good-looking to uphold his vow of chastity and obedience. The monk, after convalescing, thanks Bernabò warmly: ' "Signore, io sto bene vostra mercè e grazie, che m'avete levato grande stimolo" ' (p. 15).

[40] *Chaucer*, p. 230.

[41] Howard, *Chaucer*, p. 230.

Tanto signore e sí altero tiranno, con tanti geniti, e con tanta potenza e con tante parentele di príncipi e di regi, quanto era il Signore Melanese, in questo anno in un pícciolo punto, come ha perduto lui e tutta sua famiglia, e le famose cittá che tenea! Certo quand'io mi ricordo come io il vidi poco piú che 'l terzo anno passato, e quanto era nel supremo de la rota, e come è caduto, quasi fuori di me stesso mi trovo.

(Such a lord and such a lofty tyrant (with so many offspring, and with such power and with so many princes and kings among his relatives) as was the Lord of Milan has this year, and at one small point in time, lost both his entire family and the famous cities that he held in his grasp! Really, when I recall how I saw him little more than three years ago, and how he was on the very top of the wheel, and how he has fallen, I find myself almost beside myself.)[42]

There is a strength of feeling here that drives Sacchetti almost out of his mind: and yet that feeling is accessible only through the most commonplace of metaphors. The same metaphor wheels its way not only through the Monk's stanza, but through his entire *Tale*, which reiterates the single downward motion of Fortune. Chaucer's account of Bernabò is tailored to harmonize with this recurring pattern: the determinations of genre outweigh any impulse to personal reminiscence. The genre operative here is itself of Italian proto-humanist provenance, namely the *de casibus* form as pioneered by Boccaccio and Petrarch.[43] Ironically, this particular sacrifice of historical detail for the purposes of generic conformity is one that the pilgrimage will ultimately reject: this stanza, like this *Tale*, is all *lamento* and no *vanto*; it tells only half the story of Boethian *tragedye*.

There are a few odd historical details embalmed in the Bernabò stanza that have little direct bearing on the elaboration of the Monk's monodic theme. Chaucer, like Sercambi, notes that Bernabò perished through the offices of a 'double allye', one who was close to him in blood and marriage. But whereas Sercambi goes on to denounce this murder ('the act was cruel'),[44] Chaucer makes little of it and ends on a note of indeterminacy that foregrounds his own ignorance of the true historical record ('noot I'). There is little here, then, to suggest any private or subjective reaction on Chaucer's part to the most spectacular and (excepting the capture of King John by the English) widely-remarked fall in post-pandemic Europe. But this may itself represent an eloquent commentary on tyranny. In his remorseless effort to magnify and multiply his own bodily image through statute, statuary, and sexual intercourse, Bernabò's great enemy is death. Beyond death, his great equestrian statue becomes a funeral monument (a sarcophagus was soon added) and his name becomes synonymous

---

42 Franco Sacchetti, *La battaglia delle donne, le lettere, le sposizioni di Vangeli*, ed. Alberto Chiari, Scrittori d'Italia, 166 (Bari, 1938), p. 84. Sacchetti is writing an *epistola consolatoria* to the recently widowed Franceschina degli Ubertini. He puts aside ancient examples of the adversity of Fortune in order to cite the recent wave of murders, arson attacks and executions in Florence, the deposition and death of Queen Giovanna of Naples, and the fall of Bernabò. He then turns to the murder of Abel, remarking that 'niuna cosa . . . al mondo è nova né fu mai'.

43 See Renate Haas, 'Chaucer's Tragödienkonzept im Europäischen Rahmen', in *Zusammenhänge, Einflüsse, Wirkungen. Kongressakten zum ersten Symposium des Mediävistenverbandes in Tübingen, 1984*, ed. Joerg Fichte *et al.* (Berlin, 1986), pp. 451–65. Chaucer's Monk acknowledges 'my maister Petrak' in his *Tale* at a point when he is actually following Boccaccio (VII, 2325).

44 See Chamberlin, *Count of Virtue*, p. 81.

not with power, but with the fall from power. Chaucer's text denies the uniqueness of Bernabò's physical presence by allocating him just one stanza and then serializing this as just one *de casibus* exemplum among many.

Chaucer, in his *Monk's Tale*, does assume something of the humanist ambition to connect the past with the present, the great figures of antiquity with the recent dead, and to speak to both parties directly, in a first-person voice. But his farewell to Bernabò accentuates only his incapacity to prevent the memory of Bernabò from draining away through the cracks of history: 'But why ne how noot I that thou were slawe'. This last line on the most famous tyrant of the age seems eerily prescient of the thousands of lines waiting to be written on the death of Richard II in 1399. Richard too, we have noted, died obscurely. According to one account, he died of grief and starvation *on St Valentine's day* (nice touch); according to another he was cut down with an axe as he sat eating his dinner. The first account is of Lancastrian provenance and the second French.[45] Neither of them can be assumed to be accurate, since their interest lies not in recording the facts of history, but rather in manufacturing competing narratives of history for their own political ends. The French, like the Florentines in 1385, suddenly change their minds about their worst enemy: the more kingly and peace-loving Richard is made to appear, the more illegitimate and damnable is the pretender who usurps his place. The English rewriting of Richard's death is particularly intensive in the months following Henry's accession, but the process is still playing itself out on the London stage some two centuries later.

One of the most important narratives written during the period of Richard's demise actually exaggerates, rather than diminishes, our sense of his immediate physical presence. Richard, it is said, sometimes claimed that the laws of the land 'were in his own mouth, sometimes he said that they were in his breast, and that he alone could change or establish the laws of his realm'.[46] Such words were spoken 'with harsh and determined looks' ('voltu austero et protervo'), a phrase that sets us imaginatively within the radius of Richard's gaze (and reminds us of the stern *loking* of Chaucer's god of Love). But this evocation of

---

[45] See 'Annales Ricardi Secundi, Regis Angliae (Corpus Christi College, Cambridge, MS VII)', in *Johannis de Trokelowe, et Henrici de Blaneforde monachorum S. Albani, necnon quorundam anonymorum, Chronica et Annales*, ed. H.T. Riley (London, Rolls Series, 1866), pp. 330–31; *Chronique de la Traïson et Morte de Richart Deux Roy Dengleterre*, ed. and tr. Benjamin Williams (London, English Historical Society, 1846); Gransden, *Historical Writing II*, pp. 142–3, 190–91. The Lancastrian version of Richard's death proposes that Richard was so grief-stricken by the death of his brother, John de Holland, earl of Huntingdon, that he refused to eat; when he tried to break his fast his throat was too constricted to swallow. The French *Traïson et Mort* claims that Richard was cut down by Sir Peter Exton. Another group of chroniclers attributes Richard's death to starvation by his prison keepers; a fourth group either pleads ignorance of the cause or records two or more versions for posterity to choose from: see Louisa D. Duls, *Richard II in the Early Chronicles* (The Hague, 1975), pp. 169–82.

[46] *Rotuli Parliamentorum* 3.416, as translated in *English Historical Documents 1327–1485*, ed. A.R. Myers (Oxford, 1969), p. 410. For a sophisticated analysis of this passage, see Larry Scanlon, 'The King's Two Voices: Narrative and Power in Hoccleve's Regement of Princes', in *Literary Practice*, ed. Patterson, pp. 216–47 (pp. 218–222). The phrase *omne ius habet in pectore suo* was appropriated from Roman law by the canonists and applied to the pope: see Kenneth Pennington, 'Law, legislative authority and theories of government, 1150–1300', in *The Cambridge History of Medieval Political Thought*, ed. J.H. Burns (Cambridge, 1988), pp. 424–453 (p. 434).

Richard is written by those who are working to make him disappear; it forms part of the Articles of Deposition. Their tactic is to call attention to the absolutist pretension of identifying the princely body with the state at the very moment that the mortality of this princely body stands revealed. The Florentine chronicler Goro Dati, writing after the death of Gian Galeazzo Visconti in 1402, makes such knowledge of the mortality of the tyrant the chief source of hope for the Florentines who are struggling with him: 'for the Comune cannot die and the Duke was just one mortal man; when he was finished, so was his state'.[47]

The pretension that the king could embody his state was, of course, most famously formulated by Louis XIV of France: 'l'état, c'est moi'. Fourteenth-century Lombardy cannot be mistaken for seventeenth-century France: but the absolute state that seventeenth-century despots ruled over traces its lineages back to these Italian origins.[48] And the cruelty and ruthlessness that, for Jacob Burckhardt, was the enabling precondition of the new Renaissance individualism was first exemplified by these tyrants of Trecento Lombardy.[49] Bernabò Visconti behaved cruelly, ruthlessly, tyrannically: but his personal excesses were acted out within, and as part of, a political framework that showed much of the *infrastructural* strength of later absolutist regimes.[50] The tyranny of Richard II, on the other hand, unfolded without the supporting context of such an infrastructure. Richard could not stabilize his relations with either the merchant capitalists of London, whose financial support was crucial, or with the magnates who finally deposed him. The tyrannical style he affected in later years was both behind and ahead of its time, a doubly tragic anachronism.

'Be nat lyk tirauntz of Lumbardye' was, then, an important injunction for fourteenth-century English rulers: Lombardy was, ultimately, a long way from Westminster. The *Monk's Tale* underscores the point some time after 1385 by engorging Bernabò Visconti in a single stanza: even in Lombardy, the homeland of tyranny, the future of the individual tyrant is precarious.[51] Richard II, in his later years, became increasingly obsessed with the cult and literary record of Edward II, who was deposed, imprisoned, and murdered in 1327.[52] Richard wanted his great-grandfather to be recognized as a saint, but he might have been better advised to read the *Polychronicon*'s terse dismissal of such claims for Edward's sanctity: 'kepynge in prison, vilenes and opprobrious dethe cause

---

47 *Istoria*, pp. 97, 13–14 (p. 74): 'che il Comune non può morire e il Duca era uno solo uomo mortale, chè finito lui, finito lo stato suo'; my translation.

48 See Perry Anderson, *Lineages of the Absolutist State* (London, 1979), *passim* and p. 160.

49 See *Die Kultur der Renaissance in Italien. Ein Versuch*, ed. Horst Günther (Frankfurt am Main, 1989), pp. 15–23, 137–43.

50 'We must distinguish between the two principal meanings of a strong regime: power over civil society, that is, *despotism*; and the power to coordinate civil society, that is, *infrastructural* strength' (Michael Mann, *The sources of social Power, vol. I. A history of power from the beginning to A.D. 1760* (Cambridge, 1986), p. 477; see also John A. Hall and G. John Ikenberry, *The State* (Minneapolis, 1989), pp. 12–14. For the political innovations of western absolutist states, see Anderson, *Lineages*, pp. 15–42. For transformations in bureaucratic, agricultural, economic and religious organization under the Visconti, see Anna Antoniazzi Villa et al., *La Lombardia delle Signorie* (Milan, 1986); *Lombardia. Il territorio, l'ambiente, il paesaggio*, ed. Carlo Pirovano, 5 vols (Milan, 1981–5), vol. I; *Storia di Milano*, vols V–VI.

51 It is perhaps worth noting that only four of the twelve Visconti despots died of natural causes.

52 In 1395 Richard sent Pope Boniface IX a book of Edward's 'miracles' to support his case for Edward's canonization. This request may first have been made as early as 1387: see Anthony Steel, *Richard II* (Cambridge, 1962), p. 122.

not a martir, but if the holynesse of lyfe afore be correspondent'.[53] He might also, of course, have read the *Monk's Tale*. By the logic of this *Tale*, which is at once the dullest and most dynamic of Chaucer's narratives (it may extend itself at any moment), Edward's story is to be read as the greatest English *de casibus tragedye* of the century: before, that is, the *tragedye* of 1399, that of Richard himself.

---

[53] *Polychronicon Ranulphi Higden monachi Cestrensis; together with the English translations of John Trevisa and of an unknown writer of the fifteenth century*, ed. J.R. Lumby, 9 vols (London, 1865–86), VIII, pp. 325–7. I follow the translation of Harleian MS 2261 (rather than Trevisa) at this point.

David Wallace's essay will form part of a book entitled *Chaucerian Polity* (Stanford UP); it appears here by kind permission of Stanford University Press.

PEARL: LOVE AND THE POETICS OF PARTICIPATION

EUGENE VANCE

The opening stanzas of *Pearl* are so arresting in part because their artistry is distinct from anything else in medieval poetry – let alone the poetry of medieval England. Two closely related questions raised by these stanzas will concern me in this essay. The first, which arises with the very first word in the poem, is at least apparently semiotic: what inherent claims are made for poetic discourse when 'perle' is employed both as the sign of an inanimate jewel to represent the perfection of a deceased maiden, and as a proper noun to address her or call her into memory?

The second question, more metaphysical, extends pragmatically and discursively throughout the poem, and is concerned to ask how a mortal maiden and a pearl – indeed, how innumerable souls or pearls, all discrete and different from each other – might share in some Form of perfection, and, in more theological terms, in the whole and unlimited grace of a God (the *Idipsum*) who is single, self-identical, and infinite.

The latter question, as to how *multiple* individuals might be said to share in the being of a *single* Idea or Form, involves what Platonic philosophers and theologians have traditionally called the problem of *participation*. Since *Pearl* was written by a poet well-versed in that tradition, the alternatives proffered by its history are pertinent both to the poem itself and to any modern discussion of it. Indeed, I will claim that the doctrinal core of *Pearl* as a poem that consoles through its vision of resurrection is very much centred in a Christianized doctrine of participation.

i. 'Pearl' and the poetics of the opaque

As *incipit* (hence, as both title and first word), 'Perle' initiates a poetic process that will exploit the equivocity of the beautiful. At the most material level, the scribal hand that has embellished (as best it could) the letter P has fetishized a word sweet to the English ear, and languorous to utter – it is impossible to say 'perle' quickly. This instance of 'Pearl' is syntactically undetermined:[1] is it an exclamation? Is it the name of a person whom we are addressing or invoking – calling *into* ourselves? Is this pearl an inanimate jewel?

The initial couplet of the poem already bifurcates the referent of 'Pearl' into semantic fields that are distinct, however much their hyperboles converge in perceptions of the good, the luminous and the beautiful. On the one hand, the human Pearl whose pleasantness would delight a prince is clearly an object of

---

[1] The first four lines of the poem have been punctuated – and semanticized – in many different ways by its numerous editors.

courtly desire. Such a desire is ideologically marked, to the extent that it is mediated by a discourse that is a traditional emblem of noble rank.

On the other hand, the pearl is a conspicuously small and inanimate jewel fit to be set in gold. Such a fascination with detail and with the minute is analogous to the fetishism of the illuminated letter. To refract the desire for a maiden through the cult of an exotic gem – and thereby to cast the lover as jeweller – is to initiate an eroticism based above all on metonymy, hence, a system of pleasure in substitution. As proper sign, the pearl motivates therefore a specific mode of desire, yet as trope its figurative sense remains arbitrary and undetermined, hence, dynamic and subject to change. Thus, pearl as sign is now a written poetic word, now a lovely sound, now a proper name, now a gem that is not a gem because the pearl is a trope. Thus, Pearl is the name of an open-ended semantic process, hence, on all of these scores a token of the poetic.

However, the visions of beauty proffered by the discourses of courtliness and gemmology are not wholly congruous. The poet as gemmologist beholds in the small pearl that he has assayed ('proued') a precious object perfectly round and regular ('reken') at every point ('in vche araye'). Each of these terms connotes, here and elsewhere in Middle English (as is abundantly shown by the *Middle English Dictionary*) a kind of mathematical perfection. By contrast, the courtier's eye beholds in Pearl a more anthropomorphic perfection with curves of a different sort: 'So smal, so smoþe her syde3 were.'[2] Thus, the pearl, as perfect jewel, shines resplendently outward from a fixed point in all directions at once, while the curve of Pearl as maiden engages the searching ray of the beholder's gendered glance. Now, if all perfect curves are indeed perfect, is the concave perfection in a maiden's curves less perfect than the convex perfection of a pearl? Do they share in a *single* perfection that I see and name differently? Or do they embody different perfections? In short, how do maiden and pearl participate in a single Form of perfection?

The different aspects of perfection described in Pearl describe variations in the *persona* of the beholder as well. Thus, on the one hand, Pearl's qualities of smallness and smooth-sidedness are familiar tokens of a courtly paradigm – as is, for instance, Chaucer's Criseyde with her 'sydes longe, flesshly smothe and whyte' (*Troilus* III, 1248).[3] Purposefully, the poem does not disclose at this point that the courtly relationship expressed in this poem involves a father grieving for a small daughter, and not a distressed lover.

The gemmologist, on the other hand, has judged or assayed ('proued') an inanimate pearl whose peerless Form appears to him as nothing less than the *one* of the *one* – she is 'sengeley in synglure' (8). May such a Pearl be properly venerated? Or is she not being *im*properly worshipped (as an idol) rather than venerated (as an icon)?

To speak of the 'one of the one' is to unleash Platonic resonances indissociable from the discourse of Neoplatonism, specifically as it was so powerfully mediated to Christian culture by Dionysius the Pseudo-Areopagite. The 'one,' he says, is the most difficult of the divine names by which humans name the all-transcending God:

---

[2] *Pearl*, ed. E. V. Gordon (Oxford, 1953).
[3] Cf. *Pearl*, ed. E. V. Gordon, n. 6.

For it is complete as beyond completion in beyond-having the all, as determining every unlimited, as surpassing every limit . . . It is called one since it is singly all in once preeminence of unity; for it is the non-wandering cause of the unity of all. There is nothing among beings that is without participation in the one . . . Whatever is a being is so by *being* one. Now the one cause of all is not one among many but is before every one and many and is determinative of every one and many. There is no multitude which is in some way without participation in the one . . .[4]

So too, Pearl's perfection as sphere is another hyperbole no less charged with the semantics of medieval Platonism. In the discursive tradition of the *Timaeus* (a philosophical touchstone[5] by now securely vernacularized by Dante), to construe the virginal Pearl as a sphere of spheres is to point to nothing less than the perfection and wholeness of the primeval world as God created it:

Wherefore he made the world in the form of a globe, round as from a lathe, having its extremes in every direction equidistant from the centre, the most perfect and the most like itself of all figures; for he considered that the like is infinitely fairer than the unlike.[6]

In its perfection, this divine world-body had no need of organs because it was self-sufficient, unchanging and incorruptible – in contrast with imperfect, corruptible bodies here in our mortal realm. Its only motion was to turn on its own centre, which was soul. By doing so, this heavenly body, whose substance was comparable to gold (*Timaeus* 50), participated wholly in its own soul, since in such sacred geometry the soul was both centre and circumference:

Such was the whole plan of the eternal God about the god that was to be, for whom for this reason he gave a body, smooth and even, having a surface in every direction equidistant from the centre, a body entire perfect, and formed out of perfect bodies. And in the centre he put the soul, which he diffused throughout the body, making it also to be the exterior environment of it; and he made the universe a circle moving in a a circle, one and solitary, yet by reason of its excellence able to converse with itself, and needing no other friendship or acquaintance. (*Timaeus* 34)

The Platonic links between sphericity, wholeness and perfection had been reformulated in the thirteenth century by Robert Grosseteste, who, in his famous treatise *On Light*, considered the physical substance of light as the first corporeal Form common to all things in the universe. God created the universe from a single point of light (*lux*) that radiated outward into a perfect sphere. The created things of the outer circumference of the firmament shine with light (*lumen*) as they participate in light (*lux*) at the centre that is their source.[7]

At a rhetorical level, the alternation between the feminine and third personal pronouns (*hyr* and *hit*) in the first and second stanzas of *Pearl* corresponds,

4 Pseudo Dionysius Areopagite, *The Divine Names and Mystical Theology*, trans. John D. Jones (Milwaukee, Wis., 1980), xii. 1–2.
5 Peter Dronke, *Fabula: Explorations into the Uses of Myth in Medieval Platonism* (Leiden, 1974).
6 Plato, *Timaeus* 33, trans. B. Jowett. *The Dialogues of Plato* (New York), vol. 2, p. 16.
7 Robert Grosseteste, *On Light*, trans. Clare Riedl. *Medieval Philosophical Texts in Translation*. No. 1. (Milwaukee, Wis., 1942), pp. 10–17.

then, to two voices, or *sujets d'énonciation* (in Benveniste's terms),[8] and to diverging semanticizations of the experience of loss. On the one hand, 'Allas! I leste hyr in on erbere' (9) expresses an intensely subjective *I-her* axis fraught with a self-pity that must be both disclosed and overcome in *Pearl* as a process of grieving and of Christian consolation. On the other hand, the use of the neuter third person (or zero-person) in the next line, 'þurʒ gresse to grounde hit from me yot' (10) bespeaks an urge for distance from pain through troping the death of pearl in a conceit where cause and effect have become occluded: 'I' did not lose 'her'; rather, 'it' slipped from me into the grass. However, the exclamatory force of 'I hardyly saye', redounding as well in the five instances of the adverbial intensifier 'so', along with the persistent humanizing intrusions of 'her' upon the supposedly impersonal 'itness' of gemmology, show how tangled with emotion its discourse remains. They show too how tenuous is the transforming power of tropes.

Thus, the interplay between voices in the first two stanzas is symptomatic of a broader tension between two conventional discourses, neither of whose semantics is apt to mediate proper understanding in a poem about death and resurrection. Specifically as a poem of consolation, *Pearl* must both address and transform those visions which constitute the life of the soul as it peers darkly through the prism of language into the enigmas of the world beyond. The inadequacy of these discourses will become more patent later when we learn that Pearl is not the name of a lady but of a young child, and when we perceive that in paradise she is hardly the One of One, but one of a vast multitude of resurrected 'pearls' wedded to Christ – that is to say, sharing individually in his *whole* grace. But even at this point in the poem, the conspicuously bilingual and certainly bi-cultural[9] compound 'luf-daungere' (recalling the erotogenic figure of Danger in the *Roman de la Rose*) suggests that a northwest midland English poet is hinting at the potential of a continental courtly poetics to abort the process of Christian consolation. Conventionally, the discourse of courtly desire unfolds as a dialectics of hope and despair that remains centred in the present of uttering.[10] As the poetic word becomes an object of desire in its own right, the very process of speech sustains the desire that it also defers. Here, however, the absent object of desire is no cruel lady, rather, a maiden whose beautiful body now lies rotting in the ground. As an object of memory who is dead, Pearl is also immured in the tenses of an irrevocable time past, but her spirit has sprung into a future *not* in time – nor, indeed, any longer even in the semantics of ordinary speech.[11] In the courtly lexicon, the garden is a *locus amoenus* of erotic joy, and perhaps Pearl's oriental beauty may once have connoted a paradise of sensual pleasure; now, however, this garden, as well as the discourse that names it, has become joy's crypt. What is more, in first line of the second stanza we

---

8   Emile Benveniste, *Problèmes de linguistique générale* (Paris, 1966).
9   As William J. Courtenay notes in *Schools and Scholars in Fourteenth Century England* (Princeton, 1987), p. 156, the intellectual dominance of France had virtually ended in England by the decade of 1330–40.
10 Eugene Vance, *Mervelous Signals. Poetics and Sign Theory in the Middle Ages* (Lincoln, Nebraska, 1986), ch. 5.
11 On the ontological dissymetry of past and future tenses, see Eugene Vance, 'Le temps sans nombre: La futurité dans la *Queste* del Saint-Graal', in *Le nombre du temps*, eds., Christiane Marchello-Nizia and Emmanuèle Baumgartner (Paris, 1988), pp. 273–83.

learn of Pearl that 'it' did not really 'slip' ingenuously into the grass: rather, 'hit fro me sprang'. Perhaps the Pearl of our desire had *never* really been at home in that world of matter and of signs of which we are the willing hostages.

Thus, between the emotions of courtly love-danger and bereavement at mortality there is a world of *difference* (in the Augustinian sense) that the lover cannot properly address. The lover has brought us to his maiden's crypt on a pilgrimage, but only to tyrannize himself with memories of a joy now irrevocably past. The lover himself has become a crypt of desire:

> Ofte haf I wayted, wyschande þat wele
> Þat wont watȝ while deuoyde my wrange,
> And heuen my happe and al my hele.
> Þat dotȝ bot þrych my hert þrang ...   (14–17)

So too, the tropes of gemmology quickly exhaust their visionary potential. The 'stylle stounde' of his earthly rapture leads him even more brutally than before to the horror of materiality whereby a shining pearl fit to be set in gold is 'clad in clod' (22). Thus, the trope of the gem culminates in a jeweller's nightmare:

> O moul, þou marreȝ a myry iuele,
> My priuy perle wythouten spotte.   (23–4)

As mediated by discourse, the lover's visionary powers have thus far failed. As a first reflex, the poet now probes the once-courtly garden of the here and now, þat spot þat I in speche expoun (37), for organic metaphors that might prove consoling: perhaps, he speculates, Pearl's once beautiful 'color so clad in clod' is a seed which, by being planted, has enriched the earth with the variety and abundance of a summertime whose shining beauty as *lumen* now rivals the presence of the sun as *lux*:

> Blomeȝ, blayke and blwe and rede
> Þer schyneȝ ful schyr agayn þe sunne.   (27–8)

And, if good flows out of good, may Pearl's death not be seen as part of a natural process of decay and renewal? Such would be the lesson of August, 'Quen corne is coruen wyth crokeȝ kene'. Although the planting of seeds was an important image stressing continuity of life beyond death, here, the planted seed is not seen eschatologically, but as a figure of positive mutability in nature. Perhaps, then, to see the natural process of *becoming* as the perfection of *being* may obviate our inborn yearning for reversion from the creation back to the creator, from *lumen* back to *lux*. Through death, then, the immanent perfection of Pearl is now perhaps manifest in the abundance of Nature and in a cloying beauty that, by its very shining, covers the spot of her burial:

> ȝif hit watȝ semly on to sene,
> A fayr reflayr ȝet fro hit flot.
> Þer wonys þat worþyly, I wot and wene,
> My precious perle wythouten spot.   (47–8)

Such are the consolations of Nature, but they do not suffice. To the contrary, grief at the world once again rushes in. Pain at the incommensurability between the material and the spiritual is perhaps this Englishman's response to the claims of Nature in the *Roman de la Rose*, obeissance to whom the *Pearl*-poet seems to disdain. Rather, nothing but the supernatural 'kynde of Kryst' (55) could bring 'comfort' to the 'love-danger' that is not sexual frustration, but the deprivation of death. Indeed, we are told later by Pearl herself that to love Pearl according to the laws of nature is to love only a transient rose:

> ... if þou schal lose
> Þy ioy for a gemme þat þe watʒ lef,
> Me þynk þe put in a mad porpose,
> And busyeʒ þe aboute a raysoun bref;
> For þat þou lesteʒ watʒ bot a rose
> Þat flowred and fayled as kynde hyt gef.   (265–70)

Although the rose as sign will be put to different semiotic purposes later in the poem,[12] it is used here to stress that the grieving lover of *Pearl* will find no 'comfort' in nature, much less in the contentious thoughts of a *wreched wylle* – but only in Christ. Appropriately, the evocation of Christ's supernatural 'kynde' and the recognition of despair as a defect not only of word but of *will* closes the prologue; now it is the turn for the lover's own spirit to 'spring into space' (61) and to savour new modes of seeing, hearing and understanding through 'Godeʒ grace' (63).

Remarkably, though, as the poet crosses the threshold between nature and grace, between that 'spot that I in speche expoun' (37) and that place where 'vrþely herte myʒt not suffyse', (135), conventions of speech that had seemed to fetter his soul will not be repudiated or abandoned; rather, they will be extended and transformed.[13] Indeed, as we spring forth in this 'auenture þer meruayleʒ meuen' (64), the modes and discourses of desire become not less, but more of objects of scrutiny than before. Indeed, as in Dante, grace as Word will *transfigure* conventional speech as an instrument of the rational soul, rather than repudiate it.

ii. modes of meaning and models of participation

One way of appreciating the concerns of the *Pearl*-poet to valorize human speech as a vehicle of sacred truth and dialogue as a privileged mode of human participation in a spiritual world beyond – is to situate the poem in a history of the problem of participation itself. Let us now examine briefly some of the major permutations of that history and then relate them to *Pearl*.

The problem of participation (*metoché*) was inherent to Platonism, whose circular ontology supposed, on the one hand, a *procession* (*próodos*) of being outward from the One (or the Good, which is also co-extensive with the Beautiful) through Ideas or spiritual Forms into the multitude of sensible beings, and on the other, a *reversion* (*épistrophé*) of being back toward the One.[14] For the

---

[12] As P. M. Kean notes, *The Pearl: An Interpretation* (London, 1967), p. 169, at the poem's climax near the end (906–8), the poet will invoke the rose not as a natural symbol, but as an alchemical symbol expressing wholeness and perfection outside of nature: 'Þer lyueʒ lyste may neuer lose'.

[13] For comparisons of attitudes about discourse in other poems of Christian consolation, see R. A. Shoaf, ' "Mutatio Amoris": "Penitentia" and the Form of the *Book of the Duchess*', *Genre* 14 (1981) 63–89; and R. A. Shoaf, 'God's "Malayse": Conversion and the Structure of the Trope in *Patience*', *The Journal of Medieval and Renaissance Studies* 11 (1981) 61–79.

[14] Stephen Gersh, *Kinesis Akinetos. A Study of Spiritual Motion in the Philosophy of Proclus*

Platonist, Forms really do exist, and a worldly or sensible thing *is* that thing through participating in its Form. Immaterial Forms, then, are the 'reasons' (*aitíai*) of things that exist corporeally.[15]

However, what is meant by 'participation' is not clearly defined by Plato. As first evoked by Plato in *Parmenides* 131a, it involves understanding how multiple beings that exist (or *have* existed) in the material world may be said to 'participate' or 'share' in the higher being of a spiritual Form. Does each individual thing have its own share or separate piece of the Form? Or does it participate, rather, in the whole? If so, can the whole Form simultaneously participate in different objects and remain whole at the same time? Plato, according to Richard Patterson (p. 118), came to hold that Forms depend immediately on the Good for their existence, while material things depend on both Forms *and* the Good for their existence. It is through participation in the Good that a material thing is entitled to participate in Forms that are separate from it: 'To participate in a Form is always to exemplify some nature having a place in the intelligible order determined by the Good . . .' (Patterson, p. 131).

The question of participation remained specific to the discourse of Platonism. (Since Aristotle did believe in transcendental Forms in the first place, he regarded the whole discussion of participation as confused and as 'empty words and poetic metaphors').[16] For medieval Christian Platonism, Plotinus was a major source who nourished two distinct but complementary streams of thought, especially concerning the question of participation.

Concerned as to how a single Idea might have multiple participants, Plotinus, according to Steven K. Strange, was resolute in maintaining the autonomy and wholeness of the Idea.[17] Yet he also held that participants are not apart from Ideas, but participate directly in them. Thus, on the one hand, though the intelligible universe is utterly sufficient unto itself, never apart *from* itself, or *in* anything else; on the other hand, whatever else exists sensibly must somehow be *in* and *participate* in this true, intelligible Whole.[18] The seeming contradiction was resolved by arguing that Ideas do not proceed downward toward material being, as if unchangeable ideas created separate images of themselves by illuminating them from afar. Strange explains, 'The illumination in this case must not be conceived, Plotinus argues, in terms of light proceeding *from* a source *to* an illuminated object. Rather, we must think instead of the *light itself* as what is participated in, i.e. we must identify the power with the source of the power, so that on this analogy we will again make the participant to participate directly in the Idea'. Because an Idea cannot undergo procession toward the sensible without undergoing change, the Idea does not approach its participants: 'we instead have the participants approaching the Idea in order to participate in

(Leiden, 1973); *From Iamblichus to Eriugena. An Investigation of the Prehistory and Evolution of the Pseudo-Dionysian Tradition* (Leiden, 1978).

15 Richard Patterson, *Image and Reality in Plato's Metaphysics* (Indianapolis, 1985), esp. ch. 6. I have also benefited from personal discussions with its author.

16 Aristotle, *Metaphysics*, trans. Hippocrates G. Apostle (Bloomington, Ind., 1966), Bk. M, 1079b, pp. 220–1. For an authoritative study of participation in the Aristotelian tradition as reworked by Thomas Aquinas, see Cornelio Fabro, *Participation et causalité selon s. Thomas d'Aquin* (Louvain, Publications Univ. de Louvain; Paris, 1961).

17 I am indebted in my remarks about Plotinus's theory to a forthcoming manuscript by Steven K. Strange, of Emory University, 'Plotinus's Account of Participation in *Ennead* VI. 4–5.'

18 Here I summarize Strange's account.

it, so that we should really say that they are present to it rather than it to them . . . it is the participants that are changed or affected in coming to participate in the Idea, not the Idea itself. They move toward it, not it toward them' (Strange).

Thus, Plotinus seems to see participation as a kind of reversion of being, rather than as a procession. Strange writes, 'Every Idea is wholly present to the sensible world, without entering into it, i.e. becoming part of it: only those sensible things that have the appropriate capacity to participate in a given Idea do so participate, by somehow coming to be directly present to that Idea.' As Strange continues,

> The participant 'approaches' the Idea in 'striving' to be like it . . . It is better here to speak of *parousía* or 'presence' than to speak of participation or 'sharing', provided we realize that this relation of presence is a non-reciprocal one – hence absolute separation or independence of the Idea from participants can be maintained. (p. 20)

Such a model of participation had corollaries important to Plotinian theories of vision, hence to a tradition of visionary poetry in the West. If participation is an active (and not passive) process on the part of sensible beings striving to be informed (and defined) by the presence of the Idea, so too, seeing occurs as an active and immediate presentation of the seer to the seen, and not as an impression or trace left by a mediating ray upon the passive tablet of memory. Plotinus is emphatic:[19]

> Perceptions are no imprints, we have said, are not to be thought of as seal-impressions on soul or mind . . .
>
> In any perception we attain by sight, the object is grasped there where it lies in the direct line of vision; it is there that we attack it; there, then, the perception is formed. (IV. vi. 2.) An impression is something received passively; the strongest memory, then, would go with the least active nature. . . It is as with sense-perception; the advantage is not to the weak, the weak eye, for example, but to that which has the fullest power towards its exercise. In the old, it is significant, the senses are dulled and so is the memory.
>
> Sensation and memory, then, are not passivity but power. (IV. vi. 3)

By stressing the non-reciprocity of participation, Plotinus valorizes the soul's power to act, indeed, to fulfil itself by rising to participate in universal Soul itself, at which point it gains likeness to the supreme One. From there, the soul can move even farther beyond – from image to archetype – and this indeed is the end of the soul's journey of reversion.

iii. Augustine: the trace and human participation

Great though his debt was to Plotinus, Augustine bequeathed to the Latin West a Christian Platonism quite distinct from that of Plotinus, one stressing the abjection, rather than the (potential) divinity, of the human soul. Unlike Plotinus's, Augustine's epistemology implied above all a psychology of the trace (*vestigium*), as opposed to that of the image. Communication of divine truth occurs as an illumination granted to the human soul directly by God. This is a flash

---

[19] Plotinus, *Enneads*, trans. S. MacKenna (New York, n.d.)

without duration, but its effect subsists in the tablets of the memory as a trace or imprint. Thus, the trace that remains in the tablet of the memory is radically different (*dissimilis*) from, and inferior to, the always already hidden divine flash.[20] As a mode of participation, the trace implies passivity and sacrifice of the human will to an ineffable God.[21] Accordingly Augustine was disposed against the soul's pleasure in images and raptures in the esthetic, hence, against art in general as pleasurable representation.

But how and why in the *first place* should a self-sufficient *Idipsum* condescend to present It-Self to an unworthy human soul? Why and how should an infinite God participate in fallen humanity's abjection? This very question arises in the opening passages to the *Confessions* as Augustine aspires to invoke God in prayer:

> How shall I call upon my God, my God and my Lord, since, in truth, when I call upon him, I call him into myself? What place is there within me where my God can come? How can God come into me, God who made heaven and earth? O Lord my God, is there anything in me that can contain you?[22]

Augustine expands upon the dilemma of the sinner's participation in God a few paragraphs later, raising questions essentially the same as those of *Parmenides*:

> You fill all things, and you fill them all with your entire self. But since all things cannot contain you in your entirety, do they contain a part of you, and do all things simultaneously the same part? Or do single things contain single parts, greater things containing greater parts and smaller things smaller parts? Is one part of you greater, therefore, and another smaller? Or are you entire in all places, and does no one thing contain you in your entirety? What, then, is my God? (*Confessions* I. iii. 3)

Although Augustine finds the answer to this question in Scripture ('And they shall praise the Lord that seek him', Ps. 21:27), and although the intepretation of Scripture was, for Augustine, a valid mode for the soul to fulfil itself spiritually, and presumably to participate, in wisdom, Augustine gave great emphasis to humanity's alienation from the Creator in the created world as a 'region of difference' (*regio dissimilitudinis*).[23] 'If I err, therefore I am'.[24] Man by himself can only lie; truth comes not from him but from God.[25] So too, Augustine insisted upon the incommensurability of human language with the divine Word.[26] Poetic language is especially mendacious; nor could the inherent falsity of actors feigning to be some other person on a stage ever purvey truth.[27] Augustine's mistrust of the conventional verbal signs extended, as well, toward his fellow human beings as vehicles of truth to each other: truth itself can come only from within through God and his written Word. Human beings should never be enjoyed, but only be used as we journey to the *patria* of God.

---

[20] Augustine, *De catechizandis rudibus* ii. 3.

[21] *Confessions* VII. x. 16.

[22] Augustine, *Confessions*, trans. John K. Ryan (Garden City, NY, 1960), I. ii. 2.

[23] *Confessions* VII. x. 16.

[24] Gareth B. Matthews, *'Si Fallor, Sum'*, in *Augustine: A Collection of Critical Essays*, ed. R. A. Markus (Garden City, NY, 1972), pp. 151–67.

[25] *Confessions* XII. xxv. 34.

[26] Augustine, *De Trinitate* XV. xii–xv.

[27] Augustine, *Soliloquies* II. xvii–xviii.

Particulary in Augustine's ways of dealing with his loss of his mother in the *Confessions* we find points of comparison with *Pearl* that allow us to see how radically the English poem's model of participation differs from Augustine's.

One will recall, perhaps, that the whole narrative of Augustine's life in the *Confessions* begins with his infancy and ends with his mother's death in Book 9. To the extent that Augustine construes his life story above all in its relation to hers, Augustine superficially resembles the speaker of *Pearl* in his experience of the loss of a person whose being somehow defined his own very existence. However, Monica is never estheticized, much less, idealized. Rather, in the *Confessions*, we find a turbulent old Monica whose piety is real, but fanatic. She is good because of her dauntless faith, and good also because she has endured a bad marriage, has overcome alcoholism, and has obeyed Ambrose's orders to stop celebrating objectionable North African customs (the *refrigerium*) in Northern Italian graveyards. But she is never beautiful.

Augustine's self-narrative ends with the story of Monica's death in Ostia. In her final moments, we are told, he and his mother, 'straining out at the heart's mouth', have groped together for an understanding of eternal life with the saints. In this famous visionary moment, Augustine and Monica first pass together beyond 'all bodily things up to that heaven whence shine the sun and the moon and the stars down upon the earth' (*Confessions* IX. x. 24). Next, they encounter not Forms or Ideas, but their own inner selves, which they will transcend as well; at last, in a flash of ecstasy they reach eternal Wisdom, after which they must return to their own flesh and to the transiency of human speech, so sadly different from Christ as Word: '. . . and we turned back again to the noise of our mouths, where a word both begins and ends. But what is there like to your Word, our Lord, remaining in himself without growing old, and yet renewing all things?' (*Confessions* IX. x. 25).

After ecstasy, then, there can be only alienation in the *regio dissimilitudinis*, and Monica promptly dies and is buried alongside her husband Patricius. Augustine does not linger by this grave. Unlike grief in *Pearl*, which has become a man's way of life, Augustine's grief for Monica is intense but mercifully short. He deliberately blocks his readers from seeking in it a speculative occasion (*Confessions* IX. xii. 23). Thus, the deceased Monica – and much less, rapturous poetry about her – in no way mediate his pilgrimage to the City of God. Rather, having narrated his mother's death, Augustine abandons any concern for such external events in the *Confessions* in order to explore, through the instruments of philosophy and scriptural exegesis, the hidden mysteries of his *own* soul. For Augustine, participation in our own inner, spiritual being is our primary mode of participating in the God in whose image we are made. True, God himself will reward Augustine with a 'vision of peace', that is, with the sight of the heavenly Jerusalem where he will one day be eternally united with his mother, but his recalcitrant readers, for their part, will remain outside, 'blowing into the dust and raising dirt into their own eyes'.

For Augustine, not dialogue, but self-knowledge – that is, the turning inward and participation of the soul in its own spiritual nature – considered as a non-representational 'image' – remained the key to human participation in the divinity in whose image they have been created. Thus, for twenty years following the writing of the *Confessions*, Augustine continued in his *De Trinitate* to develop his conviction that self-reflection on the part of the tripartite human soul was a means of participation in the triune God in whose image man was made.

The Augustinian insistence on the trace placed the human subject in a relationship of passivity in the production of illuminations or vision, rather than a relationship of reciprocity and active partnership with the divine. This legacy was a negative burden on conceptions of the artistic process. For instance, for all her force and eloquence as an image-centred mystic, Hildegard of Bingen illustrates very clearly that burden: the production of her images, as she is told by the divine voice that summons her to write, is one in which she does not participate, except passively. She is a mere host, an abject receptacle whose individual will does not supposedly share in the creative process; rather, her mission is fulfilled in complete surrender followed by the labour of exegesis.[28]

iv. Love and participation in Pseudo-Dionysius

For Augustine, then, the soul's *self*-participation was the most valid mode of voluntary participation in the spiritual realm an absolutely different God. This model endured in the Latin West, and was espoused even in supposedly more rational movements of the later middle ages, as, for instance, by Peter Lombard and Thomas Aquinas.[29] However, periodically after Augustine, other models of participation also intruded upon medieval thought, and they came from a Hellenistic Platonism radically revised as a Christian theology by Dionysius the Pseudo-Areopagite, who was translated and retranslated into Latin in the ninth, twelfth and thirteenth centuries. Benefitting from the fresh Latin translation of Dionysius by the thirteenth-century English schoolman Robert Grosseteste, this strain of Platonism remained important to fourteenth-century English culture, and to the *Pearl*-poet in particular. Moreover, if this poet demonstrates artistic command of a broad speculative heritage densely informed by Scripture, by later medieval Platonism, and by certain continental vernacular masterpieces as well, it is because, as William Courtenay says, this was a time when the dominance of the schoolmen was fading in England and when the secular courts were becoming places of ambitious cultural initiatives.[30]

As a powerful counterbalance to Augustine's emphasis upon man's distance from an ineffable God, Dionysius stressed the active potential of the human soul (as Plotinus had), but also *reciprocation* on the part of an enamoured and extroverted God.

For Dionysius, as for Plotinus, all being procedes from the 'before be-ing' (*ò próon*).[31] This God-beyond-being produces being for all beings together, which is the good. The good and the beautiful are the same, and participation in the good and beautiful begins with being. Merely to exist, then, is primal participation in the good and beautiful (IV. 7). However, different beings (sensible

---

[28] Hildegard of Bingen, *Scivias*, trans. Bruce Hozeski (Santa Fe, 1986), Introduction, p. 1.

[29] D. Juvenall Merriell, *To the Image of the Trinity. A Study in the Development of Aquinas's Teaching* (Toronto, 1990).

[30] William J. Courtenay, *Schools and Scholars in Fourteenth Century England* (Princeton, 1987), p. 356.

[31] I draw freely here on the introduction to Pseudo-Dionysius the Areopagite, *The Divine Names and Mystical Theology*, trans. John D. Jones, esp. pp. 25–33.

beings, rational beings) demonstrate different capacities for participating in God. However, all participate in the one *wholly*, and not in a *part* of it, just as all the radii of a circle participate in the centre (II. 5). The One that is beyond goodness is like the centre of a circle: 'All numbers are unified in the unit; insofar as they go forth from the unit they are differentiated and made many. Again, all the lines of a circle subsist together in the centre of a circle in one unity: the point uniformly has all the straight lines in itself both among themselves and with respect to the one source from which they proceed' (V. 6).

This good is also intellectual light, and participation in it is erotic, a term Dionysius intends to be taken in the fullest human sense, though one not limited by the eros of the body. For 'this eros is not a true eros but an image of the true eros, a falling away from the true eros. The singularity of the divine and one eros is not comprehended by the many. Thus since it seems to be a more difficult name to the many it is employed in the divine wisdom for the sake of returning to and resurrecting these many to the knowledge of the true eros so as to free them from their difficulty in regards to it' (IV. 12).

Eros is a structuring principle in the cosmic process of participation: 'Eros is eminently a power of unifying, binding and joining. Before subsisting, it is in the beautiful and good on account of the beautiful and good . . . It is a [power which] conjoins equals in communion with one another, moves those who are first toward the providence of their inferiors, and founds inferiors through a return to their superiors' (IV. 12). Thus, God participates as the partner of humanity in this eros, and God's ecstasy is a downward movement of love through Christ. Simultaneously, human eros reverts upward through its own ecstasy. The interaction between Paul and Christ exemplifies this mutal convergence in an ecstasy where the axes of procession and reversion, of *ágápe* and *éros*, coincide (IV. 13). The incarnate Christ manifests God's loving participation in humanity; reciprocally, through Christ humans participate in God. Dionysius says in *On the Ecclesiastical Hierarchy* (ch. 3) that through the eucharist, the incarnate Christ is revealed to us perfectly, making communion with God and his mysteries possible to humans.

v. Participating in Pearl's participation

The Dionysian emphasis on participation as a reciprocal eroticism endured as a recessive strain of thought in the Latin West. John Scot Eriugena, the great ninth-century Platonist and translator of Dionysius speaks of participation thus:

> For every order that is established between (that which is only participated and that which is only participant) from the highest downwards, that is, from God to the visible bodies, both participates in an order above it and is participated in one below it, and therefore is both participant and participated . . . so the distribution of the natural orders has been given the name of participation but the bringing together of the distributions is called universal Love which in a kind of ineffable amity gathers all things into one.[32]

---

[32] John Scot Eriugena, *Periphyseon*, trans. I. P. Sheldon-Williams and rev. John J. O'Meara (Montréal, Washington, 1987), III. 630c–31a.

Eriugena calls the transformation in humans that comes through participation in divine love 'theosis', by which he means the deification of what is created,[33] and poets of love who espoused this brand of Platonism (as did Dante, but not Chaucer) would naturally incline to believe that theosis through the Word could mark the sphere of the poetic word as well. Thus, even though the *Pearl*-poet carries us into the terrestrial paradise whose supernatural artistry (*adubment*) surpasses the tapestries of mankind ('webbe3 þat wy3e3 weuen', 71), his own art unabashedly emulates God's sublimer works. In this world of crystal cliffs, even the Form of stone is perfectly translucent. To use the terms of Grosseteste, the *lumen* which shines from (or through) the Forms of things is therefore adequate to the *lux* that is their source. Even the trees there have silvery leaves that fairly quiver as they participate: 'Wyth schymeryng schene ful schrylle þay schynde' (80).

Indeed, it mainly is through their participation in light that the many are conjoined in the one. Thus, the lover's grief at losing his 'pryuy perle' pearl, whose being had that seemed to him *sengeley in synglure*, is confronted by a landscape virtually *covered* with the 'grauayl' of innumerable 'precious perle3 of Oryent' which combine with the colours of other gems:

> For vche a pobbel in pole þper py3t
> Wat3 emerad, saffer, oþer gemme gente,
> Þat alle þe lo3e lemed of ly3t,
> So dere wat3 hit adubbement.   (117–20).

This shared luminosity makes the light of our sun seem dark and lusterless. Still, imbued with Christian doctrines of incarnation, the poet emphasizes the commensurability of earthly and heavenly luminosities, as well as the mandate of art to celebrate a difference that is positive. Thus, metaphorical perceptions that cannot by themselves suffice as vehicles of truth are reconfigured to form powerful speculative analogies. For instance, to glance downwards in the earthly paradise at the human gems shining in the riverbottom there ('As glente þur3 glas þat glowed and gly3t', 114) is like our looking from earth *upward* into a clear winter sky at the stars shining ('staren') downward as woodsmen sleep ('stremande sterne3, quen stroþe-men slepe, /Staren in welkyn in wynter ny3t', 114–15). The transparency of a world where nature is frozen and contracted with the winter solstice is now counterpoised with the riot of summery forms and colours of before in the garden of courtly desire. As the innumerable heavenly bodies freely bestow their light on common folk, who rest from their proper hivernal labour as woodsmen, these commoners (and not courtiers) become the true visionaries. The meek inherit the earth, and the common voice of English inherits the truth.

Since *Pearl*'s poet accepts the challenge of showing how interpersonal, human love may be brought to participate in a larger divine eros, it is consistent, dramatically speaking, that this paradisial setting initially appears to be wholly centred on the resurrected Pearl as the lover's beloved object. However, since conventions of the lover's discourse must be modified before they can mediate this new understanding, it is also no surprise that its central section should be a dialogue between lovers construed as a master-disciple relationship where

---

[33] John Scot Eriugena, *Periphyseon*, I. 449b, p. 34.

speech itself remains a matter of careful scrutiny. Thus, the lover's reunion with Pearl is first evoked in terms that scarcely differ from those of his earlier memories of her as a living being: she is still 'smooth and small', she is royally arrayed; and she is fit for a duke or an 'earle' (211). Moreover, in her appearance, Pearl is virtually pearlness itself, as we learn from a very pearly portrait of 60 lines: her cloak, her crown, her dress, her collar, sleeves, her wristlet, and every hem are covered with pearls. In the middle of her breast is set a single pearl that surpasses the power of any tongue to describe it (225–6).

Although Pearl seems secure in her existence *sengeley in synglure*, here is where both the lover's feelings and his discourse must begin to change. Still the hostage of earthly understanding, the lover greets Pearl with self-pity and reproach tainted with the stereotyped Hereos Malady of the courtly lover: why, he asks, must he languish and complain alone at night in 'gret daunger' (250), while Pearl is allowed to dwell in a 'lyf of lykying ly3te,/ In Paradys erde, of stryf unstrayned' (247–8)? The ordinary cruelty of Amor having been laid at the doorstep of a seemingly unjust Christian God, Pearl is quick to correct the lover's discourse. It is to misunderstand to say that Pearl is absent because she is no longer in his midst: 'Sir, 3e haf your tale mysetente,/ To say your perle is al away' (257–8). This deluded 'joyless jeweler' is not really a 'noble jeweler'. Pearl is carefully redefining here the lexicon of courtly discourse. Instead of complaining that fate is a thief, rather, he should understand that the love that God has diffused among mortals is 'something of nothing' ('o3t of no3t', 274); moreover, by blaming the divine love that has caused Pearl to depart from him he is indeed blaming his own remedy ('bote', 274). When the lover hastens to exclaim that since she still lives, he wishes to be instantly reunited with her, Pearl once again refutes his 'jesting', saying that he speaks nonsense on three counts: the sight that he beholds is not really Pearl; the spot where she appears to be is not where they will be reunited; no living man may cross the stream that separates them. For us to love what we can see with our eyes is 'much to blame and uncortoyse' (303), and blasphemous because it implies that 'our Lorde wolde make a ly3e' (304), and it indicts God's new covenant with man as an empty pledge ('3e setten hys worde3 ful westernays', 307). In Paradise, our courtly lover has become nothing but a *médisant*! The new 'courtesy' that will bring a lover to God calls for different words (314): not words of blame for the Lord such as those that lovers in love-danger are used to declaring about Amor, rather, prayers for mercy. The new courtesy also calls for different ways of seeing – specifically, for the seeing things of earthly beauty as mere images of the true beauty that resides with God.[34]

The doctrinal core of Pearl's homily of consolation may be described as an elaborated theology of participation, but as many have noticed, it unfolds above all as a thorough revalorization of courtly conventions. For instance, the poet will extrapolate from the courtly concept of 'courtesy' (as Derek Brewer has suggested)[35] a code of deference and service valid in a spiritual configuration as well. Pearl discloses that she is now the bride of Christ and that he possesses

[34] Louis Blenkner, 'The Pattern of Traditional Images in "Pearl" ', *Studies in Philology* 68 (1971), p. 31.

[35] Derek Brewer, 'Courtesy and the *Gawain*-Poet', in *Patterns of Love and Courtesy: Essays in Memory of C. S. Lewis*, ed. John Lawlor (London, 1966), pp. 54–85.

her as his eternal queen 'in alle hys herytage' (417); she too is 'holy hysse: / Hys prese, hys prys' (418–19). Imbued as he is with feudal social models, the lover cannot grasp how Pearl can make such claims without usurping the primacy of Mary as 'Quen of Cortaysye'. Pearl's answer is that Mary does indeed preside as Queen of Courtesy, but that everyone who arrives in the 'court of þe kyngdom of God alyue / Hat3 a property in hytself beyng . . .' (445–6). Here is a moment when theology is challenging a traditional feudal ideology, and one may only wonder whether the *Pearl*-poet was not indeed committed to social reforms in his own political world.

Indeed, it is not difficult to extract from Pearl's theology of participation, as John H. Fisher has done,[36] a wholly new basis for civic participation in the body politic: *anyone* who arrives in this court is *also* queen or king of all the realm without depriving anyone else of anything: to the contrary, each is happy precisely 'of oþere3 hafying' (450). Pearl deploys the traditional analogy of the whole presence of the soul to all parts of the body to describe the participation of many humans in the whole of Christ's mystical body. This is the very doctrinal core of the new courtesy – that is, the courtesy of Paul!

> 'Of courtaysye, as sayt3 Saynt Poule,
> Al arn we membre3 of Jesu Kryst:
> As heued and arme and legg and naule
> Teme to hys body ful trwe and tryste,
> Ry3t so is vch a Krysten sawle
> A longande lym to þe Mayster of myste. . .
> So fare we alle wyth luf and lyste
> To kyng and quene by cortaysye.'   (457–68)

At this point, however, the lexicon of courtesy has been stretched beyond the lover's limits of understanding.[37] Perhaps the *Pearl*-poet knew that his readers too needed some further explanations. The lover's problem, broadly stated, remains one of understanding the participation of a limited being in the transcendent Whole: he asks how God, without dishonouring himself, can have crowned a mere child who has not lived a full life of suffering and penitence? Indeed, the lover feels cheated because he himself has suffered far more. Pearl answers that there is no 'more and lasse in Gode3 ryche' (601), and that each person is rewarded according to his specific capacity, for God is infinitely free with his whole grace to all. The innocence of a child should be no obstacle to salvation; as for those who have sinful lives, God's grace was dispensed to them as well when 'Ryche blod ran on rode so roghe, / And wynne water . . .' (646–7). God's covenant of grace includes, then, both the righteous and the innocent (671–2); yet *all* must come to him as *children* to be saved (723). Thus, the pearl mounted in Pearl's chest, the pearl of pearls, is not Pearl herself, but the pearl of salvation in Christ, and all righteous humans may participate in its being. It is now becoming clear that the singular gemmological perfection that the lover once bestowed on Pearl refers more appropriately to the 'pearl of price' from Matthew 13:45–6, which is available not only to the rich, but to all. However, such a jewel, pure and round, calls for a new kind of jeweller:

---

[36] John H. Fisher, 'Wyclif, Langland, Gower, and the Pearl Poet on the Subject of Aristocray', in *Studies in Medieval Literature*, ed. MacEdward Leach (Philadelphia, 1961), p. 152.

[37] The lover here shares the obstinacy of Jonah, as Shoaf defines it, 'God's "malyse" ', p. 272.

> This makelle₃ perle, þat bo₃t is dere,
> Þe joueler gef fore alle hys god,
> Is lyke þe reme or heuenesse clere:
> So sayde þe Fader of folde and flode;
> For hit is wemle₃, clene and clere,
> And endele₃ rounde, and blyþe of mode,
> And commune to alle that ry₃twys were.
> Lo, euen inmydde₃ my breste hit stode.   (737–40).

The lover, however, is still jealous, and balks at the idea that his own Pearl should have Christ as spouse: what about other more deserving women who have 'lyued in much stryf' (776) for Christ? Did Pearl deprive them of their more deserved marriage? Pearl now recounts the crucifixion of Christ in order to show that because his sacrifice was perfect and universal, all may participate in him as the soul's bride:

> Forþy, vche saule þat hade neuer teche
> Is to þat Lombe a worthyly wyf,
> And þa₃ vch day a store he feche,
> Among vs comme₃ nouþer strot ne stryf.
> Bot vchon enlé we wolde were fyf –
> Þe mo þe myryer, so God me blesse.
> In compayny gret, our luf con þryf
> In honour more, and neuer þe lesse.   (845–52)

Pearl's homily about grace and salvation as modes of individual participation in Christ culminates in a vision of the New Jerusalem, with its procession of virgins to the Lamb. Here as before, the whole and perfect joy of the many in the grace of the One is its most prominent feature, and the poet stresses again and again the *delyt* (now the link-word) of the many pearl-maidens as they are procede to the Lamb (himself covered with pearls) in the triumphant reversion of being to the throne of the One:

> So sodanly on a wonder wyse
> I wat₃ war of a prosessyoun.
> Þis noble cité of ryche enpryse
> Wat₃ sodanly ful, wythouten sommoun
> Of such vergyne₃, in þe same gyse
> Þat wat₃ my blysful an-vnder croun:
> And coronde wern alle of þe same fasoun,
> Depaynt in perle₃ and wede₃ qwyte;
> In vchone₃ breste wat₃ bounden boun
> Þe blysful perle wyth gret delyt.   (1096–104)

At last the lover as jeweller has found his proper jewel: not Pearl herself, but the Lamb, 'þat gaye Juelle' (1124), to whom praise is chanted that reverberates through heaven and hell. 'Ywysse, I la₃t a gret delyt' (1128).

The final glimpse of the lover's maiden in the mystical procession at last evinces desire 'luf-longing' of a new sort: to participate *with* Pearl's whole delight in co-presence to the Lamb. Though some would argue that the lover's consolation has failed, I would reply that his desire to participate individually with Pearl in a universally shared love is essential to Christianity as a religion where human love is a valid, however incomplete, mode of participating in the reciprocated love of God. For the lover of Pearl, having witnessed the delight of the Lamb even as 'Of his quyte syde his blod out sprent' (1137), the sadness of exile is no longer the love-danger of the poem's beginning. Rather, because the supreme Jewel is Christ, and because Pearl is set in this '. . . garlande gay / So wel is me in þys doel-doungoun, / Þat thou art to þat Prynseȝ paye' (1186–8). To submit to Christ's 'paye', and to 'pay' Christ, however, are easy: 'ful eþe to þe god Krystyin', and though he must now commend both Pearl to God, he remains consoled here on earth by participating in the eucharist. Through the transformed elements of bread and wine the priest reveals Christ 'vche a day', enabling all men to be his gracious servants 'And precious perleȝ unto his pay'. Poetic discourse, then, has found its proper pearl and its proper Prince. Though earthly humans may not yet participate *facie ad faciem* in the perfection of this prince, the eucharist is available to them as a valid mode of participating in the resurrected Word. The poem closes by perfecting itself in prayer, specifically, in the sign of participation *par excellence*: 'Amen. Amen'.

GRAPPLING WITH ARTHUR OR
IS THERE AN ENGLISH ARTHURIAN VERSE ROMANCE?

JOERG O. FICHTE

When I sat down ten years ago to devise a literary typology of the Middle English Arthurian verse romance I thought I had a tight grip on Arthur, but somehow within this last decade he became more and more elusive, as did the whole corpus of what is generally known as Middle English romance.[1] Although Derek Pearsall states with great conviction that this corpus 'gives the strongest impression of homogeneity', which 'is most evident in the observance of a wide range of formal and literary conventions, what we might call the "grammar" of romance',[2] he immediately proceeds to narrow down the corpus – 15th century romance and alliterative romance are omitted – and to introduce two major divisions, which are then, in turn, subdivided. If one might have expected an exposition of the 'grammar' of romance at this point, this expectation remains unfulfilled. None is provided. This omission, however, is hardly surprising, if one is familiar with Derek Pearsall's review of Susan Wittig's study, *Stylistic and Narrative structures in the Middle English Romance*, the only book which, to my knowledge, really tries to write a 'grammar' of romance based on the models provided by structural linguistics, principally the tagmemic linguistics of Kenneth Pike and Lévi-Strauss's analysis of the deep structural patterns of myth. The reviewer is critical of the approach to the subject matter under investigation and the terminology used by Wittig, stating that 'the book develops real strength in these later chapters, as the author moves away from more narrow structuralist positions and adopts a broader approach to the significant ordering of contents in the romances'.[3] Although one can sympathize with Derek Pearsall's critique of the lopsided relationship of the critical terminology introduced by Wittig in the first three chapters of her book and the actual results yielded by her analysis of formulas, motifemes and type-scenes, the book is coherent and logical in its progression from the smallest to the largest structural patterns. Thus, in terms of a structural approach to a literary form Wittig's study provides a cogent and tightly reasoned model for the analysis of the Middle English romances. Needless to say, such a study also has its limitations; it does not touch on other important aspects such as place of origin, dialect provenance, manuscript tradition, variant texts, sources, analogues, authorship, audience, etc., which would help the literary historian to form an idea of a corpus of generically related texts.
Susan Wittig based her study on twenty-seven noncyclic romances, that is, on

---

[1] Cf. Lillian Hornstein, 'Middle English Romances', in *Recent Middle English Scholarship and Criticism: Survey and Desiderata*, ed. J. Burke Severs (Pittsburgh, 1971), p. 64: 'Although the romances have never been considered difficult to understand, no one has been able to tell us exactly what they are'.
[2] Derek Pearsall, 'The Development of Middle English Romance', in *Studies in Medieval English Romance. Some New Aspects*, ed. Derek Brewer (Cambridge, 1988), p. 11.
[3] Derek Pearsall, 'Understanding Middle English Romance', *Review* 2 (1980), p. 115.

less than a quarter of the works listed in the first volume of Severs' *Manual of the Writings in Middle English*. The *Manual*, of course, is not the sole authority for what constitutes a romance and which works are to be called romances. Helaine Newstead's declaration: 'The medieval romance is a narrative about knightly prowess and adventure, in verse or in prose, intended primarily for the entertainment of a listening audience' is much too vague to be a viable and useful definition.[4] Consequently, the corpus of works assembled there under the rubric of romance has come under scrutiny from various sides. While Kathryn Hume remarks: 'The Newstead list is not sacred';[5] John Finlayson is ready to cut at least half of the works listed there because they 'do not in any way meet the paradigm proposed; that is, they are not romances in any meaningful sense'.[6] But what is a romance in any meaningful sense and should we bother to establish a definition for this amorphous group of works lumped together under the nomenclature of romance?[7] Ideally, we should have recourse to the medieval handbooks on poetry in order to find an appropriate definition of a literary genre or type. Yet, as is well known, these *artes poeticae* addressed themselves to Latin literature and not to the literary works in the vernacular. The new literary forms, such as the *chanson de geste* and the *roman*, making their appearance in the eleventh and twelfth centuries respectively, were not discussed by the rhetoricians of that age who composed handbooks designed for use in school. Consequently, the system of vernacular genres can only be an immanent and, therefore, subjective one, since the criteria applied to the definition of genres are by necessity modern ones. And there are many possibilities, as Klaus W. Hempfer's *Gattungstheorie* demonstrates, a brilliant survey of the theories from Dilthey, Brunetière and Croce at the beginning of this century to the linguistic models of textual analysis devised in the sixties and seventies. Under these circumstances, it is not surprising that the elusive corpus of narratives commonly labelled romances has been approached in a variety of ways. In spite of the many, varied attempts to define and organize these narratives, there are basically three ways of dealing with this problem: romance can either be regarded as mode or as genre or as a combination of the two.

In the wake of Northrop Frye's archetypal approach to the classification of European literature, which is divided into three *mythoi*, myth, romance and realism, critics have tried to tackle the problem of medieval romance by means of postulating an archetypal romance pattern. Critics of this persuasion like Pamela Gradon, John Stevens, Kathryn Hume, Derek Brewer and W.R.J. Barron will prefer the term 'mode' or 'experience' when speaking of romance.[8] According to this view, romance is an ahistorical category, originally linked

---

4 *A Manual of the Writings in Middle English 1050–1500*, I, ed. J. Burke Severs (New Haven, 1967), p. 11.

5 Kathryn Hume, 'The Formal Nature of Middle English Romance', *PQ* 53 (1974), p. 175.

6 John Finlayson, 'Definitions of Middle English Romance', *Chaucer Review* 15 (1981/82), p. 178.

7 Edmund Reiss, 'Romance', in *The Popular Literature of Medieval England*, ed. Thomas J. Heffernan (Knoxville, 1985), p. 109, pleads, for instance, for a corpus consisting of epic, historical, and exemplary romances, in which saints' lives, folk tales and ballads are also contained.

8 Pamela Gradon, *Form and Style in Early English Literature* (London, 1971), pp. 212–272; John Stevens, *Medieval Romance. Themes and Approaches* (New York, 1974), pp. 15–28; Kathryn Hume, 'Romance: A Perdurable Pattern', *CE* 36 (1974) 129–46; Derek Brewer,

with 'the conscious and rational development of the individual during . . . youth and early adulthood' and the 'search for identity and proving oneself, and an integration into society'.[9] Defined in these broad terms, romance includes everything from Greek romance to the Gothic novel and some forms of modern science fiction. Appealing as this concept may be, it fails to anchor the Middle English specimens conforming to this type firmly in space and time. The literary historian interested in the cultural and literary conditions leading to the rise of romance at a specific time and in a particular environment will have to look for answers elsewhere.

Those critics who approach the Middle English romances as a historical, literary form with a beginning, a peak and an ending have endeavoured to define and classify this body of texts by either theme, structure, metrical form, length, rhetorical style, mode of presentation, authorship or audience or a combination of these.[10] The majority of scholars has labelled the group of narratives so-defined a genre; others, such as Carol Fewster prefer the term ' "romance" style'.[11] Whatever the term used, the effectiveness of these enterprises depends on the chosen determinants, the tightness of the methodological grid and the stringency of the analysis. There is always a precarious balance to be maintained between over-generalization on the one hand and over-conciseness on the other, with over-generalization tending to render the definition of romance meaningless and over-preciseness to lop off too much from a corpus which, judged even by contemporary evidence, was characterized by some kind of homogeneity. Also, one has to be aware that all attempts at the definition and classification of these texts are strictly modern ones. In the absence of a normative, *ante rem* poetics, which for instance governed the production of seventeenth century French tragedy, and because of the relative dearth of any usable contemporary commentaries, these attempts at a generic classification of romance are *post rem*.

What is truly needed, however, is the determination of groups or families of texts *in re*, as suggested by Hans Robert Jauss.[12] Literature should be treated as a dialectical process of production and reception. Thus, the relationship of a single text to a series of texts and its passive or active reception leads to the formation of a horizon of expectations, which is either validated or violated. By horizon of expectations Jauss means an intersubjective system of expectations which governs the production and the reception of any literary text. In other

---

'The Nature of Romance', *Poetica* 9 (1978) 9–48. W.R.J. Barron, *English Medieval Romance* (London & New York, 1987).

9 Kathryn Hume, 'Romance: A Perdurable Pattern', p. 132.

10 Cf. A.B. Taylor, *An Introduction to Medieval Romance* (London, 1930); Laura Hibbard, *Medieval Romance in England: A Study of the Sources and Analogues of the Non-cyclic Metrical Romances*, rev. edn. (New York, 1963); Hanspeter Schelp, *Exemplarische Romanzen im Mittelenglischen* (Göttingen, 1967); Dieter Mehl, *The Middle English Romances of the Thirteenth and Fourteenth Centuries* (London, 1968); Velma Bourgeois Richmond, *The Popularity of Middle English Romance* (Bowling Green, Ohio, 1975); Utz Dürmüller, *Narrative Possibilities in the Tail-Rime Romance* (Berne, 1975) and L.C. Ramsey, *Chivalric Romances: Popular Literature in Medieval England* (Bloomington, Ind., 1983).

11 Carol Fewster, *Traditionality and Genre in Middle English Romance* (Cambridge, 1987), p. 150.

12 See Hans Robert Jauss, 'Theorie der Gattungen und Literatur des Mittelalters', in *Grundriss der romanischen Literaturen des Mittelalters*, I (Heidelberg, 1972), pp. 107–38.

words, the structure of the individual work always mediates between an immanent concept of genre and a literary series. The formation of the immanent
poetics of a genre, therefore, is a continual process because every new work is
not only an addition to the corpus but it also enhances our understanding of the
rules and regulations governing the other works comprising this corpus. As
literary historians we are, of course, in the enviable position of looking back on
a literary development – here, incidentally, I disagree with Jauss who insists on
ignoring one's own historical situatedness because he wants to escape the
positivist-historicist paradigm. I believe that we must accept the historical nature of the literary situation, a situation which presents itself as a diachronic
process. We can follow this process which starts with the origin of a new genre,
continues with its variation, expansion, correction and mechanization, and ends
with its displacement by a new genre or literary form. Applied to the genre of
the Middle English romance, this means a period from the thirteenth to the
sixteenth century, when the genre was replaced by either ballads or long prose
narratives, as Derek Pearsall has shown.[13] Although the older works are still
copied, there are no new compositions.

Any definition of the genre *in re* must proceed from a consideration of the
scant evidence we have: the use of the term 'romaunce', the catalogues of
romance heroes in contemporary works, and the intertextual relationship between specimens of the same literary type. Since Reinald Hoops and Paul
Strohm have conducted an exhaustive examination of the first two points, I can
be brief.[14] Although the term 'romaunce' had a variety of meanings – a classical
Roman story, a French story, an English translation or adaptation of either a
classical Roman or a French story in poetry rather than prose, and reading
matter in prose or verse – a closer look at the works listed by Hoops reveals a
surprising similarity in theme, form, and style. With the exception of four
romanticized histories, a love allegory, a saint's life, a Passion poem, a penitential treatise and Minot's *Poems* the term 'romaunce' was used for works featuring an aristocratic protagonist in pursuit of adventures. They were written in
verse (mostly rhymed couplets or tail rhyme stanzas). And they made use of a
popular style or idiom, which we have come to associate with this genre. It
appears, in other words, that the term 'romaunce' was also used for the purpose
of generic identification.

Furthermore, we have various catalogues of romance heroes and a brief
description of their exploits, as in *The Laud Troy-Book*,[15] *Richard Coer de
Lyon*[16] and the *Cursor Mundi*[17] which demonstrate that the authors of these
works were thinking in terms of a certain literary type. In addition to conquests
and deeds of arms, the author of the *Cursor Mundi* mentions 'ferlys' (11) and

---

[13] Derek Pearsall, 'The English Romance in the Fifteenth Century', *E&S* 29 (1976) 56–83.

[14] Reinald Hoops, *Der Begriff 'Romance' in der mittelenglischen und frühneuenglischen
Literatur* (Heidelberg, 1929) and Paul Strohm, 'Origin and Meaning of Middle English
Romaunce', *Genre* 10 (1977) 1–28.

[15] *The Laud Troy Book*, ed. J. Ernst Wülfing, EETS OS 121, 122 (1902, 1903), ll. 11–26.

[16] *Der mittelenglische Versroman über Richard Löwenherz*, ed. Karl Brunner, Wiener Beiträge
zur englischen Philologie (Vienna & Leipzig, 1913), ll. 7–20 and ll. 6725–34.

[17] *Cursor Mundi*, ed. Richard Morris, EETS OS 57, 59, 62, 66, 68, 99, 101 (1874–1893), OS 99,
ll. 1–26.

'aunters' (12) and the besotting influence of love (17–18). The stress is on theme, not on form or style.

And, finally, there is the evidence of intertextual relations, which can take various forms. We can check the English translations against their French sources; we can compare and contrast the items in manuscripts containing a large number of romance type narratives (the Auchinleck MS, BL MS Egerton 2862, Lincoln's Inn MS Hale 150, BL MS Cotton Caligula A ii, the two Thornton MSS, etc.);[18] we can study the various versions of the same romance; and we can look for responses to the romance type. Chaucer's *Tale of Sir Thopas* is a celebrated case in point because his parody of the theme, form and style of the popular romance narratives helps to move the conventions of the genre into focus. It is anagnorisis in the worst possible sense because although the features Chaucer ridicules by overuse are not all contained in any one romance to this degree, one instantly recognizes them as characteristic of the ' "romance" style', to use Carol Fewster's term once more. The horizon of expectations is constituted by these romances, the knowledge of which is necessary to recognize the literary parody carried out in *Sir Thopas*. Thus, parody can be a valuable aid in the identification of genre markers. The horizon of expectations, however, is also conditioned by our familiarity with other Chaucerian romances. The *Tale of Sir Thopas* could take its place in a series of texts marked 'Chaucerian romance', which would include such works as the *Knight's Tale*, *Troilus and Criseyde*, the *Squire's Tale* and the *Wife of Bath's Tale*. Seen from this point of view, the possibilities of generic variation become apparent. A philosophical treatise on the questions of determinism, free will and man's responsibilities in a divinely ordained cosmos presented in the guise of romantic story, an almost psychoanalytical analysis of the nature of love, an oriental tale of wonder and sentiment, an Arthurian story suitably debased to fit the teller's interest in female domination, and a parody of the popular romance style – these are Chaucer's experiments with the romance genre. We are struck, of course, by the disparity of subject matter and treatment, but then a series of texts consisting of *Guy of Warwick*, *Emare*, *The Sege of Melayne* and *The Weddynge of Sir Gawen and Dame Ragnell*, all lumped together in the *Manual*, will appear equally disparate. Hence, the questions presenting themselves with ever greater urgency are: Is there a meaningful way of defining and delimiting this vast corpus of heterogeneous texts? How can it be distinguished from other literary forms? And can we subdivide it into recognizable types or families?

To answer these questions, our *in re* approach to the problem will have to be supplemented by a *post rem* analysis; that is, we shall have to use the tools of literary criticism, and doing this implies the development of a heuristic model which will serve as the basis for the study of the total corpus of Middle English romance. The design of such a model has two obvious advantages: it creates the proper methodological basis from which the analysis can proceed, and it serves as poetological touchstone by which the variations can be tested. Since such a model will consist of a catalogue of criteria suitable to the analysis of the available material, I would suggest a paradigm comprising the following four major categories: first, structure divided into intrinsic and extrinsic structure;

---

[18] Cf. Gisela Guddat-Figge, *Catalogue of Manuscripts Containing Middle English Romances* (Munich, 1976).

second, authorship and presentation; third, content and meaning; and fourth, authorial intent and reception. These four major headings could be subdivided into a number of subordinate constituent parts which would facilitate a more detailed analysis of the literary type under discussion. Needless to say, such a detailed analysis would exceed the scope of this tentative investigation.

The intrinsic structure of verse romance derives its unity from the personality of the exemplary, knightly protagonist, whose actions in the form of knight errantry and quest, which determine the extrinsic structure of the romance narrative, are mostly accidental. The authorship of the romances is generally anonymous; its presentation was by a professional entertainer who recited it to a listening audience. The content, i.e. the *matière*, of romance is characterized by tests through battles, loss, exile, love etc. And its meaning, that is, its *sens*, is the affirmation of the existing class structure by the success and vindication of the alienated knightly protagonist. The authorial intent is to entertain and to teach, to entertain by means of a story of high adventure and love, and to teach by presenting an exemplary figure whose moral excellence and deeds of valour are worthwhile of imitation. Conversely, the reception should be accordingly. Moreover, the audience's participatory identification with the values presented in the romances should strengthen the acceptance of the role of these values in society. In short, romance is a conservative genre.

There have been a number of attempts to distinguish the text corpus of romance from other literary forms.[19] Although these attempts are not always convincing because of the criteria used and the often blurred boundaries between the various types of texts which make clear identifications difficult, I recognize the need for such divisions. Without wanting to spend much time on this problem, let me introduce some criteria which might be helpful: the aristocratic status of the protagonist; the comic narrative structure; the earthly telos; the fictional status of both hero and story; and the coherent, sequential organization of the narrative material. Taken in this order, these properties distinguish the romance from the fabliau, the *chanson de geste*, the saint's life, the chronicle or history, and the ballad.

After defining and delimiting romance as a generic type, let me tackle the most difficult task, the establishment of meaningful groups within the vast corpus. Many attempts have been made, of which those using the criteria of quality or theme have been the least successful. A more obvious division into epic romance and lyric romance has been proposed by Derek Pearsall, 'the former more prosaic, realistic, historical and martial, the latter more emotive, more concerned with love, faith, constance and the marvellous'.[20] The question, of course, presents itself whether the epic type based on the French *chanson de geste* is a romance at all. John Finlayson would deny this, as he likewise rejects another group of romances long recognized as a fairly homogenous group of texts as alien to the spirit of romance: the exemplary or homiletic romances. Kathryn Hume's threefold division by 'the hero and the background against

[19] Cf. Dorothy Everett, 'A Characterization of the English Romances', in *Essays on Middle English Literature*. ed. Patricia Kean (Oxford, 1955), pp. 15–22; Kathryn Hume, 'The Formal Nature of Middle English Romance', pp. 169–80; F.N.M. Diekstra, 'Le roman en moyen anglais', in *Le Roman*, Typologie des Sources du Moyen Age Occidental, 12, ed. J. Ch. Payen and F.N.M. Diekstra (Turnhout, 1975), pp. 69–127.

[20] Derek Pearsall, 'The Development of Middle English Romance', p. 16.

which he works out his destiny' is an interesting attempt because it accounts for the differences in historical situatedness.[21] She distinguishes a Type A – the amor-clad folk tale –, in which the hero is all, the locale unimportant; a Type B, where the hero is displayed against a significant background, usually a swatch of history or pseudo-history; and a Type C – the histories, 'whose events overshadow any hero the story might possess'.[22] One is, of course, inclined to ask if Type C can still be called a romance. In the face of these classificatory difficulties it seems brazen to revert to the time-honoured division first proposed by Bodel, who distinguished three *matières* 'de France, et de Bretaigne, et de Rome la grant'.[23] Let me say immediately that I don't subscribe to this division because the matters of France and Rome, which include any subject from antiquity, are too diffuse to make for a meaningful category. I will argue, however, that some matters are so homogenous in character and treatment as to warrant consideration as a special group. This holds true, for instance, for the English adaptations of the Anglo-Norman ancestral romances or the group of homiletic romances. I also believe that the *matière de Bretaigne* is unified enough by Arthur, his knights and a specific setting as to generate a horizon of expectations which would warrant a separate classification of this type. W.R.J. Barron has made the treatment of Arthur in Middle English Arthurian literature the touchstone of his attempt to look for a community between texts. Thus, he isolates thematic features such as a nationalistic spirit and a dynastic element as being characteristic of the English renderings of the matter of Britain.[24] Valuable as these observations may be, shared thematic concerns alone are insufficient to establish a community between a group of widely divergent texts. We must be careful to respect generic boundaries and a text's relationship to actual events, that is, Layamon's *Brut* and *Golagrus and Gawain* should not be lumped together because a contemporary audience hearing or reading these two works would have done so with an adjusted set of expectations generated by its knowledge of genres. The *Brut* is a chronicle, a non-fictional work; *Golagrus and Gawain* is a romance, a fictional work. Thus, it seems important to divide the corpus of Arthurian literature first and assign the individual works to their appropriate classes and to do so by paying attention to the historical development of the corpus. In order to facilitate this distribution, we might resort to the traditional, Ciceronian categories of *historia*, *argumentum* and *fabula*.[25] *Historia*, let us recall, designates a truthful account of something which actually happened, or was believed to have taken place – this qualification is important. *Argumentum* refers to a feigned account of something which could have happened, but didn't. Such narratives are characterized by verisimilitude. And *fabula*, finally, is a narrative which is told concerning things which are neither true nor governed by verisimilitude. And since these texts bear the moral stigma

---

[21] Kathryn Hume, 'The Formal Nature of Middle English Romance', p. 161.

[22] *Ibid.*, p. 161.

[23] Jean Bodel, *Roman des Saisnes*, ed. Fr. Michel (1839), ll. 6–7.

[24] W.R.J. Barron, 'Arthurian Romance: Traces of an English Tradition', *ES* 61 (1980) 2–23.

[25] Cicero, *Rhetorica ad Herennium*, ed. and trans. Harry Caplan (Cambridge, Mass., 1954), pp. 22–24: 'Id quod in negotiorum expositione positum est tres habet partes: fabulam, historiam, argumentum. Fabula est quae neque veras neque veri similes continet res, ut eae sunt quae tragoediis traditae sunt. Historia est gesta res, sed ab aetatis nostrae memoria remota. Argumentum est ficta res quae tamen fieri potuit, velut argumenta comoediarum'.

of folly or vanity, authors continually try to escape condemnation by stressing the verisimilitude, truthfulness or historicity of their accounts.

Applied to Middle English Arthurian literature this means a chronicle tradition, a tradition of historiographic fiction, and a fictional, poetic tradition. Obviously, the chronicle tradition is based on Geoffrey of Monmouth's seminal pseudo-historical work, the *Historia Regum Britanniae*, and Wace's courtly translation, the *Brut*. The credibility of Geoffrey's account was not damaged by William of Newburgh's scathing indictment of Geoffrey, who had 'dressed up fables of Arthur, taken from primitive fictions of the Britons and added to by himself, adorned with the Latin tongue, in the honest name of history'.[26] Layamon, Robert of Gloucester, Robert Manning, the anonymous author of the *Brut*, Thomas Castleford and John Harding incorporated the Arthurian 'history' into their chronicles written between the first quarter of the thirteenth and the third quarter of the fifteenth century.[27] Only Ranulph Higden was sceptical of the veracity of Geoffrey's account, which earned him the stern rebuke of his translator, John Trevisa, who justified the inconsistencies by an argument drawn from the Bible: 'Seint Iohn in his gospel telleþ meny þinges and doynges þat Mark, Luk, and Matheu spekeþ nouȝt in here gospelles, ergo, Iohn is nouȝt to trowynge in his gospel. He were of false byleve þat trowede þat þat argument were worþ a bene. . . . So þey Gaufridus speke of Arthur his dedes, þat oþer writers of stories spekeþ of derkliche, oþer makeþ of non mynde, þat dispreveþ nouȝt Gaufrede his storie and his sawe, . . .'[28] Here, the truthfulness of Geoffrey's Arthurian history is forcefully reasserted.

The Middle English tradition of historiographic fiction can be traced to three sources, the *Roman de l'estoire du Graal* and the *Merlin* by Robert de Boron and the French Vulgate Cycle. All three compositions were attempts to reintegrate the mechanized post-classical model, which replaced Chrétien's ahistorical, fictional one, into the process of history. This development was aided by two unsolved problems in Chrétien: the unresolved Lancelot/Guinevere relationship in the *Chevalier de la Charrette* and the grail story in the *Conte du Graal*. Both fragments occasioned continuations inimical to the spirit of Chrétien's fictional accounts: the connection of the now vastly expanded Lancelot story with the story of Arthur's fall taken from the Geoffrey of Monmouth/Wace tradition, and the invention of the history of the holy grail and the creation of a spiritual grail kingdom as an alternative to the flawed concept of the worldly Table Round. Thus, the connection of these themes from Chrétien, developed in the form of a vast prose cycle which spanned history from the Last Supper to Arthur's death, was the almost logical consequence of these historicizing efforts. In England this tradition was continued by *Arthour and Merlin*, *Arthur*, the prose *Merlin*, Lovelich's *Merlin* and *History of the Holy Grail*, *Joseph of Arimathie*, the stanzaic *Morte Arthur*, the alliterative *Morte Arthur* and by Malory's *Morte Darthur*. All these works are imaginative poetic elaborations of the historical 'facts' as they are presented in the chronicles and histories.

[26] William of Newburgh, *Historia Rerum Anglicarum*, Rolls Series (London, 1884), p. 12.

[27] See Karl Heinz Göller, *König Arthur in der englischen Literatur des späten Mittelalters* (Göttingen, 1963), pp. 23–40.

[28] *Polychronicon Ranulphi Higden Monachi Cestrensis; Together with the English Translations of John Trevisa and of an Unknown Writer of the Fifteeth Century*, eds. Churchill Babington and Joseph Rawson Lumby, 9 Vols. Rolls Series 41, 1–9 (London, 1865–86), 5, 337, 339.

The fictional tradition of Arthurian writings, finally, is represented in Middle English literature by fourteen romances and five ballads. Since the body of Arthurian romance is rather heterogeneous, literary historians have traditionally been hesitant to assign these works to a separate group, distinguished from the other romances by its recurrent cast of characters only. In France and Germany, of course, the *Artusroman* has long been recognized as a specific literary type characterized not by a set of figures, but by an identical structural model.[29] A look at the corpus of English Arthurian romance, however, reveals a surprising variety of features which have traditionally been used as criteria for the classification of romance. Metrics is a case in point. Eight romances are written in tail rhyme stanzas, three in rhymed couplets, two in rhymed alliterative stanzas, and one in stanzas of unrhymed alliterative lines followed by a bob and wheel. In length these works vary from 541 to 4032 lines. Their place of origin is mostly the Midlands and the North including Scotland. All seem to have been composed for oral presentation from a period extending from the early 14th century to roughly 1500. Only one of these romances, *Ywain and Gawain*, is a translation of a work by Chrétien and thus occupies a special place because any changes made by the English adapter are indicative of his understanding or lack of understanding of the classical model. A second group of works consists of romances once removed from the classical type by either some lost intermediary (*Sir Perceval of Galles* and *Libeaus Desconus*) or a post-classical source (*Golagrus and Gawain* and *The Jeaste of Syr Gawayne* both based on episodes from the *Continuation* of the *Conte du Graal* and *Lancelot of the Laik* based on an episode from the French Vulgate Cycle). *Golagrus and Gawain*, an alliterative poem, would better fit into the third group of alliterative romances together with *Sir Gawain and the Green Knight* and *The Awntyrs off Arthure*, two works which are likewise critical of the Arthurian system of values, as is the Scottish *Lancelot of the Laik* which could also be placed into a group of 'Alliterative Arthurian romance and Arthurian romances of Scottish origin'. Regional origin apparently plays a role. A final group consists of short romances, usually treatments of one episode, which make use of folklore motifs: *Syre Gawene and the Carle of Carlelyle*, *The Weddynge of Sir Gawen and Dame Ragnell*, *The Turk and Gowin*, and *The Avowing of King Arthur*. Some of these have been transmitted in two versions of which the second one is a reduction of the first, sometimes in the form of a ballad (*The Grene Knight*, *The Carle off Carlile* and *The Marriage of Sir Gawaine*). The spirit of these short pieces tends to be burlesque or grotesque.

When I tackled the matter ten years ago, I suggested a classification by means of a structural analysis, which revealed that the intrinsic structure of Chrétien's Arthurian romance reappeared in the Middle English specimens, although in a

---

[29] Cf. Hildegard Emmel, *Formenprobleme des Artusromans und der Gralsdichtung* (Bern, 1951); Hans Fromm, 'Doppelweg', in *Werk-Typ-Situation: Studien zu poetologischen Bedingungen in der älteren deutschen Literatur*, ed. Ingeborg Glier, Gerhard Hahn, Walter Haug and Burghart Wachinger (Stuttgart, 1969), pp. 64–79; Walter Haug, 'Die Symbolstruktur des höfischen Epos und ihre Auflösung bei Wolfram von Eschenbach', *DVLG* 45 (1971) 668–705; Paul Zumthor, 'Le Roman courtois: essai de définition', *Etudes littéraires* 4 (1971) 79–90 and Beate Schmolke-Hasselmann, *Der arthurische Versroman von Chrestien bis Froissart* (Tübingen, 1980).

variety of modifications.[30] Today I want to concentrate on one essential locale: King Arthur's court, the paradigmatic function of which will be the focus of attention in the following exemplary part of my presentation. The treatment of the court both as an actual place and as an abstract concept will be made the touchstone for determining the limits of the transformational abilities of Arthurian romance.

I shall begin with *Ywain and Gawain* because it is not only one of the earliest English Arthurian romances but also the only one based on a work by Chrétien. Although reduced in length and altered in theme – troth being substituted for love – the English romance retains the extrinsic structural pattern of its source. On the other hand, thematic change is immediately noticeable in the introduction, one of the most elaborate descriptions of King Arthur's court found in English Arthurian romances dating from the first half of the 14th century. Chrétien's knights and their ladies speak of Love, its joy and its sorrow, a topic which prompts the author to deplore the decline of love in contemporary society where the self-styled subjects of Love's order have made a mockery of it. For this the English adapter substitutes a different topic. His lords and ladies speak of deeds of arms, of hunting, and of knightly exploits. And his complaint turns into a *laudatio temporis acti*: formerly truth and faith reigned everywhere; now they cannot be found at all. This glorification of the past is bracketed by two encomia to Arthur, who 'Of al knightes . . . bare þe prise' (11).[31] With him there was 'his curtayse cumpany' (43), which was the 'flowre of chevallry'. (44).

These important changes, that is – the casual dismissal of love, which in Chrétien functions as the second determinant after King Arthur, and the pronounced *laudatio temporis acti* – are symptomatic of the altered conception of the nature of Arthur's court found in English Arthurian romance. In those most closely akin to their French counterparts, like *Ywain and Gawain*, the court symbolizes the best to be found in human society. It functions as a centre of chivalry and fulfils a normative role. In contrast to the almost utopian conception in Chrétien, however, the English work presents the court and its virtues as a thing of the past. Of course, Chrétien also uses the past tense, when speaking of Arthur's court, but he does so in a different sense, as this quotation will illustrate: 'Por ce me plest a reconter / Chose, qui face a escouter, / Del roi, qui fu de tel tesmoing, / Qu'an an parole pres et loing; / Si m'acort de tant as Bretons, / Que toz jorz mes vivra ses nons;' (33–38) [So it pleases me to relate a matter quite worthy of attention concerning the king, whose reknown was such that men still speak of him far and near; and I agree with the Britons that his name will live on forever].[32] For Chrétien Arthur, and by implication his court, represent an omnipresent ideal and model. The court's ethos is constantly valorized by the exploits of its members who are chosen or challenged to prove themselves by *aventure* and quest. And with the return of the victorious protagonist, the court demonstrates again and again not only its superiority but also its uniqueness, which it derives from its special ontological status as utopian

---

[30] Joerg O. Fichte, 'The Middle English Arthurian Verse Romance: Suggestions for the Development of a Literary Typology', *DVLG* 55 (1981) 567–90.

[31] All quotations are taken from *Ywain and Gawain*, ed. Albert B. Friedman and Norman T. Harrington, EETS OS 254 (1964).

[32] Kristian von Troyes, *Yvain (Der Löwenritter)*, ed. Wendelin Foerster, 2nd ed. (Halle, 1926), p. 2, ll. 33–38.

fiction. In *Ywain and Gawain*, however, the court is regarded as a historical reality. In contrast to Chrétien, who simply informs us that King Arthur celebrated the feast of Pentecost, the English author fixes this event in historically verifiable time. It took place after the king had conquered Wales and Scotland.[33] Thus, both the court and the story to be told are located in the continuum of history. This history, of course, is not just a succession of events, but a *magistra vitae*. Like many other phenomena from the past, the court and its special circumstances serve an exemplary purpose. In this case, Arthur's court is a model of truth and faith, something illustrated by the ensuing action. The English author is intent on showing how an excellent knight, once he has inadvertently broken his troth, will now have to demonstrate his truthfulness and reliability by undertaking a number of adventures. Ywain is thus turned into an exemplary figure who illustrates by his conduct that the members of Arthur's court 'tald of more trewth þam bitw[e]ne / þan now omang men here es sene' (33–34).

To recapitulate, then, Arthur's court in *Ywain and Gawain* is a historical place. It is more perfect than present institutions, a model worthwhile of imitation, although its moral perfection seems unattainable in view of the deterioration in human relationships that has occurred in the meantime. Still, a story developed from such a historical setting must by necessity emphasize the exemplariness of the past. Thus, in contrast to Chrétien who devises a purely fictional model of King Arthur's court – a model, moreover, which contains many ambiguities and unresolved issues – the English author endeavours to provide historical authenticity for his fictional source. And in doing so, he robs the court of its unique identity, which it derives in Chrétien from its ahistoric, literary status.

The setting in the most interesting specimen of Arthurian romance in England, *Sir Gawain and the Green Knight*, is also consciously integrated into the process of history. At the opening of the work the author takes great pains to portray this history from the fall of Troy to the beginning of King Arthur's reign in a grand epic sweep. And at the conclusion of his narrative he follows the reverse procedure, leaving King Arthur's court and ending with the siege of Troy. Once the author has reached the point in time he has chosen for his setting of the romance story, we get a very unusual description of Arthur's court. It is a place of wonders, adventures, and strange happenings. The court, careless and mirthful, is presided over by a young king, who is called 'childgered', that is, 'boyish' or even 'childish' and is as well impetuous or reckless. There is much carousing and merrymaking at this Christmas season. The knights and their ladies, all 'fayre folk in her first age' (54), are festively entertained.[34] Games are played and tournaments are fought. Everyone is in high spirits. There is a decided lack of the stateliness and ceremoniousness so characteristic of

---

[33] Tony Hunt, 'Beginnings, Middles, and Ends: Some Interpretative Problems in Chrétien's *Yvain* and Its Medieval Adaptations', *The Craft of Fiction: Essays on Medieval Poetics*, ed. Leigh A. Arrathoon (Rochester, Mich., 1984), p. 91 suggests some historical parallel: 'There is a constellation of elements which may point to the figure of Arthur as a symbol for Edward I. 'þe Kyng of Yngland, / þat wan al Wales with his hand / and al Scotland' (ll. 7–9) may evoke Edward's conquest of Wales in 1274–86 and his attempted subjugation of Scotland with the Scottish campaign of 1296 or the taking of Stirling Castle in 1304'.

[34] All quotations are taken from *Sir Gawain and the Green Knight*, ed. R.A. Waldron (London, 1970).

Chrétien's description of Arthur's court assembled at high feast days. And, thus, it is not surprising that in *Sir Gawain* Arthur himself initiates the action by his wish for either a marvellous story or an extraordinary occurrence. This motif is common in French post-classical Arthurian romance, where Arthur often refuses to eat until some adventure occurs (as in *Jaufre, La Vengeance Raguidel, Les Merveilles de Rigomer, Floriant et Florete* and, of course, the *Livre de Caradoc,* one of the *Gawain*-poet's putative sources). However, seen against the background of Chrétien's model plot, Arthur's wish for *aventure* negates the very meaning of the court in which all conflicts should be resolved. If Arthur eagerly waits for a challenge from the outside, then he is looking for confrontation in order to find some sort of *raison d'être* for his court and himself. Thus, the justification of the court derives from self-initiated adventures rather than from its status as an ideal social body, the existence of which is constantly valorized by its capacity for neutralizing and integrating the antagonistic forces confronting it. In the French romances this contradiction is usually not recognized. The desire for adventure expressed by the king as the highest representative of the court only functions as a device to initiate the action. Upon Arthur's wish some challenger appears and some knight takes on a now meaningless adventure.

The author of *Sir Gawain and the Green Knight,* however, is aware of this contradiction and he uses it to unmask the hollowness of Arthur and his court. With the sudden appearance of the Green Knight the mood changes, for now the reputation of the Round Table will be put to a test. The representative of an elfish counterworld is unimpressed by the court's glittery façade. Almost mockingly he recounts the rumor – 'as I haf herd carp' (263) – that Arthur's court is considered to be the best of the land. He enumerates all the virtues and accomplishments the court is renowned for in order to demonstrate quickly that such praise is undeserved. When none of the 'berdles chylder' (280) is ready to play his little Christmas game with him, he asks contemptuously: 'Where are now your pride and your conquests, your ferocity and your wrath and your big words? Now the revel and the renown of the Round Table is overcome by one word of one man's speech' (311–14).

When Gawain later on accepts the challenge, the author presents us with an exemplary knight. He is the personification of the courtly ideal combining both chivalric and Christian virtues. Bertilac calls him the 'fautlest freke' (V, 2363), the most faultless man, for in comparison to other men, he is like a pearl among peas. Still, he fails. In order to save his life, he keeps the green girdle – a shortcoming for which he is nicked in the neck, but also excused by his host. One would expect Gawain to be content with this judgement. The recognition of his failure, however, precipitates a deep personal crisis which the hero cannot master. Moreover, Gawain's self-appraisal is made in strictly moral terms from an exclusively Christian vantage point, reminiscent of the moral norms propagated in the *Queste del Saint Graal* of the Vulgate Cycle where the validity of a secular courtly ethos is negated. Consequently, his reintegration into the Table Round is impossible because the court lives by insufficient moral standards. Thus, in the final analysis, Gawain's failure and humiliation must be equated with the devaluation of the Arthurian ideal. The counterworld prevails; even more, the ostentatious courtliness of Bertilac's world has proved to be superior to Arthur's court. But then Bertilac's castle belongs to a fairy world while Arthur's court is firmly integrated into a historical process in decline. Whoever added the Garter motto 'Hony Soyt Qui Mal Pence' may have meant it as note of farewell to an outmoded concept of chivalry which as an imitation of art never had more than a propagandist meaning in real life. At the end of the poem the court of King Arthur becomes curiously blurred with that of Edward III.[35]

As I mentioned before, Chrétien's courtly romances served as the literary model for compositions in both France and England. One of the continuators was Renaut de Beaujeu, whose *Le Bel Inconnu*, written about 1200, enjoyed great popularity in the Middle Ages: we find versions of it in Germany, the *Wigalois* by Wirnt von Grafenberg, and in Italy, the anonymous *Carduino*. There is also an English treatment, *Lybeaus Desconus*, known to Chaucerians from the *Tale of Sir Thopas*. This English adaptation represents another of the possible responses to the model. Here, there is no attempt made to situate Arthur's court in the process of history. Yet, there is also no realization on the part of the English author of its special ideological status. In *Lybeaus Desconus* the court is simply a place in some exotic world where the knights of the Round Table congregate around King Arthur. Young men seeking knighthood must go there in order to receive the official accolade. It is also a place to which damsels in distress will turn to find a champion. And last but not least, it is a place which provides the necessary funds for a young man who has distinguished himself on Arthur's behalf. In short, the nature of the court is completely utilitarian. It serves no other purpose. Thus, after taking the armour from a slain knight, the Fair Unknown (Gawain's illegitimate son) can go there, make his request, and receive instant knighthood. No qualifications are necessary – noble birth (a fact known only to the audience) and appropriate attire seem to be sufficient. Once this is done, the young man can be sent out on his first mission. This happens in spite of the vociferous protests by the young lady seeking help. Although the court should guard its reputation, Arthur has absolutely no concern for the image of the Round Table. Thus, he flatly refuses to provide the damsel in distress with a well-tried knight such as Lancelot, Perceval or Gawain, once he has decided to let Libeaus Desconus have the adventure. The threat that news of this choice will harm the reputation of his court does not make him reconsider his rash decision. Arthur, of course, has to be proven right. Consequently, the young man sends back the defeated adversaries as prisoners to Arthur's court. And after this has happened a few times, Arthur congratulates himself for having made Libeaus a knight of the Round Table (V, 1263–68).[36] He has made a 'prophytable', a 'worthy' choice. In reality, of course, there was no choice; rather, the knighting of Libeaus was an automatic procedure. He came there to demand knighthood, just as he will return there, once he has liberated the damsel in distress, in order to be married at King Arthur's court. Again, the court is conceived of as an institution providing important social services – it has lost its ethical function as the ideal centre of the Arthurian world. In a sense, it has degenerated into a mere stage prop designed to equip the young man desirous of adventure with the essential prerequisite: a certificate of knighthood, to which first money and then a marriage license are added later on. Any court could provide this stamp of approval – the fact that it is Arthur's court is

[35] For Edward's imitation of Arthur see Juliet Vale, *Edward III and Chivalry: Chivalric Society and Its Context 1270–1350* (Woodbridge, 1982).

[36] All quotations are taken from *Lybeaus Desconus*, ed. M. Mills, EETS OS 261 (1969).

only due to the romance's source which featured an Arthurian setting, but in the English adaptation this has no special significance.

A final response to Chrétien's model found in English literature is that of parody or burlesque. This attitude is best expressed in *The Weddynge of Sir Gawene and Dame Ragnell*, one of those many short romances in which Gawain serves as the protagonist. As in *Lybeaus Desconus*, the setting here is strictly unhistorical – there is no attempt made to situate the story within a precise historical context. The locale, however, is that of Inglewood Forest and Carlisle – geographical fixed points frequently found in these brief 15th-century Arthurian narratives. The author of *The Weddynge of Sir Gawene and Dame Ragnell* was obviously familiar with the structural features characteristic of the classical model, for otherwise the playful inversion of its salient features could not be explained.

Although the work appears at first sight to be a serious treatment of Arthurian *matière* – the king's exalted position is immediately stressed in the introduction – the romance turns out to be a burlesque of the genre. In order to save his life, the unarmed King, caught by his archenemy, Sir Gromer Somer Jour, must discover within a year's time what women love most. This demand signals the decline of the action to a subcourtly level, because with the exception of *The Tale of Florent* in Book I of Gower's *Confessio Amantis*, this popular motif was never treated in any serious context in Middle English literature. Arthur's task determines the nature of the ensuing 'quests'. In a clearing in Inglewood Forest the King meets a frightfully ugly hag who promises to provide the life-saving answer if she is rewarded for her services by marrying Sir Gawain. Although Gawain graciously accedes to this request, the crisis is not resolved. On the contrary, the situation for both Arthur and the court is rather precarious, since the old hag insists on a public marriage and, moreover, she proves to be an embarassment because of her boorish behaviour: 'The king of her had great shame' (V,515).[37] The concept of courtliness so intimately associated with Arthur's court is threatened by this intruder, who despite the entreaties by Arthur and the laments by all the knights and ladies of the Round Table insists on a public wedding. The ceremony is announced but turns into a wild orgy. Thus, the courtly feast, the symbolic expression of joy and harmony, becomes grotesquely perverted. The ugliness of the whole scene is punctuated by an *effictio* describing in great detail the ungainliness of the old woman. The wedding of the protagonist, in Chrétien one of the salient points in the development of his narratives, a moment in which personal relationships become social bonds, turns out to be the nadir of this story. The scene is so much dominated by the impossible behaviour of the old hag that even the one missing page of the manuscript could not have remedied the negative impression. And then, her frank exhortation: 'A, Sir Gawen, sin I have you wed, / Shewe me your courtesy in bed;' (V,629–30) illustrates once more her blatant misinterpretation of the concept of courtesy. The author cleverly manipulates the image of Gawain as a potent lover found in post-classical Arthurian romances for his purpose of

---

[37] All quotations are taken from *The Weddynge of Sir Gawene and Dame Ragnell*, ed. Laura Sumner, *Smith College Studies in Modern Language* 5 (1924).

comic devaluation.[38] Thus, on a much lower level here, we find the same argument Bertilac's wife had used in *Sir Gawain and the Green Knight*, even though in that romance Gawain had successfully parried the thrust by pointing out that courtesy means loyalty to one's host and lord. The present Gawain, however, does not have to be asked twice. At his wife's request to give her at least a kiss, he responds: 'I wolle do more / Then for to kisse . . .' (V,638–39). Gawain's readiness to fulfill his wife's bidding is, of course, part of the disenchantment process, but it is also a further example of the inverted value system characteristic of this tale. The final section of the story bears this out. After the transformation of the ugly hag into a radiant beauty, Gawain falls so deeply in love with his wife that he ceases to perform his knightly duties. Instead of proving his excellence in tournaments, he spends all his time in bed with his wife. This classical dilemma which leads to the personal crisis in Chrétien's *Erec* is solved here quite differently. The author grants Gawain five years of pleasure and then lets the lady die in order to finish his tale. The inclusion of this incident proves once more the author's primary interest in the inversion of traditional Arthurian motifs, a tendency everywhere apparent in this burlesque romance.

The treatment of Arthur's court in Middle English Arthurian verse romance takes on its most radical form in *The Weddynge of Sir Gawen and Dame Ragnell*. In this 15th-century work we reach the end of a development which from its very inception had occurred in England under conditions different from those in France. Although the English adapter of Chrétien's *Yvain* took great pains to stress the excellence of King Arthur's court and its normative function, he also deprived it of its special status as a literary model by making the court part of an historical process. Wittingly or unwittingly, he destroyed the concept of its uniqueness so prominent in Chrétien's romances. Once this was done, the way was open for individual interpretations of the function and the meaning of Arthur's court. Although the authors of the romances presuppose a familiarity with its image and reputation on the part of their respective real or implied audience, they use this knowledge for their own purposes. Thus, the norms formulated by the individual authors have replaced the validity of the original model, a change paradigmatic for the development of Arthurian romance in England.

[38] Cf. B.J. Whiting, 'Gawain: His Reputation, His Courtesy and His Appearance in Chaucer's *Squire's Tale*', *MS* 9 (1947) 189–234 and Beate Schmolke-Hasselmann, pp. 86–115.

ROCKY SHORES AND PLEASURE GARDENS:
POETRY vs. MAGIC IN CHAUCER'S *FRANKLIN'S TALE*

V. A. KOLVE

In taking as my subject the rocks and gardens of *The Franklin's Tale*, I promised the convenors of this symposium – no doubt to their great relief – that I would say almost nothing about love or marriage. Though no one would deny the interest or importance of the tale's exploration of those themes, the 'marriage debate' which Kittredge discovered in *The Canterbury Tales* – a debate he declared opened by the Wife of Bath's Prologue and concluded by the Franklin's Tale – has been so endlessly replicated in the pages of twentieth-century criticism there is surely little more needing to be said. We have argued so long about Chaucer's view of the Franklin's 'conclusion' that it's only in the classroom, or in books addressing the general reader, that we dare broach the question again without embarrassment. All likely positions having been expressed, what remains is largely a matter of casting one's vote – and I am content to give my proxy to two members of this symposium, Jill Mann and Helen Cooper. Both have written persuasively about Chaucer's view of love and marriage in *The Franklin's Tale*.[1]

I want to focus instead on the tale's other great subject – that of magic and illusion-making – and on the clerk of Orléans, its master practitioner. If we study him carefully, he may lead us to another subject still – more hidden, but no less urgent – a meditation (in these terms) on the poetic art itself, and on the ethical responsibilities of fiction. I have long thought that the best guide to medieval poetic is the practice of poets, closely read and sympathetically imagined – not the handbooks of poetic or rhetorical art, not the theological defenses of certain preferred kinds of poetry, not the *accessus* (or introductions) to classical texts read in the schools, interesting and useful as all those ancillary texts may be. In *The Franklin's Tale* I think one can see Chaucer carefully mapping out his own best sense of what a poet *is* and *does* against a world of alternative possibilities. And because I have an on-going interest in the relation of literature to the visual arts in the later Middle Ages, I shall use a number of

---

[1] Jill Mann, 'Chaucerian Themes and Style in the *Franklin's Tale*', pp. 133–53 in *Medieval Literature: Chaucer and the Alliterative Tradition* (vol. I, pt. 1 of The New Pelican Guide to English Literature), ed. Boris Ford (Harmondsworth, 1982); Helen Cooper, *Oxford Guides to Chaucer: The Canterbury Tales* (Oxford, 1989), pp. 230–45. The 'goodman of Paris' (*Le Ménagier de Paris*), writing (ca. 1392) to instruct his young wife in the nature of marriage, describes the love that should unite a married couple so: 'And all their special pleasure, their chief desire and their perfect joy is to do pleasure and obedience one to the other, if they love one another'. The fact that mutual obedience in marriage seems to him neither fantastical, wicked, nor darkly humorous, is enough to dismiss those readings of the tale that claim *any* sympathy for its premises is romantic and 'non-medieval'. I quote Eileen Power's translation in her *Medieval People* (New York: 10th ed., 1963), p. 105; she offers an informed and sympathetic introduction to the French book.

pictures to illustrate (perhaps even illuminate) the moral/aesthetic issues Chaucer raises in this tale.

The novelty of my reading might be said to depend upon a single phrase – 'in his studie, ther as his bookes be' (line 1207, repeated with only slight variation at line 1214) – a phrase, so far as I can discover, that has not been closely thought about before. It indicates the place where the clerk demonstrates his magic at Orléans, and thus establishes one of the three major places of this story – the rocks, the garden, the study – through which the narrative moves, and upon which its meaning depends. If each of these *loci* carry iconographic meaning, as I shall attempt to prove, their dialectical relationship may likewise matter. Not for the first time in Chaucer's work, but here in an especially brilliant fashion, poetic practice becomes a form of theory.

Among these three 'places', it is only the clerk's study that has failed to attract sustained critical attention. But its importance depends upon the two others, and so it is with them – with the rocky coast of Brittany and the pleasure garden sited on its banks – that I must begin.

Erwin Panofsky, in his pioneering studies of iconography in the visual arts, long ago excluded most landscape painting (landscapes painted for their own sake, 'independent' landscapes) from his purview. Such painting, he said, like the depiction of food and wine and flowers in still-life (*nature morte*), represents a late development in the history of art, and is notable for its freedom from cultic, textual, conventional or symbolic meaning.[2] Landscapes, in particular, do not become an independent subject until the 16th century, and remain rare for a century thereafter.[3] In poetry, however, the matter is far different. Medieval romancers had long before found ways of justifying the detailed representation of landscape – using it to mirror (and thus explore) the inner psychological

---

2 Erwin Panofsky, *Studies in Iconology: Humanistic Themes in the Art of the Renaissance* (Oxford, 1939; repr. New York, 1972). Panofsky alludes to these later kinds of painting (independent landscape and *nature morte*) in setting out his three-part analysis of how we come to understand the sense of a work of art: (1) a *pre-iconographic* recognition of primary or natural subject matter (recognizing an apple as an apple, a hill as a hill); (2) an *iconographic* recognition of secondary or conventional subject matter – images, stories, allegories, generally text-based, which must be learned and correctly identified; and (3) an analysis of 'intrinsic meaning or content', which he elsewhere calls *iconological*, and which finds in the artifact 'those underlying principles which reveal the basic attitude of a nation, a period, a class, a religious or philosophical persuasion – unconsciously qualified by one personality and condensed into one work' (pp. 3–17; I quote from p. 7). Panofsky believed that in European landscape painting, still-life and genre, 'the whole sphere of secondary or conventional subject matter is eliminated' (p. 8). For problems with this leap from the first to the third kind of analysis, see Jean Arrouye, 'Archéologie de l'iconologie', in *Pour un Temps: Erwin Panofsky*, ed. Jacques Bonnet (Paris, 1983), pp. 71–83, esp. 73–74.

3 Paris, Bibl. Natl. MS fr. 1586, a sumptuous manuscript containing the complete literary works of Guillaume de Machaut, made ca. 1350, may offer (on fol. 103) an early precursor. It illustrates the enchanted garden of *Le Dit du Lion* as a kind of wild forest alive with animals and birds, thus providing (in the judgment of François Avril) 'one of the oldest independent landscapes in European painting'. But this picture too is linked to literature, and would not have been painted without that (pre)text. Avril publishes it in colour in his *Manuscript Painting at the Court of France: The Fourteenth Century (1310–1380)* (New York, 1978), pl. 26; see pp. 36, 84, 90 for details. See Reindert L. Falkenburg, *Joachim Patinir: Landscape as an Image of the Pilgrimage of Life*, trans. Michael Hoyle, *Oculi* 2, (Amsterdam/Philadelphia, 1988), for the claim that Patinir (ca. 1485–1524) created the first 'autonomous landscapes'.

experience of their characters.[4] They moved outward to move inward, describing or invoking a landscape simply because it could stand for something larger. Almost never (apart from school exercises imitating set-pieces from classical poetry) was landscape description valued as an end in itself.[5]

It was in this vein that Charles Owen, Jr. some years ago taught us to recognize the degree to which the rocks along the Breton coast take on symbolic meaning within the Franklin's story.[6] Their significance, he noticed, is largely pyschological. When Dorigen's husband, Arveragus, is away in England on a two-year campaign, the rocks (which threaten the safe passage and harbouring of shipmen and seafarers) come to represent in her mind all 'the menace of natural forces to her husband's life'. Her marital happiness gets caught upon a question: How shall he ever return to her safely, with those rocks so threatening there? Grieving and despairing, she invests the rocks with meaning far beyond any specific or intrinsic danger:

> 'Eterne God, that thurgh thy purveiaunce
> Ledest the world by certein governaunce,
> In ydel, as men seyn, ye no thyng make.
> But, Lord, thise grisly feendly rokkes blake,
> That semen rather a foul confusion
> Of werk than any fair creacion
> Of swich a parfit wys God and a stable,
> Why han ye wroght this werk unresonable?
> For by this werk, south, north, ne west, ne eest,
> Ther nys yfostred man, ne bryd, ne beest;
> It dooth no good, to my wit, but anoyeth.
> Se ye nat, Lord, how mankynde it destroyeth?
> An hundred thousand bodyes of mankynde
> Han rokkes slayn, al be they nat in mynde,
> Which mankynde is so fair part of thy werk
> That thou it madest lyk to thyn owene merk.
> Thanne semed it ye hadde a greet chiertee
> Toward mankynde; but how thanne may it bee
> That ye swiche meenes make it to destroyen,
> Whiche meenes do no good, but evere anoyen?
> . . .
> This rokkes sleen myn herte for the feere.'   (865–84; 893)

This meditation on a landscape – characterized by Chaucer in line 844 as 'hire derke *fantasye*' – is a kind of truncated theodicy, one that questions the ways of God to man, but cannot get beyond a formulation of the question itself. In Dorigen's mind, the rocks come to stand for everything in the world that seems counter to human values, threatening to human enterprises, and inimical to the happiness of two lovers – a man and woman who (in a very modern way) have invented their own ceremony and covenant of marriage.

---

4 In Arthurian literature above all: e.g., the fierce penitential landscape Gawain travels through in his Advent quest for the Green Castle, in Fitt II of *Sir Gawain and the Green Knight*.
5 See, e. g., Chapter 10, 'The Ideal Landscape', in Ernst Robert Curtius, *European Literature and the Latin Middle Ages*, trans. Willard R. Trask (New York, 1953).
6 'The Crucial Passages in Five of the *Canterbury Tales*: A Study in Irony and Symbol', *JEGP* 52 (1953) 294–311; little more than two pages (295–97) are devoted to *The Franklin's Tale*, but they are remarkable in their insight.

Figure 1: The rocky coast of Pedmark (Penmarc'h) in Brittany.
(Photo: Ellin M. Kelly)

In fact, the rocks are not quite adequate to the heavy significance Dorigen would lay upon them. The story will ultimately make that clear, as would a visit to the place where Chaucer sets his story: Pedmark – modern Penmarc'h – on Finistère in Brittany. Since few Chaucerians seem ever to have journeyed to the site, I reproduce (courtesy of Professor Ellin M. Kelly) a photograph of it here (**Figure 1**): a low beach covered by black rocks, low enough (perhaps) to be coverable by a very high tide, and one may see some greater rocks far out from the coast (*les roches de Penmarc'h*). But (as will soon be clear) Chaucer's site in other major details does not correspond at all.[7] We are dealing with an invented landscape, with a meaning to be determined.

Chaucer takes care to show us the larger scene first, part of it through Dorigen's eyes:

> Now stood hire castel faste by the see,
> And often with hire freendes walketh shee
> Hire to disporte upon the bank an heigh,
> Where as she many a ship and barge seigh
> Seillynge hir cours, where as hem liste go.   (847–51

[7] **Figure 1:** I am grateful to Professor Kelly for sharing with me her first-hand knowledge of the site. *The Riverside Chaucer*, 3d ed., ed. Larry D. Benson (Boston, 1987), p. 897 (n.801) contains relevant bibliography, and notes that 'the nearest high shore is at Concarneau, 35 km. away'. Chaucer may have simply taken the name Pedmark from a source – written or oral – and invented the rest, or he may have conflated some personal knowledge of the site with that of other parts of the Finistère coast, where cliffs and rocks meet the sea much as they do in his description of the place: see, e.g., Michel Renouard and Hervé Champollion, *Bretagne* (Rennes, 1984), pp. 64–65 (which shows a modern ship wrecked against rocks), 68–69 (with its solitary figure standing high, overlooking the sea), and 70, 72–73, 77, 78 (all in handsome colour). Bernard Henry and Marianne Henry, *Villages de Bretagne* (Paris, 1985), includes a view, in colour, pp. 84–85, looking down upon the Penmarc'h and Saint-Guénolé; it is taken from the lantern of the present lighthouse (p. 87), there being no 'bank on heigh' available (then or now). Michel Renouard, *Nouveau guide de Bretagne* (Rennes, 1982), pp. 226–27, offers a useful description of the town; his colour plate, pp. 40–41, (not of Penmarc'h) again offers something much closer to the landscape of Chaucer's poem.

This sea-traffic is represented as sailing without impediment, a marine-scape of boats moving freely 'wherever it pleases them to go', no rocks mentioned. And the whole is seen from a bank *high above*, a walk-with-a-view where she and her friends promenade for pleasure's sake ('hire to desporte'). It is the absence of a certain ship, not danger to *all* ships, that comes to obsess her – and with that narrowing of emotional focus comes the first notice of the 'grisly feendly rokkes blake' (in the meditation quoted above). Their meaning is more attributed than intrinsic – an important fact, as other details soon make clear.

For just as there had been no mention of the rocks when Arveragus left for England, so there is no mention of them when he returns safely home – though his homecoming preceeds by some considerable time (perhaps two years) Aurelius' visit to the clerk of Orléans and the rocks' subsequent 'removal'. The return is narrated in just half a line – he 'is comen hoom' (1089) – and marital happiness is renewed. The rocks, in short, pose little *real* danger in the poem: they are absent from our first view of the seacoast, they are absent in the notation of Arveragus' return, and they are 'apparently' absent for a week or two, when Aurelius claims his reward. Their importance is iconographic rather than literal: they are made to stand for something by the human mind.[8] Chaucer allows Dorigen to create her own 'iconography of the rocks', and then (by means of narrative) discover how little general truth she has understood in their terms. Her first conclusion is despair.

And so her friends lead her to the poem's second major 'place' – a garden 'ther bisyde' 'ful of leves and of floures', where

> . . . craft of mannes hand so curiously
> Arrayed hadde this gardyn, trewely,
> That nevere was ther gardyn of swich prys
> But if it were the verray paradys.
> The odour of floures and the fresshe sighte
> Wolde han maked any herte lighte
> That evere was born, but if to greet siknesse
> Or to greet sorwe helde it in distresse,
> So ful it was of beautee with plesaunce.   (909–17)

Unlike the world outside its walls – which has come to be symbolized by the rocks – the garden contains nothing not delightful. It is a human artifact, made by 'craft of mannes hand', from which all that is harsh, threatening, and ugly has been excluded.[9] Medieval pleasure gardens were made intentionally reminiscent of Eden – 'the verray paradys', with its trees, birds, animals, and four

---

8 The rocks may draw something of their symbolism from a tradition that declared this world a tempestuous 'sea of fortune', with Fortune's House set on a rocky island in its midst; Chaucer knew versions of the tradition from (*inter alia*) Boethius's *Consolation of Philosophy*, Alain de Lille's *Anticlaudianus*, Jean de Meun's continuation of the *Roman de la Rose*, and Guillaume de Deguileville's *Pelerinage de la vie humaine*. I have written on the tradition at some length, with pictorial evidence, in my *Chaucer and the Imagery of Narrative* (Stanford, 1984), pp. 325–33. See Guillaume de Lorris and Jean de Meun, *The Romance of the Rose*, trans. Charles Dahlberg (Princeton, 1971), pp. 118–22 (ll. 5921–6174) for the relevant passage, and fig. 30 for an illustration; John V. Fleming, *The* Roman de la Rose: *A Study in Allegory and Iconography* (Princeton, 1969), fig. 31, publishes another. But I do not think this powerfully relevant: in *The Franklin's Tale* the rocks must be seen as no more than rocks, if we are to assess the changing meanings Dorigen attributes to them.

9 See Derek Pearsall and Elizabeth Salter, *Landscapes and Seasons of the Medieval World*

rivers. And they were made intentionally reminiscent as well of the enclosed garden and fountain of *The Song of Songs* – a garden at once the symbol and the habitation of Christ's beloved.[10] Because of these textual relationships, such gardens readily carry iconographic meaning, as Panofsky would have been the first to recognize: medieval gardens communicate a symbolic significance only dimly potential in natural landscape itself. The garden, we may say, welcomes and expresses all that is young and beautiful and happy; to other conditions it offers consolation and cure. **Figure 2**, from an English manuscript of Marco Polo's *Li Livres du Graunt Caam*, made ca. 1400, shows the 'garden paradise' of the Old Man of the Mountain, illustrating a text that brings together this whole complex of ideas – some of them no doubt based on travellers' accounts of real gardens they had seen in Persia, India, and the exotic East.[11] It illustrates Book I, chap. 22 of the work, which describes a 'luxurious garden, stored with every delicious fruit and every fragrant shrub that could be procured', that lies between two lofty mountains, maintained by a Persian chief who worships Mahomet. The description is worth quoting at some length: 'Palaces of various sizes and forms were erected in different parts of the grounds, ornamented with works in gold, with paintings, and with furniture of rich silks. By means of small conduits contrived in these buildings, streams of wine, milk, honey, and some of pure water, were seen to flow in every direction. The inhabitants of these palaces were elegant and beautiful damsels, accomplished in the arts of singing, playing upon all sorts of musical instruments, dancing, and [other skills] especially those of dalliance and amorous allurement. Clothed in rich

(Toronto, 1973), esp. Chap. 4 ('The Enclosed Garden'). Their citations of Chrétien de Troyes' *Cligès* and Boccaccio's *Decameron*, pp. 76 and 82, are particularly apposite here.

[10] See Teresa McLean, *Medieval English Gardens* (New York, 1980), pp. 120–27, on this double heritage of the medieval love garden. In her judgment, the *hortus conclusus* of *The Song of Songs* ultimately 'overshadowed its archetypal partner, the Garden of Eden, and became the dominant image of Paradise and Love. . . . it was an earthly garden as well as a heavenly one and, like Eden, was interpreted both representatively and allegorically, as an image of human and of divine love' (p. 121). Paul F. Watson, *The Garden of Love in Tuscan Art of the Early Renaissance* (Philadelphia, 1979), is useful, esp. Chapter 6 on the characteristic architecture and activities of the garden. Marilyn Stokstad and Jerry Stannard, *Gardens of the Middle Ages* (Lawrence, Kansas, 1983), offer many images. John Harvey, *Mediaeval Gardens* (Beaverton, Oregon, 1981) surveys changing ideas of the garden from classical times through the high Middle Ages. But especially recommended is *Medieval Gardens*, intro. Elisabeth Blair MacDougall (Washington, D.C., 1986), a collection of essays published by the Dumbarton Oaks Research Center, rich in learning and intellectual surmise: the essays by Paul Meyvaert, Anne Hagopian van Buren, Marilyn Stokstad, John V. Fleming, Derek Pearsall, and Brian E. Daley are of particular relevance here. For illuminations showing Eden as a walled garden with turfed bench or with fountain, see, e.g., Millard Meiss, *French Painting in the Time of Jean de Berry: The Boucicaut Master* (New York, 1968), figs. 380 and figs. 379, 381 respectively. For a French translation of *The Song of Songs* in which the bride and bridegroom are shown as elegant medieval lovers strolling in a walled garden, see London, Brit. Lib. MS Royal 15.D.III, fol. 297v.

[11] **Figure 2**: Oxford, MS Bodley 264, fol. 226 (a turn-of-the-century addition to the famous Flemish manuscript containing the *Romance of Alexander* in French, finished by its illuminator in 1344 and owned by Thomas, duke of Gloucester, d. 1397). I quote from *The Travels of Marco Polo* (New York, n.d.), pp. 48–50, a volume furnished with medieval illustrations. For the equivalent material in *Mandeville's Travels*, ed. M.C. Seymour (Oxford, 1967), see pp. 200–2.

Figure 2: A garden-paradise (English, ca. 1400). Oxford, MS. Bodley 264, fol. 226.
(By permission of the Bodleian Library)

dresses they were seen continually sporting and amusing themselves in the garden and pavilions, their female guardians being confined within doors and never suffered to appear'. The garden seems infinitely desirable, until we learn that the Old Man of the Mountain has formed this garden for political reasons. It is his custom to tell the young men of his kingdom that, if they are brave and utterly obedient in his service, he can admit them to paradise. He makes good on his word by drugging them, bringing them into this garden where sensual and erotic pleasures overwhelm them for four or five days, and then drugging them again before returning them to ordinary life. From that time forward they are his to command, for the experience has ravished them. They do not recognize the garden as a false paradise.

The standard medieval pleasure garden – the garden of romance literature and courtly relaxation – shares many of these charms, and is potentially (if not necessarily) as dangerous. It is characteristically a place of *artificial* beauty, set apart from the real world by garden walls, entered by a narrow gate, and ruled by geometry – however natural the trees and grasses and flowers in formal beds within those walls. Little is untouched, untrained, or untutored in this world. Here love talk and witty conversation replace earnest discourse, music and song often replace speech, and dance makes an art of motion. The God of Love's 'carole' being danced in the late fourteenth-century *Roman de la Rose*

Figure 3: The God of Love's carol-dance in the *Roman de la Rose*
(French, late fourteenth-century). Oxford, Bodley MS. Douce 332, fol. 8v.
(By permission of the Bodleian Library)

illustration reproduced as **Figure 3**[12] – we must imagine for ourselves the garden walls, previously described and depicted – offers a kinetic image of those values: social, highly patterned, it expresses life and love in idealized terms, protected and free from care. As in the garden of *The Franklin's Tale*, the governing mood – and mode – is *play*.[13]

Two of the three signifying locations in *The Franklin's Tale* are thus set in binary opposition to each other: what one includes the other excludes, and vice versa – a juxtaposition of settings whose conflicting claims as registrations of truth will be tested by the action played out between them. In fourth-century Egypt, the desert father Abraham defended his monastic vocation in terms of a similar dialectic, likewise expressed in terms of landscape. 'We are not ignorant', he wrote, 'that in our land there are fair and secret places, where there be fruit trees in plenty and the graciousness of gardens . . . . But we have despised all these and with them all the luxurious pleasure of the world: we have joy in this desolation, and to all delight do we prefer the dread vastness of this solitude . . . .'[14]

Within the bounds of *The Franklin's Tale* – a highly specific fiction – Chaucer had no reason to put his elegant, courtly young people to such a choice.

---

[12] **Figure 3:** Oxford, Bodley MS Douce 332, fol. 8v. As is often true in 14th-century MSS of the *Roman*, once the walled garden has been depicted, it may or may not reappear in illustrations of the action that takes place within it; for a picture from this same MS that shows the garden walls, see Otto Pächt and J.J.G. Alexander, *Illuminated Manuscripts in the Bodleian Library Oxford*, Vol. I (Oxford, 1966), pl. XLVII, fig. 619a; cf. fig. 612. Bryan Holme, *Medieval Pageant* (London, 1987), pp. 64–65, publishes (in colour) two late 15th-century Flemish illustrations to the poem that show dancing and music-making within the garden-walls proper; John V. Fleming, 'The Garden of the *Roman de la Rose*: Vision of Landscape or Landscape of Vision?', in *Medieval Gardens*, reproduces one of these (Paris, Bibl. Natl. MS fr. 19153, fol. 7) in black-and-white, and includes a valuable discussion of the geometry (square vs. round) of the poem's garden; see also his fig. 2. Figure 12 of the present essay is also relevant.

[13] Emphatically established in *The Franklin's Tale* by ll. 849, 897, 900, 905, 988, 1015.

[14] From the *Collationes* of Cassian of Marseilles, 'Of Mortification', spoken by the abbot Abraham in response to Cassian's confession that he was homesick for all the pleasures of life that he had left behind; trans. by Helen Waddell, *The Desert Fathers* (1936; Ann Arbor, 1957), p. 160.

Figure 4: A harbour with rocky cliffs (Netherlandish, ca. 1470).
Detail from a panel painting 'Madonna and child with an anonymous
benefactress and St Mary Magdalen', Liège, Musée Diocésain.

But as the maker of many fictions – not all of them (like this one) set 'in pagan
times', not all of them courtly romances – Chaucer knew that *for the poet* every
fiction implies some decision of this kind. The implications of this antithesis
(garden/desert here standing in for garden/rocks) go deep. Artistic and ethical
choice overshadow each other, in ways that become clear only when we have
left the rocks and the garden for the tale's other major setting: the magician's
study in Orléans.

But first we must pause to notice (again with Charles Owen, and affirmed by
many after him) a narrative reversal that greatly complicates the meaning of
these two opposed settings in *The Franklin's Tale*. Once Dorigen has made her
rash promise – linking her destiny to Aurelius for the first time – the iconic
values of the harsher location – the *locus non amoenus* – change. From this
point forward, the happiness of Dorigen's marriage *depends* upon the rocks
remaining in place; they have become foundational to it, an essential guarantee
of her fidelity in love. The garden, as an image for the joy that is possible in this
world, is *secured* by the rocks' continuance.[15] It is now their disappearance that
would be terrible.

---

[15] In Chaucer's *Knight's Tale*, Emily's walled garden *adjoins* the knights' prison tower, creating

In real terms, we notice that upon Arveragus's return the rocks shrink once again to their proper size in the larger landscape of the poem, little more problematic (we may guess) than the juxtaposition of harbour, cliff and pleasure garden shown in **Figure 4**, a detail from a fifteenth-century Burgundian painting now in Liège.[16] Only Dorigen's rash promise to Aurelius preserves her sense of the rocks' significance as an iconographic force within the tale.

Aurelius, believing with Dorigen that removal of those rocks is an 'impossible' (1009), falls into a love-sickness near to death. He lingers so for two years and more, until his brother proposes a remedy – and brings the action of the poem to its third significant setting. Thinking back on his days at the university at Orléans – where 'yonge clerkes' were famously 'lykerous / To reden artes that been curious' (1119)[17] – Aurelius's brother remembers seeing a book of 'natural' magic on the desk of a fellow student. Through such magic (it occurs to him) Aurelius might accomplish the impossible task, and lay claim to the love Dorigen foolishly vowed.

Natural magic ('magyk natureel') – the key term here – was a large and inclusive concept. Though in the present context it probably means little more than astrology, predictive or manipulative in kind, we can only be certain that it excludes magic dependent on diabolic powers [**Figure 5**], the sort shown in this English illustration (mid-fourteenth century) of a clerk observing the heavens, his one hand on a book, the other gesturing toward a demon just below.[18] Whatever the 'magyk natureel' Aurelius thinks he's buying – and whatever exact brand the clerk of Orléans will use to make the rocks seem to go away – it is not of this demonic sort.

But it *is* magic – that is Chaucer's word for it – and it is further complicated by the speech that follows, in which Aurelius's brother recalls still other evidence for thinking that some such solution might suffice. (Virtually every detail will matter to my argument). Aurelius's brother muses thus:

> "My brother shal be warisshed hastily;
> For I am siker that ther be sciences
> By whiche men make diverse apparences,

a comparable iconographic setting. There too an apparently binary opposition (life's possibilities, imagined at two extremes) first reverses its values, and then reveals at its core a profound unity. See my analysis of this setting in *Chaucer and the Imagery of Narrative* (Stanford, 1984), Chap. III.

[16] **Figure 4**: From a panel-painting by the Master of the view of St Gudule, 'Madonna and child with an anonymous benefactress and St Mary Magdalene', ca. 1470, in Liège, Musée Diocésain. The full painting, of which this is only a tiny detail, is reproduced in colour, p. 14 (fig. 2), in Walter Prevenier and Wim Blockmans, *The Burgundian Netherlands*, trans. Peter King and Yvette Mead (Cambridge, 1986).

[17] J. Burke Severs, 'Chaucer's Clerks', in *Chaucer and Middle English Studies in honour of Rossell Hope Robbins*, ed. Beryl Rowland (London, 1974), pp. 146–47, notes 'two well-known facts concerning the University of Orléans' in Chaucer's time: that its curriculum was entirely devoted to law, both canon and civil; and that it was 'a hotbed of astrological and magical studies, not formally, but informally'. He quotes a 1396 French text that refers to this double reputation, honourable for law, scandalous for 'nigromancie' (the devil finds his disciples there).

[18] **Figure 5**: London, Brit. Lib. MS Royal 6 E. VI, fol. 396v, from an encyclopedia, *Omne Bonum*. A related miniature, with two devils, is reproduced in colour by Francis King, *Magic: The Western Tradition, Art and Cosmos* (New York, 1975), fig. 16.

Figure 5: Black magic: a clerk studies the heavens with demonic assistance
(English, mid-fourteenth century). London, Brit. Lib. MS. Royal 6 E. VI, fol. 396v.
(By permission of the British Library)

> Swich as thise subtile tregetoures pleye.
> For ofte at feestes have I wel herd seye
> That tregetours withinne an halle large
> Have maad come in a water and a barge,
> And in the halle rowen up and doun.
> Somtyme hath semed come a grym leoun;
> And somtyme floures sprynge as in a mede;
> Somtyme a vyne, and grapes white and rede;
> Somtyme a castel, al of lym and stoon;
> And whan hem lyked, voyded it anon.
> Thus semed it to every mannes sighte."   (1138–51)

Aurelius's brother recites this catalogue of illusions ('apparences') with excitement and wonder – and Chaucer surely meant his first audiences to wonder at them too, though perhaps in a specially qualified way. For, as Laura Hibbard Loomis long ago demonstrated, at least some part of these marvels recapitulates an actual event, a great feast given in 1378 by the French king Charles V in honour of his uncle, the Emperor Charles IV of Luxembourg. The visit is recorded in a deluxe manuscript of the *Grandes Chroniques de France* – in unusually detailed prose, as well as in the miniature reproduced here [**Figure**

Figure 6: Entertainment at a royal feast, Paris, 1378
(Charles V's *Grandes Chroniques de France*). Paris, Bibl. Natl. MS. fr. 2813,
fol. 473v. (By permission of the Bibliothèque Nationale)

6].[19] It shows the royal personages seated beneath canopies ornamented with
fleur-de-lys, the bearded Emperor on the left, the King of France in the middle,
and the Emperor's son and heir, Wencelas, on the right. A short play, the siege
and conquest of Jerusalem by Godefroy de Bouillon, is being enacted before
them as an *entremès*, an entertainment between courses at a banquet. On the

---

[19] **Figure 6**: Paris, Bibl. Natl. MS fr. 2813, fol. 473v. See Laura Hibbard Loomis, 'Secular
Dramatics in the Royal Palace, Paris, 1378, 1389, and Chaucer's "Tregetoures" ', *Speculum*
33 (1958) 242–55; she prints the prose description of the feast on p. 246 (and on pp. 249–50
Froissart's account of a 1389 *entrémes* intended to stage the Siege [or Fall] of Troy, but
abruptly cancelled by royal command due to dangerous overcrowding of the hall). Avril,
Manuscript Painting at the Court of France, pl. 34, publishes the picture in colour (commentary, p. 107), as does Charles Sterling, *La peinture médièvale à Paris 1300–1500*, I (Paris,
1987), p. 247 (commentary and other illuminations from the MS, pp. 245–49).

right a castle is being scaled, with one soldier already hurled down from its fortifications. From the left a ship (no doubt with hidden wheels)[20] sails toward them, those wheels hidden by painted waves. A black-clad monk, Peter the Hermit, who preached the First Crusade, is its only remaining passenger, the others being already engaged in the assault. Though the picture records something worth wondering at – the feast was so famous there is every likelihood Chaucer knew of it[21] – that 'something' worthy of wonder has nothing to do with magic as we normally define it. It represents instead a triumph of the mimetic, scenic, and mechanical arts, joined together to create an 'apparence'. The 'subtile tregetours' to which Aurelius's brother attributes this spectacle were in fact 'actors, craftsmen, artisans mecaniques, who, in effective unison, produced spectacular results'.[22] Yet it's also clear he thinks of the spectacle as a kind of magic, brought to mind by memory of the clerk's book 'of magyk natureel'. Something rather subtle – or very muddled – is going on.

The picture before us documents perfectly well the 'water and a barge' in the brother's recital, as well as a castle made to seem 'al of lym and stoon'. The boat and waves could be easily 'voided' – pulled out of sight – when the eating and drinking resume, and so too perhaps the castle itself, though its position to the side may indicate it was built to remain in place throughout the feast. The other 'wonders' he catalogues have historical equivalents as well: actors dressed in lion costumes, pre-Fabergé mechanical flowers that close and unclose, lifelike models of grapes and vines, can all be paralleled in medieval accounts of courtly entertainments, state pageantry, and royal entries.[23] Medieval romances describe other 'wonders' still, many of them well within the range of such art: mechanical giants, for example, and magic storms; bronze singing birds, and a golden stag operated by means of a bellows.[24] The Sketchbook of Villard de Honnecourt, dating from the second quarter of the thirteenth century, shows [**Figure 7**: above left] a wheel-and-pulley mechanism labelled 'How to make an angel keep pointing his finger toward the sun', and [bottom left] another device,

---

[20] The 1378 account tells us that the pageant-structures were moved about by men concealed within them, and the 1389 account specifies the use of hidden wheels. See Loomis, pp. 244, 250.

[21] Loomis, p. 244, describes some possible ways in which Chaucer might have heard of the 1378 feast, and on p. 247 does the same for that of 1389.

[22] Loomis, p. 244.

[23] William Tydeman, *The Theatre in the Middle Ages* (Cambridge, 1978), p. 71ff., discusses other medieval and early-Renaissance occasions graced with spectacular effects, including, e.g., the coronation banquet of Martin I of Aragon in Saragoza in 1399.

[24] See Merriam Sherwood, 'Magic and Mechanics in Medieval Fiction', *SP* 44 (1947) 567–92. The gifts brought to King Cambyuskan in *The Squire's Tale* – a brass horse, a glass mirror, a golden ring, and a naked sword, each of which has 'magic' properties – deserve mention here. (They serve, moreover, as a prelude to the Franklin's treatment of magic, for his tale both succeeds and in a sense completes the Squire's). The gifts excite much speculation, including the following comment concerning the horse of brass: 'it is rather lyk / An apparence ymaad by som magyk, / As jogelours pleyen at thise feestes grete' (217–19). But there too Chaucer refuses to settle for so easy an explanation, dismissing it in lines 220–24 (together with other rumours and guesses) as typical of 'lewed peple' attempting to understand matters beyond them. Helen Cooper, 'Magic that Does Not Work', *Medievalia et Humanistica* n.s. 7 (1976) 131–46, writes interestingly about magic in medieval romances, including *The Franklin's Tale* (on p. 141).

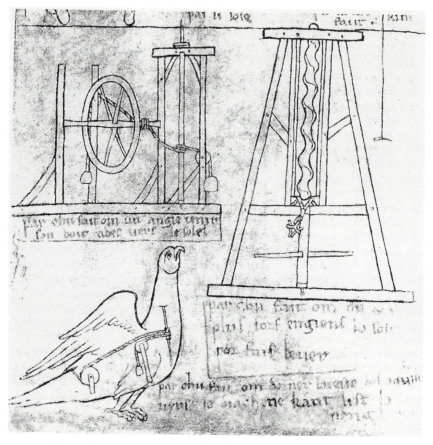

Figure 7: Automata from the Sketchbook of Villard de Honnecourt
(French, ca. 1225–50). Paris, Bibl. Natl. MS. fr. 19093, fol. 22v (detail).
(By permission of the Bibliothèque Nationale)

for the inside of an eagle lectern, labelled 'How to make the eagle face the Deacon while the Gospel is being read'.[25]

Automata of this kind were often confused in the popular mind with magic and the occult, not just in the Arab world where they seem to have originated,[26] but in Western Europe as well. Though their real nature would have been clear to Chaucer and to many in his courtly audiences – as the brother's reference to 'tregetours' and noble 'feestes' makes clear – we should honour the fact that

---

[25] **Figure 7:** Paris, Bibl. Natl. MS fr. 19093, fol. 22v (detail). For a convenient facsimile and translation of the whole book, see *The Sketchbook of Villard de Honnecourt*, ed. Theodore Bowie (Bloomington, 1959); the page before us appears there as pl. 59. It shows in addition (top row, not reproduced here) 'How to make a saw operate itself; How to make a crossbow which never misses', and (to the right, in our detail) 'How to make the most powerful engine for lifting weights'.

[26] See Naomi Miller, 'Paradise Regained: Medieval Garden Fountains', pp. 143–44 n. 23, in *Medieval Gardens* (Dumbarton Oaks), for a basic bibliography.

Chaucer makes no explicit mention of machines. The rhetorical emphasis of the passage is, instead, overwhelmingly on mystery and illusion: 'Thus *semed it* to every mannes sighte.'

That is the first of the 'magic shows' in the tale – a retrospective report, based on memory and hearsay:

> "For ofte at feestes *have I wel herd seye*
> That tregetours withinne an halle large
> Have maad come in a water and a barge,
> And in the halle rowen up and doun." (1142–5)

The second show takes place in the tale's real time, in Orléans at the house of the clerk, and is in several ways grander and more mysterious by far. Again, the passage needs to be read in its full detail:

> He shewed hym, er he wente to sopeer,
> Forestes, parkes ful of wilde deer;
> Ther saugh he hertes with hir hornes hye,
> The gretteste that evere were seyn with ye.
> He saugh of hem an hondred slayn with houndes,
> And somme with arwes blede of bittre woundes.
> He saugh, whan voyded were thise wilde deer,
> Thise fauconers upon a fair ryver,
> That with hir haukes han the heron slayn.
>   Tho saugh he knyghtes justyng in a playn;
> And after this he dide hym swich plesaunce
> That he hym shewed his lady on a daunce,
> On which hymself he daunced, as hym thoughte.
> And whan this maister that this magyk wroughte
> Saugh it was tyme, he clapte his handes two,
> And farewel! Al oure revel was ago.
> And yet remoeved they nevere out of the hous. . . . (1189–205)

Chaucer's rhetoric serves to *link* the two 'magic shows', describing each as a random list of wonders, and emphasizing their common evanescence: both can be 'voided' in an instant, at their presenters' will (1150, 1195). For a long time critics took their cue from that rhetorical parallelism, treating the two shows as one, seeking a single explanation for all their singular detail, and accepting both (despite the Loomis essay) at face value, as 'magic' capaciously defined. Such wonders, after all, are to be expected in romances; the 'tregetoures' tricks merely make more credible the show. But two recent essays – inspired by Loomis, but going well beyond her – seek to deny the 'magic' of these shows altogether, reducing them to entertainments of an entirely conventional, non-mysterious kind.

Anthony Luengo, in 'Magic and Illusion in *The Franklin's Tale*',[27] sees both shows as 'stage magic' – a 'theatre of illusion' made mysterious by astrological jargon alone. The clerk of Orléans is a 'tregetoure' whose magic show depends on 'skillfully constructed and lavishly decorated mobile pageant wagons upon which actors and mechanical figures [play] out a simple scenario'. 'One can reasonably assume', he goes on, 'that the members of Chaucer's audience would have recognized the 'automates' for what they were', 'a common part of both

---

[27] In *JEPG* 77 (1978) 1–16; I quote from pp. 1, 4, 7, 9, 16.

indoor and outdoor dramatic entertainments in England and on the Continent', contrivances that were highly mobile – 'being wheeled and manually drawn or pushed from within' – and making use of 'stock motifs, the most popular being those of the castle, the forest, and the ship at sea'. That presumed recognition on the part of Chaucer's courtly audience becomes for Luengo the key to reading the poem: because neither the Franklin nor the characters in his fiction are of the court, they do not understand what they're talking about or witnessing within the tale. 'In confusing scientific astrology with black magic, [the Franklin] betrays his ignorance of contemporary thought. In failing to recognize a theatrical presentation, he betrays his ignorance of courtly entertainment'. In Luengo's reading, this failure 'to separate appearance from reality' is the real subject of the tale, an ironic exposure of the pretensions and limitations of its teller.[28]

Mary Flowers Braswell, in 'The Magic of Machinery: A Context for Chaucer's *Franklin's Tale*',[29] puts her emphasis less on actors and pageant wagons than on automata: ingenious machines meant to amuse the rich and noble, machines whose history as an art form is too little known. 'A bastard genre', she calls it, 'not completely espoused either by art historians or by technologists'.[30] Braswell reminds us that Chaucer was a scientific writer, responsible for a treatise on the astrolabe and very likely the author of another on the equatorie of the planets. His responsibilities as Clerk of the King's Works in 1389, and as Commissioner of Walls and Ditches along the Thames from Greenwich to Woolwich in 1390, would have necessitated some knowledge of mechanics and machines. And his role as courtier and court/poet would have given him access to many elaborate rituals and entertainments – among them (in Braswell's well-chosen example) the experience of watching a mechanical golden angel bend down to offer Richard II his crown during his coronation ceremony.[31] Such things, she says rightly, were 'an integral part of late medieval culture. On the simplest level, a manor lord could entertain his dinner guests by means of a magic trick: red wine turning white, a cooked chicken dancing in a pan, or four and twenty blackbirds emerging live from a pie and flying into the room. In church, Eucharistic doves with moveable wings, such as that in the Cloisters Museum in New York, might have given new impetus to the Mass. Pageant wagons, ferocious dragons with moveable tongues, propelled by

---

[28] As will soon be clear, I think that this blurring of several kinds of 'magic' into a single category is essential *to the tale and its issues*, urgent and interesting in its own right. I don't think it's meant to characterize the Franklin as ignorant, provincial, or confused. A good deal of modern criticism to the contrary, I suspect the poet would have acknowledged a deep kinship with the Franklin – the pilgrim whose social class and aspirations, temperament, courtesy, and *savoir faire* seem most to resemble what the life-records (and other poems) suggest were Chaucer's own. Chaucer does not offer his Franklin as a pattern of Christian perfection – the portrait is full of light satiric touches – but neither does he present him as his (or our) moral and intellectual inferior. The Franklin is a great 'housholdere'' – a man of property, with responsibilities in the world – and he fills that role in ways that bring to Chaucer's mind St Julian, patron saint of hospitality, as well as a Roman philosopher who taught that pleasure is happiness. I think Chaucer would have been amused at how austerely some modern critics judge the Franklin, all the while living (as Chaucer did, and as most of us do) as amply as we can. Chaucer found the more innocent forms of hypocrisy endlessly diverting, but he did not write from out of them.

[29] Braswell, in *Mosaic* 18 (1985) 101–10.

[30] Ibid., p. 101.

[31] Ibid., p. 105.

wheels, like that from the *Luttrell Psalter*, probably sent audiences scurrying
. . . . But magic frequently required much more enterprise than this. When the
mechanical clock was invented in the fourteenth century, for example, its mechanism was often used to make inanimate objects seem alive'. At the very highest
levels of medieval culture, she argues, *'artists created magic* by designing
automata'.[32] [my emphasis]

This sort of thing alone, according to Braswell, constituted 'the magic of the
late Middle Ages'.[33] For her – as for Luengo – the magic of *The Franklin's Tale*
is something to be *seen through*, a series of marvels requiring of us nothing
more than accurate recognition and classification.

I shall argue against that view, but before I do, let me join Braswell in bringing
into this discourse the most attractive evidence for believing that contemporary
automata *might* explain it all: the artful amusements of the noble park at Hesdin
in Artois. Built by Count Robert II in the late thirteenth century, and extensively
renovated by Philip the Bold around 1390 – more or less at the time Chaucer was
writing *The Franklin's Tale* – Hesdin had been for generations the favourite
castle of the Dukes of Burgundy. Amid its extensive grounds and gardens
(including a garden called *li petit paradis*) there was located a Pavilion – a kind
of royal fun-house – renowned for automata and 'magic' devices. A sixteenth-
century copy of an earlier tapestry or painting, thought to show a wedding held
at Hesdin in 1431 [**Figure 8**], includes a version of the Pavilion depicted at the
rear.[34] Records tell us that this structure, built upon marshy land with a river
running beneath it, was filled with contraptions – including (I quote from Braswell's lively summary) 'stuffed monkeys covered with hair, which were
chained to a dais, though they contained some mechanism which allowed them
to descend from the platform and frighten the guests. At the vestibule was an
automated lion. The walls sported large mirrors which distorted the images of
the guests, and hidden under the floor were jets of water which sprayed the
hapless visitors from below [ladies were special targets]. Trick windows spurted
water when opened and mechanical birds in a cage spit on those who came too
close'.[35] Anne van Buren, who is editing the Hesdin archives, notes with wry
amusement that 'whatever the Duke's hapless guests may have thought of
them', in the records these devices 'are regularly called *ouvraiges ingenieux et
de joyeuseté et plaisance'*.[36] Hesdin castle, standing elsewhere in the park, contained a room famous for wall paintings depicting Jason and the Golden Fleece,

[32] Ibid., pp. 102–03.
[33] Ibid., p. 108.
[34] **Figure 8**: Versailles, Musée des Beaux-Arts du Château (Photo Giraudon): the lost original is
thought to have been by Jan van Eyck. It is reproduced in colour as fig. 256 (p. 292) in
Prevenier and Blockmans, *The Burgundian Netherlands*, and as fig. 78 in Elisabeth Dhanens,
Hubert and Jan van Eyck (New York, 1980). On it, see Anne Hagopian van Buren, 'Un jardin
d'amour au parc d'Hesdin, et le role de Jan van Eyck dans une commande ducale', *Revue du
Louvre* (1985). Van Buren's exhaustive study of the Hesdin records (which extend from 1288
to 1536), soon to issue in a book, will significantly extend and secure our knowledge of the
Park's history.
[35] Braswell, 'The Magic of Machinery', p. 103; for a fuller account, translated from a 1433
record of refurbishings, see Richard Vaughan, *Philip the Good: The Apogee of Burgundy*
(London, 1970), pp. 138–39.
[36] Anne Hagopian von Buren, 'The Model Roll of the Golden Fleece', *The Art Bulletin* 61
(1979) 359–76; I quote from p. 372.

Figure 8: The Pavilion at Hesdin, with festive courtiers (possibly a 1431 wedding)
before it. (Sixteenth-century copy of a lost original.)
Versailles, Musée des Beaux-Arts du Château.
(Photo Giraudon/Art Resource, New York)

as well as for mechanisms capable of still other astonishing effects: lightening, thunder, snow and rain. The English printer William Caxton, proud of having personally visited the castle, described the room that held these paintings so:

> well wote I that the noble Duc Philippe firste foundeur of this sayd ordre [of the Golden Fleece] / dyd doo maken a chambre in the Castell of Hesdyn / where in was craftyly and curiously depeynted the conqueste of the golden flese by the sayd Iason / in which chambre I haue ben and seen the sayde historie so depeynted. & in remembraunce of Medea & of her connyng & science he had do make in the sayde chambre by subtil engyn that whan he wolde it shuld seme that it lightend & then thondre / snowe & rayne. And all within the sayde chambre as ofte tymes & whan it shuld please him. which was al made for his singuler pleasir.[37]

It's doubtful that *real* snow falling through the ceiling at Hesdin castle would have charmed anyone, but a room with imitation snowstorms (machines strewing flour) was enough to make it famous throughout Europe.

Most of the devices at Hesdin, van Buren has established, date from the late 13th century, not from the late 14th-century renovation – and thus long predate Chaucer's tale. Among aristocratic audiences, at least, they were widely known, and Chaucer might have heard of them from many sources. He had, at the very least, read testimony to the charms and attractions of the Park in Machaut's *Remède de Fortune* (ca. 1340), a poem on which he drew in writing his own *Book of the Duchess*, *Anelida and Arcite*, and *Troilus and Criseyde*. In Machaut's poem the despairing lover retreats into the Park of Hesdin, which he describes so (783–822):

> 'I went along thus for a while, ever lost in my thoughts, until I saw a very beautiful garden called the Park of Hesdin. . . . And when I'd succeeded in entering and found myself all alone, I bolted the lock on the wicket. I walked along among the plantings, which were more beautiful than any I'd ever seen, nor will I ever see any so beautiful, so fair, so agreeable, so pleasing, or so delightful. And I could never describe the marvels, the delights, the artifices, the automata, the watercourses, the entertainments, the wondrous things that were enclosed within. . . .'[38]

Chaucer knew at least this much of the Hesdin wonders; he may well have known more.

Instructed by all this beguiling evidence from Paris feasts, English royal entries, and Hesdin fun houses, we might well conclude that the magic shows of

---

[37] Quoted by Van Buren, 'The Model Roll', p. 370. For the whole preface (and a more recent text, quoted here) see *The Prologues and Epilogues of William Caxton*, ed. W.J.B. Crotch, EETS OS 176 (1928), pp. 33–34. Van Buren succeeds in reconstructing what these paintings might have been like. Medea *as magician and sorceress* would seem to be the crucial link between the room's 'magic' machines and the Jason narrative painted on its walls.

[38] The catalogue of delights reads so in Machaut's French: 'Et les merveilles, les deduis, / Les ars, les engins, les conduis, / Les esbas, les estranges choses . . ..' For both text and translation (here from pp. 210–13), and an authoritative study of the poem's tradition – '[it] is probably the most important French love poem of the fourteenth century, and it may also be the best' (p. 32) – see Guillaume de Machaut, *Le Jugement du roy de Behaigne and Remede de Fortune*, ed. James I. Wimsatt and William W. Kibler, The Chaucer Library (Athens, Georgia, 1988). They reproduce as colour frontispiece an illumination showing the poet within the walled park of Hesdin, writing a complaint against Fortune and her wheel.

The Franklin's Tale have been accurately and sufficiently described. But I think there are good reasons not to do so, the first of which is simple indeed: it makes both the Middle Ages and the tale itself entirely too neat and tidy.

We must remind ourselves that the medieval centuries, for all their high intellectual and theological aspirations, were also centuries of superstition, imperfect knowledge, and widespread credulity. The Church had its own several varieties of 'white magic' – the sacred transformation of substance at the heart of the Mass, the demonic struggle implicit in the rituals of exorcism, the demonstration of power over natural law in the miracles of the saints.[39] And the distinction between natural magic and black magic, dear to scholars then as now, was in fact variously drawn. Richard Kieckhefer's distinguished recent study of *Magic in the Middle Ages* summarizes the period so:

> At the popular level the tendency was to conceive magic as natural, while among the intellectuals there were three competing lines of thought: an assumption, developed in the early centuries of Christianity, that all magic involved at least an implicit reliance on demons; a grudging recognition, fostered especially by the influx of Arabic learning in the twelfth century, that much magic was in fact natural; and a fear, stimulated in the later Middle Ages by the very real exercise of necromancy, that magic involved an all too explicit invocation of demons even when it pretended to be innocent.[40]

If you add to this account a widespread tendency to attribute to occult or magical powers any operation or mechanism not well or widely understood, even automata and the machinery of theatrical illusion become magical.[41] And while I believe (along with most previous writers on the subject) that Chaucer was skeptical of most of what was called magic – as he was of practical alchemy, to name another semi-magical 'science' – I suspect he did not dismiss it as confidently as we dismiss it in our twentieth-century lives. Chaucer leaves too much of the tale's magic mysterious – especially the apparent removal of the rocks – for the mystery not to signify.

Concerning *that* event, certainly, Chaucer shows himself reluctant to pay magic any real respect: he is contemptuous of both the profession and its practice (1131–34, 1261–96). But he never explains it all away: 'thurgh his magik' – the magic of the clerk – 'for a wyke or tweye, / It semed that alle the rokkes were aweye' (1295–96). Something *seems* to have happened – or, to put

---

[39] Valerie I.J. Flint, *The Rise of Magic in Early Medieval Europe*, forthcoming from Princeton Univ. Press, 1991, studies the Church's accomodation of practices originally condemned as magical.

[40] Richard Kieckhefer, *Magic in the Middle Ages* (Cambridge, 1989), pp. 16–17. There is a most interesting discussion of the several kinds of magic in *The Chess of Love*, trans. Joan Morton Jones (Ph.D. Diss., University of Nebraska, 1968), a late 14th-century or early 15th-century commentary on *Les Echecs Amoureuse*, pp. 288–304; it deserves to be better known, and richly confirms the view that magic must be taken seriously in the study of medieval culture. (The poem and its commentary still await publication in the original French).

[41] Kieckhefer, pp. 101–02 and passim ('the allure of machines combined with the mystery of the unexplained', p. 107). On the blurring of categories see also van Buren, 'Reality and Literary Romance', in *Medieval Gardens*, pp. 128–29, 132–33, and cf. this contemporary account of a great *Passion* play staged in Valenciennes in 1547: 'The machines (*secrets*) of the Paradise and of Hell were absolutely prodigious and could be taken by the populace for magic' [there follows a long list of machines and wonderful actions], in A.M. Nagler, *A Source Book in Theatrical History* (New York, 1952), pp. 47–48.

it another way, a *real* illusion has been created. For historical reasons, if for no other, we should not sweep the magician's study too clean.

But there is a more precise reason still for not thinking the tale's magic to be only a matter of automata, pageant wagons, and human actors. It derives from the fact (ignored in most critical writing on the tale) that the two magic shows are not similar in kind. Their ontological status – the ground of their being – is different, and the difference matters greatly.

The first 'show' (to recapitulate briefly) seems to me perfectly well glossed by the material I have been presenting. It invokes entertainment of a kind sometimes presented at great feasts or other noble occasions, invented by 'tregetoures' whose skill lay in bringing together human actors, automata, and 'mansions' or pageant-wagons of a kind familiar from the medieval stage. There is nothing mysterious about any of this *in mode*, however ingenious its machines, or metaphorically 'magical' their effects. Entertainments of this kind were valued as artful precisely because they were not the real thing – because they were *other* than the effect they imitated. Such shows are part of the history of pageantry, mime and masque; they do not invoke forbidden powers or exercise forbidden arts. Their intention is to surprise and delight; they 'deceive' mechanically, not ontologically.

The tale's second magic show is different. Whereas the first is simply a poetic catalogue, some heresay remembered by Aurelius's brother ('ofte at feestes have I wel herd seye'), the second happens within the *real time* of the narrative, and in a particular place. It is not set in a grand royal hall (like the Palais de la Cité in Paris, where the 1378 feast was held, attended by some 800 knights)[42] or in a rich and costly pavilion such as that at Hesdin (with its automated rooms and corridors and galleries). Chaucer locates it instead in a house in Orléans – a 'wel arrayed' house, no less no more, with a single squire to serve the supper. The clerk seems prosperous enough, as clerks go, but there is no suggestion that he commands great wealth or great space, nor is there a single circumstantial detail meant to evoke wonder: the setting is domestic and homely. The show that takes place there, in contrast, is truly fabulous, exceeding in sweep and scope anything reported from distant banqueting halls.

The clerk first shows them 'Forestes, parkes ful of wilde deer', where they witness the death of a hundred harts, their antlers the greatest ever seen, some slain by hounds and others by arrows, bleeding from grievous wounds. That vision 'voyded', he shows them falconers 'upon a fair ryver', slaying heron with their hawks, and following that, a company of knights jousting upon a plain. It is only after these visions – these three demonstrations of power – that he directly addresses Aurelius's desire, showing him 'his lady on a daunce, / On which hymself he daunced, as hym thoughte'. The vision is described paratactically, revealing its subject in two stages, the second more intimate and erotic than the first: it's as though Aurelius first sees his lady (Dorigen) dancing with others [**Figure 9**] – the illumination is taken from a MS of Machaut's *Remède de Fortune*[43] – and only then *himself* dancing with her in that dance. As soon as that final voluptuous illusion is achieved, it too is voided: the clerk of Orléans

[42] Loomis, 'Secular Dramatics', p. 243.
[43] **Figure 9**: Paris, Bibl. Natl. MS fr. 1586, fol. 51; reproduced in colour by Avril, *Manuscript Painting at the Court of France*, pl. 24.

Figure 9: A courtly dance in the Park at Hesdin, illustrating Machaut's *La Remède de Fortune* (French, ca. 1350). Paris, Bibl. Natl. MS. fr. 1586, fol. 51. (By permission of the Bibliothèque Nationale)

claps his hands and 'Al oure revel was ago'. 'And yet', the story continues (in some crucial lines, which, following Chaucer's lead, I have held back until this moment),

> And yet remoeved they nevere out of the hous,
> Whil they saugh al this sighte merveillous,
> *But in his studie, ther as his bookes be,*
> They seten stille, *and no wight but they thre.*   (1205–8)

To underscore the importance of that notation, Chaucer has the clerk himself repeat it just seven lines later, in a complaint that is really a concealed boast, intended to remind the Bretons how much he has shown them in a very short while:

> To hym this maister called his squier,
> And seyde hym thus: "Is redy oure soper?
> *Almoost an houre* it is, I undertake,
> Sith I yow bad oure soper for to make,

> Whan that thise worthy men wenten with me
> *Into my studie, ther as my bookes be.*"   (1209–14)

Unlike the privileged guests at Hesdin, Aurelius and his brother (and we, in the act of imagining the tale) have not been touring a noble pavilion or castle. We are in an intimate space – a scholar's study, with books – and the ontological nature of what happens there is far from clear. If Aurelius 'sees' the things he is said to be shown, then *magic of some kind* is being worked in that place, unlikely to be dependent on complicated machines, hidden mechanisms, or concealed attendants working levers and bellows, winches and weights.

Braswell (to my mind) pays insufficient attention to both the setting and Aurelius's response to the magic in her explanation of this second show. 'This continuous change of scene', she writes, 'could easily have been accomplished by a fourteenth-century device employing the principle of a mill wheel. Such a tool could make a globe spin or a stage turn, thus creating continuous changes in scene . . . . [Or] perhaps the deer, the falconers, the knights and the dancer were all parts of a medieval pageant that has not survived'.[44] Such a show might indeed have been mounted, in the fashion of the Paris *entremès*, and it might indeed have evoked wonder. But not in a clerk's study, and not with any hope of deceiving Aurelius *in the way he is deceived.*

Aurelius is not shopping for machines, automata, or travelling players. He wants *real magic* – nothing less will remove the rocks – and he is *convinced* by this demonstration that the clerk has that power. For 'real' magic (if there is such a thing) a room of any size will do. And the books are the key to its meaning. The magician must be a figure of power, authority and mystery, a man *capable* creating convincing illusion.

As I see it, the subtext of the tale requires no less, for Chaucer means to define himself against this figure, to set himself in contest with him. We are asked to imagine the clerk among his books, creating illusions of a courtly, chivalric kind, because it can bring to our minds another image, similar in many ways: the image, so deeply familiar from Chaucer's early works, of the poet himself 'in his studie, ther as his bookes be', afflicted with insomnia, dulled by his work at the counting house, grieving over his own unhappiness in love, but 'dreaming' poems that grow out of those books – dreams that likewise violate the logic and the laws of the waking world with magical flights, astonishing visions, golden eagles that speak. I think Chaucer invented the magic of Orléans – so very different from that which he found in Boccaccio's *Filocolo*, his most proximate source[45] – as a means of assessing the mystery and grandeur of his own craft, the making of fictional poems. The image of a magician in his study is meant to evoke the image of a poet among his books, a comparison that is for poetry as troubling as it is exalting.

By unleashing this magic in such a setting, and by describing in even less than the clerk's 'space of an hour' its four spectacular illusionary events, Chaucer

---

44 Braswell, 'The Magic of Machinery', p. 106.
45 The *Filocolo* account tries to imagine *real* magic, magic that is, within terms of the story, successful. It does not undercut it with reference to easier, less mysterious arts (banquet entertainments, stage devices, automata), nor does it limit its setting to a study full of books; Theban, the magician, travels all over the world, by magical means and with magical speed, to gather what is necessary to make a garden bloom in January.

makes *us as audience* see them too – in our mind's eye, the eye with which we imagine fictions – just as surely (and just as mysteriously) as Aurelius is said to do. Chaucer's 'bookish art' allows both poet and audience to imagine the real and the unreal, the natural and the naturally impossible, and to do so (what is more) with a facility greater than anything magic has ever aspired to. Chaucer's double interest in the Orléans magic show can be read very clearly in its voiding movement, as he writes of the clerk, 'He clapte his handes two, / And farewel! Al oure revel was ago'. The possessive 'oure' (intentionally or accidentally) marks the fact that the creator of what we have just 'seen' is unwilling to remain outside the charmed circle at this moment of maximum power. And the force of this most unexpected pronoun reminds us that we too stand within it. It is 'oure revel' – a cooperative enterprise – that is 'a-go'. Like Aurelius and his brother, we 'see' what the artist would have us see without moving from the room where we read or listen, the room – perhaps – where our own 'bookes be', and where our own role in the creation of literary illusion is most readily acknowledged.[46]

In making that claim, I ground myself not only upon evidence from the tale itself,[47] but upon a long Western tradition connecting magic and poetry – a tradition whose earliest expression (in Greek, Roman, Celtic and Germanic culture) must be passed over here.[48] Let us look instead at its later (metaphorical) expression in a text Chaucer knew, the *Poetria Nova* of Geoffrey de Vinsauf, written ca. 1210. Near the beginning of that treatise, Geoffrey carefully notes the limitations of 'natural order' in narrative, restricted (by definition) to a single way of organizing a story, moving strictly and sequentially from beginning to end. In contrast, he tells us, the high art of poetry offers eight different ways of ordering such material:

> Art can draw a pleasant beginning out of either [the end or the middle of a work]. *It plays about almost like a magician*, and brings it about that the last becomes the first, the future the present, the oblique direct, the remote near; thus rustic matters become polished, old becomes new, public private, black white, and vile precious.[49]

---

[46] For a later but powerful expression of this same phenomenon, see the engraving Gustave Doré made as frontispiece to his edition of *Don Quixote*. The Don sits in a chair with books stacked or thrown all about him waving a sword in one hand and reading from one of his favourite romances in the other; the air is full of his literary imaginings – knights, horses, goblins, damsels in distress – figures from books who are as real to him (that is his problem) as life itself. It can be seen, e.g., in *Gustave Doré: Das graphische Werk*, 2 vols., ed. Gabriele Forberg (Munich: 1975), I, 454.

[47] Two critics have touched briefly on such a reading before me: Samuel Schuman, 'Man, Magician, Poet, God – An Image in Medieval, Renaissance, and Modern Literature', *Cithara* 19 (1980) 40–54, who writes about Chaucer (pp. 40–43), Shakespeare and Nabokov; and Derek Pearsall, *The Canterbury Tales* (London, 1985), p. 154, who describes (in passing) the magic show at Orléans as 'an almost gratuitous exhibition of Chaucer's delight in his own poetic powers'.

[48] See, e.g., Morton W. Bloomfield and Charles W. Dunn, *The Role of the Poet in Early Societies* (Cambridge, 1989); Marc Drogin, *Biblioclasm: The Mythical Origins, Magic Powers and Perishability of the Written Word* (Savage, Maryland, 1989); and, with reference to the visual arts, Ernst Kris and Otto Kurz, *Legend, Myth, and Magic in the Image of the Artist* (New Haven, 1979), esp. Chap. 3 ('The Artist as Magician').

[49] Ernest Gallo, *The Poetria Nova and Its Sources in Early Rhetorical Doctrine* (The Hague, 1971), pp. 20–21 (ll. 120–25). Geoffrey's *praestigiatrix*, rendered by Gallo as 'magician', is translated as 'conjurer' by Margaret F. Nims, *Poetria Nova of Geoffrey of Vinsauf* (Toronto, 1967), p. 20. *An Early Commentary on the Poetria nova of Geoffrey of Vinsauf*, ed. Marjorie

In Geoffrey's concluding examples, values and identities are invoked as well as temporal sequence, for the magic of poetry is capable of transforming them all.

Geoffrey de Vinsauf addresses us from the high road of art, where poetry is related to magic only metaphorically. Its imaginative reorderings and transformations are praised simply as acts of power, without social or moral consequence, ideational rather than 'real'. But Chaucer in his last great work speaks to us from the pilgrim road to a cathedral, and so cannot celebrate for long the illusion-making at Orléans as though it were virtuoso entertainment merely. The clerk's final illusion – offering Aurelius a vision of himself and Dorigen together in a dance – marks the end of Chaucer's sympathy, a rupture in his imaginative identification with an allied art. Things swiftly take a sinister turn as the magician/clerk transforms himself into a shrewd business man, demanding a ruinous price for making the rocks seem to disappear, and shortly after moves into something worse, a set of calculations and operations apparently competent to alter something foundational in the created world.

Chaucer makes only a half-hearted attempt to imagine what the magician actually does, dismissing it *as false poetry*, a confusing techno-babble that reduces to one of two possibilities – 'apparence or jogelrye' – its details and language of little interest to him: 'I ne kan no termes of astrologye'. This third magic-show, the apparent removal of the rocks, borders on blasphemy and presumption, and is castigated by the poet as 'japes', 'wrecchednesse', 'supersticious cursednesse', 'illusiouns and swich meschaunces / As hethen folk used in thilke dayes'. Though this catalogue of scorn takes proper measure of the event – the most such a magician can do is make the world *seem* briefly other than it is – we quickly discover that even in such reduced terms there is implicit a world of moral danger. In what follows, Chaucer defines his poetic art by its difference, proving himself no trafficker in appearances-for-their-own-sake, no vendor of easy fantasies, no lousy juggler, no clerk of Orléans.

The art of poetic illusion originates in, and addresses itself to, the *phantasy* – in medieval faculty psychology that power of the mind (generally located in the brain's second 'cell' [**Figure 10**])[50] that is able to process sensory images stored in the imagination (located in the first cell) and combine them into images of things never seen – a human torso on the body of a fish, let us say, or (to use an example from Roger Bacon's treatise on magic) a machine with wings that can

---

Curry Woods (New York, 1985), pp. 28–29, specifies both ('He praises the subtlety of art and says that this ART PLAYS LIKE A MAGICIAN that is, a sorcerer' / 'PRESTIGIATRIX, id est uenefica'), continuing 'A *prestigium* is a kind of subtle magic trick [*quedam subtilitas magice artis*] that makes something seem other than what it is, as is said about this art.. . .' A related phrase, *praestigiae verborum*, specifically signified the deceptive use of words. That Chaucer knew the early part of Geoffrey's treatise can be reasonably presumed: ll. 43–47 furnished him an important stanza near the end of Book I of the *Troilus*, beginning 'For everi wight that hath an hous to founde' (l. 1065 ff).

50 **Figure 10**: From Triumphus Augustinus de Anchona, *Opusculum perutile de cognitione animae*, an anatomy text revised by Allesandro Achillini, Bologna, 1503, sig. f. [viii]. See my *Chaucer and the Imagery of Narrative*, Chapter I, for extensive discussion of the role of mental imagery in medieval accounts of how we experience literature; figs. 5–7 are diagrams of brain function. In the picture reproduced above, the three cells have each been assigned two functions: (1) 'common sense' (receiving impressions from all the senses) and imagination; (2) phantasy and estimation; (3) memory and motion [*motiva*].

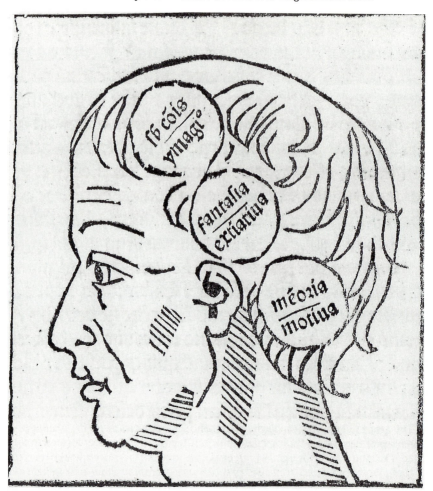

Figure 10: A three-cell diagram of the brain (*fantasia* in the middle cell), from
Triumphus Augustinus de Anchona, *Opusculum perutile de cognitione animae*,
rev. Achillini (Bologna, 1503), sig. f. [viii].
(By permission of the British Library)

fly.[51] But *phantasia* is also a name for the *deceptive* power of the mind: the
power that lets us imagine, and sometimes tricks up into believing, something
we particularly desire or fear is real. At the culmination of his magic show, the
clerk creates an illusion so pleasant and so convincing – Dorigen in a dance –
that Aurelius thinks himself *included* within it. But the magician's art is as
remarkable for its exclusions: Dorigen's husband and her love for him, the
rocks, all care for society, all thought of a future. He offers the young knight a

---

[51] *Roger Bacon's Letter Concerning the Marvelous Power of Art and of Nature and Concerning
the Nullity of Magic*, trans. Tenney L. Davis (Easton, Penn., 1923), p. 27.

Figure 11: A portrait of Sorrow (*Tristesse*) tearing her hair, from the *Roman de la Rose* (French, ca. 1330). London, Brit. Lib. MS. Add. 31840, fol. 5. (By permission of the British Library)

most dangerous illusion – desire fulfilled, in a world without moral consequence.

Once the bargain has been made, the clerk/magician must go further, using his art to conform the coast of Pedmark to the landscape of a lover's fantasy (first Dorigen's, now Aurelius's). The narrative outcome of that third magic-show is well known to everyone in this audience, and need not be rehearsed here. I shall focus instead on Chaucer's resolution of the more hidden issues it raises: the power and peril of illusion-making within poetic fiction.

The clerk of Orléans, in presenting us with an alternative ending to the fiction – Dorigen and Aurelius together, carefree, in a dance – removes one of the iconographic centres of the tale: the rocks in the sea, and all the hard meanings that Dorigen has laid upon them, however temporary her reasons for doing so. By creating the 'appearance' of removal, the clerk in effect rewrites *The Franklin's Tale* from within – presenting the world all as 'garden'. In bringing the poem back to a more truthful relation to reality, Chaucer profoundly distinguishes his 'art poetical' from the 'art magical' of Orléans.

For central to Chaucer's art in this tale is the conviction that both rocks and garden symbolize something essential in human life. Either alone, chosen as the single landscape of the soul, has its dangers. If you address yourself too exclusively to the rocks – Dorigen's great error – you may fall into blasphemy and despair: life will lose its savour, suicide can seem an appropriate response. She experiences despair during Arveragus's long absence (817–36) and turns to thoughts of suicide (1346–1458) when Aurelius tells her it is time to keep her

Figure 12: The Lover admitted into the Garden, from the *Roman de la Rose* (French, beginning of the fifteenth century). London, Brit. Lib. MS. Egerton 1069, fol. 1. (By permission of the British Library)

promise, the rocks having been removed. On this latter occasion, she becomes (one might say) Sorrow itself [**Figure 11**], as that emotion was understood in the *Roman de la Rose*.[52] Too much sadness (*Tristesse*), we learn near that poem's beginning, excludes one from Love's adventure, and for that reason *Tristesse* is depicted (together with other sins against Love) on the *outside* of the love garden. In **Figure 12**, her portrait decorates the wall to the right of the entry gate:[53]

> Sorowe was peynted next Envie
> Upon that wall of masonrye. . . .
> Her roughte lytel of playing
> Or of clypping or kissyng;

---

[52] **Figure 11**: London, Brit. Lib. MS Add. 31840, fol. 5, ca. 1330, illustrating the *Roman de la Rose*. In expression of her nature, *Tristesse* tears at her hair and gown, and scratches savagely her face.

[53] **Figure 12**: London, Brit. Lib. MS Egerton 1069, fol. 1, showing the Lover admitted by Lady Idleness, porteress of the gate. (On the wall, from far left, we see images of Covetousness, Avarice and Envy, other sins that exclude one from the garden). The picture is from the beginning of the 15th century; it can be seen in colour in Harvey, *Medieval Gardens*, pl. III B. For the verbal portrait of 'Sorowe' I quote above, see *The Romaunt of the Rose*, ll. 301–48 (*Riverside Chaucer*, p. 690); the translation may be Chaucer's own.

For whoso sorouful is in herte,
Him luste not to play ne sterte,
Ne for to dauncen, ne to synge,
Ne may his herte in temper bringe
To make joye on even or morowe,
For joy is contrarie unto sorowe.

Though Dorigen cannot quite bring herself to suicide, she spends a day or two thinking luxuriously upon it: it is, one might say, her only joy. . . .

To that troubled vision – that 'derke fantasye' – the garden offers an authentic and valuable antidote. It is a place of beauty, comfort and joy, where psychological and moral equilibrium can be restored. But if you focus too exclusively on the garden – as Aurelius does in his love fantasy, as the friends of Dorigen do who would comfort her, and as Dorigen did earlier, for one crucial moment – you may fall into other kinds of danger: carelessness, folly, infidelity, adultery, each more perilous than the other.

The rocks, in short, genuinely matter to the moral economy of the tale.[54] Though they do not literally injure anyone or anything, the poem would be something very different without them. For just as Chaucer seems to have had only a limited interest in the emotional histrionics of young lovers, so the poetry proper to pleasure gardens or gardens of love engaged him very little. Nor does he seem to have cared much more for poetry focused exclusively upon a harsher moral landscape – the poetry of rocks and barrenness, suffering and death. Like the painter of a fifteenth-century diptych from the upper Rhine [**Figure 13**], Chaucer sought in this tale to express a dialectical truth, setting the two side by side, in appropriate scale and balance. The left wing of the diptych shows a dead man laid out upon a wintry bank whose grass is brown, and whose trees are bare and broken; the river and sea are frozen, and one sees in the far distance ruined houses and towers, high rocks and cliffs; the only road up the mountain enters a man-made cave. The right wing shows, in contrast, an elegant young man and woman in courtly conversation, seated in sunshine on green grass and soft herbs, with children (or *putti*, the idea of children) playing below. Behind them one sees green trees and fields, prosperous houses and castles, and the same high mountain, but here made accessible by a road winding upward through broad meadows.[55] The frame of the diptych separates these two paintings, determining the mood and season of each, but we slowly realize they share the same landscape, the same rocky mountain, perhaps even the same foreground. What seems divided and antithetical is in fact a complex unity: the beautiful and the ugly, the comfortable and the austere, the courtly and the macabre inhabit the same world. In *The Franklin's Tale* Chaucer does not allow his young people to escape into a garden without paying some price – some growth in wisdom and character whose roots are not to be found in that privileged and

---

[54] They seem to be Chaucer's own invention, without parallel in either of the Boccaccio versions of the story. See Geoffrey Chaucer, *The Canterbury Tales: Nine Tales and the General Prologue*, ed. V.A. Kolve and Glending Olson (New York, 1989), pp. 393–406, for translations of both the *Filocolo* and *Decameron* texts. The longer (*Il Filocolo*) version is the more likely source.

[55] **Figure 13**: a panel painting in the Germanisches Nationalmuseum Nürnberg, from about 1480; on it (and for a colour reproduction) see the museum guidebook, *Führer durch die Sammlungen* (Munich, 1980), item 134 (described as an allegory of life and death).

Figure 13: An allegory of human life (panel painting from the upper
Rhine, ca. 1480). Germanisches Nationalmuseum, Nurnberg.
(Photo courtesy of the museum)

protected place. But neither does he demand of them (in the manner of the desert father Abraham, quoted earlier) that they forsake all garden values once harsher truths are known. When Arveragus returns from England, and Dorigen's first grief is at an end, the courtly life *fittingly* resumes: he 'daunceth, justeth, maketh hire good cheere; / And thus in joye and blisse I lete hem dwelle' (1098).

The *real* magic in *The Franklin's Tale*, as many have said before me, is that which transforms selfishness into generosity, debt into forgiveness, and courtly loving into courteous living. That 'magic' is made morally attractive – and psychologically credible – by the poet, not the magician. A poet can make rocks disappear quite easily. But it is only in literature that such magic happens.

In his dream-vision visit to *The Hous of Fame*, Chaucer describes at great length (l. 1193 ff.) a motley company installed on and about the castle's outer walls, composed of 'alle maner of mynstralles / And gestiours that tellen tales / Both of wepinge and of game, / Of al that longeth unto Fame', accompanied by harpers and musicians of every sort. Among them he discovers a company even more diverse, 'jugelours, / Magiciens, and tregetours', 'charmeresses', 'sorceresses', 'And clerkes eke, which konne wel / Al this magik naturel', including Medea, Circes, Simon Magus, and even a specific English magician, 'Colle tregetour' who is able by sleight-of-hand to produce miniature windmills from under walnut shells. It is a wild and turbulent group, uncomfortable company for an ambitious young poet, but we must not think it a private nightmare, unrelated to social categories. Everyone in this comany offers some artful form of illusion and 'apparence', and John Southworth's recent study of *The English Medieval Minstrel* amply confirms their linkage in such a throng. The medieval word 'minstrel', he tells us, like the Latin *mimus*, *histrio* and *joculator*, which it translated, was used indiscriminately for 'musicians – composers, instrumentalists and singers – oral poets and tellers of tales (often to a musical accompaniment), fools, jugglers, acrobats and dancers; actors, mimes and mimics; conjurors, puppeteers and exhibitors of performing animals – bears, horses, dogs, even snakes'. 'For all the variety of names used, few distinctions are made by the chroniclers between the different types of entertainer. The consequent, terminological confusion undoubtedly reflects a large degree of versatility and flexibility of role on the part of the performers, but is also an indication of the low esteem in which they were generally held – especially by clerics'.[56]

As in *The Hous of Fame*, so in *The Franklin's Tale*. Through a memorial recital of the entertainments at a recent Paris feast, and by setting the Orléans magic-show in a clerk's study 'there as his bokes be', Chaucer again acknowledges his own relation to these other arts, locating his own craft somewhat ruefully among them – an act of humility (we may believe), attended by a certain pride. Though the tale has much to say about love and marriage, it suggests as well a poetics of illusion, in which the truth-telling potential of poetic fiction can be distinguished from other forms of 'magic' and 'apparence', despite all that those arts might seem to have in common.

---

[56] John Southworth, *The English Medieval Minstrel* (Woodbridge, Suffolk, 1989), esp. Chapters I and II. I quote from pp. 3, 10–11. A.A. Prins, 'Notes on the Canterbury Tales (3)', *English Studies* 35 (1954) 158–62, on the meaning of 'tregetour', remains valuable.

Index